A Force for Good

A Force for Good

How the American News Media Have Propelled Positive Change

RODGER STREITMATTER

ROWMAN & LITTLEFIELD
Lanham • Boulder • New York • London

Published by Rowman & Littlefield
A wholly owned subsidary of The Rowman & Littlefield Publishing Group, Inc.
4501 Forbes Boulevard, Suite 200, Lanham, Maryland 20706
www.rowman.com

Unit A, Whitacre Mews, 26-34 Stannary Street, London SE11 4AB, United Kingdom

British Library Cataloguing in Publication Information Available

Library of Congress Cataloging-in-Publication Data

Streitmatter, Rodger.
   A force for good : how the American news media have propelled positive change /
Rodger Streitmatter.
      pages cm
   Includes bibliographical references and index.
   ISBN 978-1-4422-4510-5 (cloth : alk. paper) — ISBN 978-1-4422-4511-2 (pbk. :
alk. paper) — ISBN 978-1-4422-4512-9 (electronic)
   1. Press—United States—Influence. 2. Press and politics—United States.
3. Journalism—Political aspects—United States. 4. Journalism—Social aspects—
United States. I. Title.
   PN4888.I53S74 2015
   302.230973—dc23
                                                            2014046658

♾️™ The paper used in this publication meets the minimum requirements of
American National Standard for Information Sciences—Permanence of Paper
for Printed Library Materials, ANSI/NISO Z39.48-1992.

Printed in the United States of America

I dedicate this book to my grandchildren, Eli, Noah, and Liam Streitmatter, and Max, Charlie, and Emma Galardini, in the hope that they all will become "forces for good" in their lifetimes.

Contents

Introduction

American journalism is a punching bag.

That is, this country's news media are relentlessly criticized. They're constantly slammed for being too negative and too sensationalistic, and too profit-oriented, too liberal, and too biased. Other items on the seemingly endless list of faults are that the Fourth Estate isn't patriotic and that it fails miserably in reflecting the nation's diversity—especially when it comes to women, persons of color, and poor people.

Much of this criticism is deserved. There's no doubt, in other words, that American journalism has often failed the public that it's supposed to be serving.

At the same time, though, I believe this persistent railing against the news media has obscured the fact that journalism has made many positive contributions to the country's well-being. And so, I've written this book to illuminate a few examples of the myriad instances in which news outlets have helped the United States become a better place.

A Force for Good: How the American News Media Have Propelled Positive Change is driven by the thesis, simply put, that journalism has improved this country in an impressively broad range of areas.

Chapter 9 shows the role that newspapers played in breaking the color barrier in professional baseball. From the moment Jackie Robinson signed on to play with a Brooklyn Dodgers farm team in 1945, these journalistic voices did everything they could to make sure the public would welcome him once team officials moved him up to the majors. The papers not only praised Robinson's athletic prowess but also depicted him as a squeaky-clean role model—the *New York Times* calling him "a high-class citizen in every respect."

Chapter 12 highlights how news organizations helped popularize the birth control pill. Newspapers and magazines of the late 1950s and early 1960s transformed this obscure medication, originally used to treat rare menstrual disorders, into a cultural phenomenon that was soon having remarkable consequences. Within half a dozen years after the country's leading news outlets began celebrating the pill as a medical marvel, the nation's birthrate had plunged 24 percent and the frequency of sexual intercourse had soared an astonishing 40 percent.

Several of the sixteen case studies in this book focus on TV news. Chapter 13 documents how the networks covered the U.S. space program's effort, during the 1960s, to put a man on the moon before the Soviets did. Specifically, TV news consistently painted the launches in rose-colored hues and depicted the men inside the spacecraft as national heroes. This flattering coverage contributed to the American public's obsession with the Space Race, which meant NASA received the funding it needed to complete its history-making lunar landing.

Now that you have a sense of what *A Force for Good* is about, I need to add a caveat that speaks to one thing this book *isn't* trying to say. The easiest way to understand this point is to notice the word "propelled" in the title. This particular verb choice means this work takes the position that the American news media have—to borrow a pair of synonyms for propelled—"pushed" and "driven" social change. What this book isn't arguing is that journalism was solely responsible for the positive changes that are described in the various case studies.

For example, chapter 14 looks at how news outlets gave extensive coverage, during the 1980s, to the effort to secure a formal apology and monetary reparations for Japanese Americans who'd been forced into internment camps during World War II. The stories and editorials discussed in the chapter illustrate that the country's journalistic voices steadfastly championed that proposal. But, ultimately, it was Congress and the president who enacted the legislation that gave those wronged Americans at least a portion of the justice they deserved.

When my students read this book in draft form, a few of them were surprised at its consistent emphasis on the news media, pointing out that other forces also were at play in many of the phenomena being described. Those astute young people were onto something.

Chapter 3, on the Fourth Estate's role in putting child labor laws into place during the early twentieth century, for instance, doesn't explore the contributions that church leaders made to that initiative. Likewise, the chapter 7 case study about news outlets alerting readers to the dangers of smoking doesn't have a lot to say about the scientists who conducted the research studies that the journalists later showcased on their front pages.

Fortunately, other scholars have published works that go into detail about those church leaders and those scientists. What no one has previously written, however, is a book that focuses specifically on the news media's role in the phenomena highlighted here. That's the unique perspective that *A Force for Good* offers.

One existing work that shares similarities with this one is *Mightier than the Sword: How the News Media Have Shaped American History*. I wrote that book in 1997 and have created three more editions of it since then. *Mightier than the Sword* chronicles journalism's influence on the American Revolution, the Abolition Movement, the Watergate scandal, and a dozen or so other major events in this nation's history. *A Force for Good*, by contrast, looks at topics that aren't classified as historic milestones but are what can be seen as *cultural phenomena*. These incidents often had enormous impact on society, and yet they don't make the cut when scholars list the landmark moments that have charted this country's evolution.

The final point in this introduction involves the phrase "positive change" in this book's title. I chose those words because they're appealingly vague, which means they gave me a wonderful degree of latitude in the topics I was able to write about. And this freedom helped me create a work that I hope you find readable—perhaps even, on occasion, compelling.

Chapter 1, for example, examines how a spirited young woman feigned mental illness so she would be committed to an insane asylum and could then report on the activities taking place inside that institution. Nellie Bly's daring adventure ultimately led to improvements in how some of the most vulnerable members of society were being treated.

Chapter 16 shines the spotlight on another creative and high-energy woman, this one named Ellen DeGeneres. It documents the important role the news media—including many online venues—played in turning this personable comedian into one of the most admired women in America today. By doing that, the Fourth Estate simultaneously redefined how the public perceives women who love women.

From reforming mental institutions in the 1880s to changing what people of the 2000s think of lesbians—that's just an initial taste of the variety of cultural phenomena that come to life in *A Force for Good*.

Securing Humane Care for the Mentally Ill

In August 1887, the New York Times *ran a two-paragraph news item suggesting that staff members at the Women's Lunatic Asylum may have been mistreating the patients who resided in the city-operated institution. The article prompted the* Times *to write an editorial, four days later, questioning the truth of the claims because "of the mental or moral unsoundness" of the patients who made them. "It would be as much a mistake to assume that there is nothing in these stories," the editorial stated, "as to assume that they are all literally true."[1]*

Two months after the article and editorial appeared, the New York World *published a blockbuster two-part series—the headlines above the pieces read "Behind Asylum Bars" and "Inside the Madhouse"—that went far beyond suggestions. The exposé detailed precisely how patients at the facility were being mistreated, told by a twenty-three-year-old undercover reporter who'd observed the abuse firsthand. Nellie Bly's articles didn't just cause a national sensation but also propelled officials to improve how mentally ill citizens were being treated.*

The journalist who later adopted the pen name Nellie Bly was born Elizabeth Cochran in the tiny town of Cochran's Mill, Pennsylvania, in 1864. Her father was a wealthy mill owner who sent his daughter to private school. During her teenage years, Elizabeth wanted to portray herself as more sophisticated, so she added an "e" to the end of her family name to make it "Cochrane."[2]

In 1885, Elizabeth Cochrane read a column in the *Pittsburgh Dispatch* that characterized the proper role for the American woman. It stated, "Her sphere is defined and located by a single word—home."[3]

Incensed by the column limiting the scope of a woman's life so narrowly, Cochrane fired off a rebuttal. *Dispatch* managing editor George Madden didn't print the letter, but he was so impressed with its author's spunk that he offered her a part-time job writing for his paper.[4]

It was considered unseemly at the time for a woman to work for a newspaper, so editors typically obscured a female writer's identity behind a *nom de plume*. Madden chose to call his newest recruit "Nellie Bly," and, for her first series of articles, she opted to write about the plight of young working women.[5]

ENTERING THE NEWSPAPER WORLD

In those stories, Bly focused on the women's personal lives. In one highly provocative piece, she introduced her readers to the concept of "catching a mash." This involved, Bly explained, a woman meeting a man casually, such as on the streetcar, and then going with him to a neighborhood bar. The couple would next get drunk together, the reporter continued, and the woman would inevitably—in the euphemistic term of the day—"fall."[6]

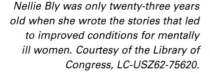

Nellie Bly was only twenty-three years old when she wrote the stories that led to improved conditions for mentally ill women. Courtesy of the Library of Congress, LC-USZ62-75620.

These early stories included spicy direct quotes from Bly's sources. In one piece, the reporter told how she'd asked a young woman, "Why do you risk your reputation in such a way?" This question was followed by the source's own words: "I go home at night tired of labor and longing for something new, anything good or bad to break the monotony of my existence."[7]

Bly's series of eight articles attracted such a strong following that Madden hired her full-time to write stories aimed specifically at female readers. She then covered the city's annual flower show, wrote a profile of the first American woman to own an opera company, and tried her hand at fashion writing by detailing the latest trends in shoes, dresses, and evening wraps.[8]

GROWING RESTLESS

The ambitious Bly quickly tired of writing such stories, however, and repeatedly complained to her editor that she wanted to report on broader topics—and on ones that would get her name on the front page. In early 1886, she quit her job with the *Dispatch*, later writing that she was "too impatient to work along at the usual duties assigned women on newspapers."[9]

A month later, Bly's name was back in the pages of the paper, this time as the author of a series titled "Nellie in Mexico." She'd traveled south of the border to see what it was like to live in a foreign country. She soon discovered that corruption was rampant in Mexico, so she gathered evidence by talking to officials and copying incriminating documents. She then returned to Pittsburgh and wrote hard-hitting articles that exposed various misdeeds, including Mexico City politicians jailing an editor who'd criticized the government.[10]

The series gave Bly her first taste of substantive reporting, and she immediately hungered for more. And so, in the spring of 1887, she left Pittsburgh and headed for the U.S. city with more newspapers than any other. She wrote a note to her coworkers at the *Dispatch*, stating, "I am off for New York. Look out for me."[11]

GOING UNDERCOVER TO DO GOOD

Nellie Bly's plan was to work for the *New York World*. Since Joseph Pulitzer had bought the paper four years earlier, he'd catapulted its circulation from 20,000 to 200,000 by exposing fraud and fighting public evils. Pulitzer's critics denounced the paper as cheap and vulgar because of its multicolumn drawings and dramatic headlines, but the innovative publisher defended the techniques, saying they attracted subscribers who then read and supported his progressive editorials.[12]

It took Bly four months in the big city to talk her way into getting an appointment with the *World*'s managing editor, John Cockerill. The meeting was worth the effort, as she came away with the green light to pursue the story that ultimately would make her a legend in American journalism—and a national celebrity.[13]

Her proposal was to get herself committed to the Women's Lunatic Asylum—the place where the *New York Times* story and editorial had suggested, two months earlier, that staff members might be treating patients improperly. Once inside, she planned to provide a firsthand account of what happened at the institution. It was a harrowing task for a young woman who'd never been anywhere near such a facility, but Bly threw herself full-bore into the challenge.[14]

EXPOSING DOCTORS AS INCOMPETENT

The enterprising reporter was on her own to figure out how to get inside the asylum. Cockerill didn't give her any guidance except that she should use the alias "Nellie Brown," which was the person he'd have released from the institution after ten days.[15]

Bly's first step was to stand in front of a mirror and practice how to look like she was mentally ill. "I remembered all I had read of the doings of crazy people, how first of all they have staring eyes," she later wrote. "And so I opened mine as wide as possible and stared unblinkingly at my own reflection."[16]

Once she perfected her facial expressions and mannerisms, she dressed in old clothes and moved to a boarding house where poor working women lived. She talked incoherently to the other residents, which made them—partly because her large gray eyes appeared so vacant—decide she was mentally ill. By the next morning, her fellow boarders called the police, saying they feared she'd soon become violent. The officers then took Bly before the local magistrate. After chatting with the young woman, who stood only five feet three, a kindly judge announced, "Poor child, she is well dressed and a lady. Her English is perfect, and I would stake everything on her being a good girl. I am positive she is somebody's darling." He then sent her to a doctor.[17]

Then followed a series of four medical exams, each by a different physician employed by the city and each ending with a diagnosis of insanity. "Positively demented," one doctor pronounced. "I consider it a hopeless case. She needs to be put where someone will take care of her." That physician also concluded that Bly was a drug addict, even though she'd never used drugs of any kind. During the sessions, she didn't do anything but stare blankly and speak in a rambling style, repeatedly asking what had happened to the trunks where she kept her clothes.[18]

The last of the medical exams took place after she'd spent a night at Bellevue Hospital, and the doctor asked, "Do you ever hear voices at night?" Nurses at the hospital had gossiped until the wee hours of the morning, so Bly said honestly, "Yes, there is so much talking I cannot sleep." Based on that response, she was committed to the Women's Lunatic Asylum.[19]

EXPOSING PATIENT FOOD AS INEDIBLE

On September 22, 1887, Bly was taken to the facility located on Blackwell's Island (now Roosevelt Island) in the East River. She and several other women were transported to the asylum, which consisted of several stone buildings, on a horse-drawn wagon.[20]

Her first activity was eating supper, which consisted of prunes, buttered bread, and tea. Before Bly even had a chance to sit down at the communal table, however, another patient took all her prunes—the nurses watching over the room saw the theft but didn't do anything about it. "I tried the bread," Bly later wrote in the *World*, "but the butter was so rancid that one could not eat it."[21]

Bly was very hungry by the next morning, so she was sure she'd gulp down anything that was put in front of her. She initially thought it was a good sign when she saw that the bread wasn't buttered this time, but she quickly changed her tune: "I found a spider in my slice of bread, so I did not eat it." This time Bly managed, she wrote, "to choke down the tea."[22]

Other patients told Bly, later in the morning, that lunch was the major meal of the day, which she was glad to hear because she was famished. She immediately ate—in two bites—the single boiled potato she was given. She also tried to eat the chunk of beef offered as the main course, but she thought better of it because the meat was spoiled.[23]

During Bly's ten days in the asylum, she survived mostly on bread and weak tea. The specific detail about the asylum's food that disturbed her the most was what she discovered one day when she and fellow patients were passing by the kitchen where meals were prepared for the doctors and nurses. Bly and the others looked through the window, and, "There we got glimpses of melons and grapes and all kinds of fruits, beautiful white bread and nice meats."[24]

EXPOSING LIVING CONDITIONS AS INHUMANE
Bly began to learn, after arriving at the asylum, that patients were not only forced to eat substandard food but also to endure any number of other appalling circumstances.[25]

One early revelation came when the women were given their weekly bath. Bly was herded into a large room, along with the forty other residents of her ward, that contained a single tub. When the nurses told Bly to take off her clothes, she pleaded for privacy. They told her that if she didn't undress herself, they'd do it for her, "and it would not be gentle." When Bly didn't move, the nurses forcibly stripped her—while the other patients watched.[26]

"One by one they pulled off my clothes," she wrote in her exposé. "At last everything was gone excepting one garment. 'I will not remove it,' I said vehemently, but they took it off." Rather than stand naked in front of the crowd of women, she jumped into the tub.[27]

Bly next wrote, "The water was ice-cold, and I again began to protest." By this point, the nurses were angry that the new patient wasn't cooperating. "Suddenly, I got, one after the other, three buckets of water thrown over my head—ice-cold water, too—into my eyes, my ears, my nose and my mouth. I experienced the sensation of drowning as they dragged me—gasping, shivering and quaking—from the tub."[28]

Now the reporter was standing naked in front of the other women. When she looked around the room for something to dry herself off with, she found only two coarse towels for all the patients to use. Sharing the towels was a major concern to her—as was the fact that one woman after another was placed in the tub without the water being changed—because she spotted large, open sores on several of the patients. So Bly used her own underskirt to dry herself.[29]

After the chaos and humiliation of the bathing ordeal, Bly couldn't wait to get into bed and go to sleep. Her first indication that she wouldn't have a restful night came when two nurses entered the sleeping area. Both women had large keys attached to their belts, and the keys clanked loudly as they struck against each other. "The nurses made no attempt at quietness," Bly wrote. The women reappeared periodically throughout the night, each time waking her and the other patients so none of them slept more than an hour at a time.[30]

EXPOSING TREATMENT AS ABUSIVE

Bly's harshest indictment of the asylum came in describing how the nurses dealt with the patients.[31]

The intrepid reporter was introduced to the uncaring treatment on the first night when patients assembled to go into the dining room for supper. Instead of asking the women to pair off and form a line, the nurses barked orders as if they were prison guards disciplining hardened criminals. "Get in line!" one nurse yelled, followed by another one shouting, "Keep in line!" When Bly described the scene, she added vivid details. "As the orders were issued," she wrote, "a shove and a push were administered, and often a slap on the ears."[32]

As the days passed, Bly came to see that this treatment was mild compared to the abuse the nurses later doled out. One example unfolded after a mentally ill woman named Urena Little-Page arrived on the ward. She was clearly frightened to be in the new setting, so she began to cry. Rather than comfort her, the nurses screamed that she should be quiet. "She grew more hysterical every moment," Bly wrote in the *World*, "until the nurses pounced on her and slapped her face. This made the poor creature cry the more, and so they choked her." The nurses then took Little-Page into another room. "They dragged her out, and I heard her terrified cries hush into smothered ones," Bly wrote. "After several hours' absence, she returned, and I plainly saw the marks of their fingers on her throat for the entire day."[33]

Another instance of physical brutality involved a patient Bly described as "pretty" and "delicate." Mrs. Cotter was sometimes delusional, and one day she thought she saw her husband coming up the walk. She then broke out of the line where she was supposed to stand and ran toward the apparition. The nurses punished Mrs. Cotter by striking her with a broom handle, Bly reported. This caused the woman to become agitated, so the nurses tied her hands and feet together and submerged her entire body in a tub filled with cold water. When Mrs. Cotter still resisted, the nurses beat her head against the floor and pulled clumps of hair out of her scalp—by the roots—until she finally fell into a coma.[34]

Although Bly witnessed numerous instances of physical abuse, she wasn't harmed beyond being forced to sit for entire days on a hard bench, constantly being reprimanded for not sitting up straight and for asking "to walk around to take the stiffness out." She also wrote that the nurses frequently "called me vile and profane names." Bly speculated that she was treated relatively well because she wasn't, in fact, mentally ill and therefore didn't complicate the lives of the nurses, other than when she protested having to undress in front of the other women.[35]

CREATING A NATIONAL SENSATION

Ten days after Bly entered the asylum, an attorney from the *World* had her released. The next Sunday, her article titled "Behind the Asylum Bars" was published, and it was followed a week later by "Inside the Madhouse." Together, the two pieces totaled 30,000 words. They were illustrated with a dozen line drawings, including one of Bly standing in front of a mirror practicing her vacant stare and another of her being examined by a doctor.[36]

New York's other papers printed excerpts from Bly's blockbuster stories, giving credit to the *World*—along with unstinting praise for the reporter's courage and creativity. The *New York Sun* even went so far as to showcase a piece about Bly, headlined "Playing Mad Woman," by placing it on page one.[37]

Dozens of other papers throughout the United States also provided their readers with versions of Bly's shocking exploits—from the *New Haven Evening Register* in Connecticut and the *New Orleans Daily Picayune* in Louisiana to the *Fort Worth Daily Gazette* in Texas and the *Salt Lake Herald* in Utah. The stories emphasized how a comely twenty-three-year-old "girl" had outsmarted a long string of doctors and nurses to reveal the shameful practices taking place inside the asylum.[38]

PROPELLING POSITIVE CHANGE

The *New York World* made it clear that its goal in publishing the series was larger than merely gaining notoriety for itself and its reporter. "The enterprise was projected by The World not as a journalistic triumph alone or in chief," the paper said in an editorial, "but in the interest of humanity and with the object of accomplishing a needed reform." Changes had to be made, the paper continued, to ensure that mentally ill New Yorkers were properly cared for. "The World demands that the system shall be changed."[39]

City politicians, feeling enormous pressure from the *World* and its readers, responded quickly. Less than two weeks after Bly's exposé was published, Mayor Abram Hewitt called for a grand jury to investigate the Women's Lunatic Asylum. Members of that group then convened, calling Bly as their star witness. The jurors also visited the facility to examine the conditions with their own eyes, with Bly serving as their tour guide.[40]

The grand jury next met with officials of the Department of Public Charities and Corrections, the city agency that oversaw the asylum. Recommendations called for reform measures very much in line with correcting the problems Bly had written about in her articles—better food, improved living conditions, and compassionate treatment of patients. Department officials also replaced several nurses with new ones, who were paid higher wages and were monitored more closely. The price tag for these changes was sizeable, but no one objected when the department's budget for the next year was increased by a stunning 57 percent.[41]

City officials credited the reforms to their concern for the well-being of the less fortunate. Observers who'd been following developments during the last several months knew, however, that the changes wouldn't have taken place if it hadn't been for the reporting by a woman who, not so long before, had been described by a judge as a "poor child" and had been diagnosed by a doctor as "positively demented."[42]

Waging War on Urban Slums

Millions of desperately poor immigrants flooded into the United States during the 1880s, with a critical mass of them settling in New York City. This glut of newcomers pushed the already high population density in the city's most poverty-stricken areas to a crisis level, causing an untold number of health and sanitation problems. Many neighborhoods in America's largest metropolis became unfit for human habitation, as they were breeding grounds for diseases such as typhus, cholera, and smallpox—fully half the children were dying before their fifth birthday.

After learning about these tragic realities, journalist Jacob Riis made it his life's work to improve the conditions in the country's urban slums. He published his words and photos in some of the leading publications of the day—most notably the New York Tribune *and* Scribner's *magazine—and in a book. Riis's powerful prose and compelling images didn't merely shock the public but also prompted efforts to clean up the country's worst neighborhoods.*

Jacob August Riis was born in Ribe, Denmark, in 1849. The boy's father, a schoolteacher, taught his son English by having him read the literary works of Charles Dickens.[1]

Young Jake enjoyed writing, but he didn't think he could turn those interests into a livelihood. So he chose to become a carpenter. Once he finished his apprenticeship in that trade, he immigrated to the United States. At age twenty-one, he traveled to New York City in the steerage section of a steamship.[2]

After five unhappy years as a carpenter, Riis set his sights on following his passion by becoming a journalist. He was hired, in 1874, by the editor of the weekly *South Brooklyn News*, to work as a reporter.[3]

This was also a period of change in Riis's personal life. In 1876, he returned briefly to Denmark and married his childhood sweetheart, Elisabeth Giortz. The couple then set up housekeeping in New York.[4]

A year after he married, Riis landed a job with the *New York Tribune*. This was a major boost in his career, as the paper was one of the three largest dailies in the city.[5]

GETTING A CLOSE-UP VIEW OF THE SLUMS

Riis's editor at the *Tribune* assigned him to cover police news. He worked out of an office on the Lower East Side of Manhattan. Most of the people living in the area were poor, and the crime rate was the highest in the entire country.[6]

The young reporter grew intrigued by the world he was writing about, finding the human drama that unfolded in the dark alleys and run-down

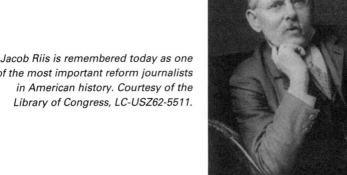

Jacob Riis is remembered today as one of the most important reform journalists in American history. Courtesy of the Library of Congress, LC-USZ62-5511.

apartment buildings to be both fascinating and appalling. He saw countless murder victims in the streets and often visited the nightmarish prison where inmates were confined to unimaginably tight spaces. Riis also spent time in the poorhouses and at the city's mortuaries, where the dead bodies lay side by side in long rows.[7]

In his reporting, Riis consistently went beyond the basic facts of a story, hoping to communicate the misery that was part of daily life in the slums. Typical of his articles was one that began "George Weiss, age forty-six, a German tailor, hanged himself in the rear tenement at No. 217 Avenue A yesterday morning." Riis persuaded the police to let him see the suicide note that Weiss had written and then shared its content with his readers. "I am starving and without means to satisfy my hunger," Riis quoted the dead man as saying. "I am going to kill myself forthwith. Farewell."[8]

Riis devoted many articles to describing the horrendous problems facing the destitute residents of the area he covered. In one piece about a family living in a cramped apartment, he wrote, "The father's hands were crippled from lead poisoning. He had not been able to work for a year." Other members of the family were also suffering: "A contagious disease of the eyes, too long neglected, had made the mother and one of the boys nearly blind. The children cried with hunger." The family subsisted on $2 a week—$48 in today's dollars—that their parish priest gave the mother.[9]

After only a few years of reporting such stories, Riis began to see himself not merely as a detached observer but as someone who had the ability to bring about social change. In other words, he wrote his stories with the goal of inspiring the public to demand that the inhuman living conditions in the tenement buildings—which he often referred to as "dens of death"—be improved.[10]

A decade into working for the *Tribune*, however, he'd grown disappointed that his writing wasn't having the impact he'd hoped it would. Many years later, he looked back on that period and said, "I wrote, but it seemed to make no impression."[11]

PIONEERING AS A PHOTOJOURNALIST

One morning in 1887, Riis was at home reading the paper when he came upon a particular article. The content made him so excited that he yelled out with such exuberance that he startled his wife and four children.[12]

The piece reported that two chemists had discovered a method of taking photos using what the article labeled a "flashlight." Riis instantly recognized that this method, which involved igniting a powder made of magnesium and calcium chlorate, meant that he could take photos in the dark tenements and alleyways in the slums. And those images, he was convinced, would show the dire living conditions with such stark realism that people who saw them would be propelled to undertake the reform efforts he wanted to see.[13]

Riis, who'd never taken photos before, then set out to master the innovative method. At the same time, he also trained himself to use something called "magic lantern" technology. This system allowed a photographic slide to be blown up and projected onto a screen large enough for a large audience to view.[14]

Later that year, Riis began working what amounted to two full-time jobs— one paid, the other not. For the first, he continued to report for the *New York Tribune*; for the second, he took photos of the slums. He used those images as the centerpiece of lectures he gave to educate the public about the need to clean up America's poor urban neighborhoods.[15]

Riis gave his first presentation in January 1888, which several dozen people attended. Communication scholars consider that event a historic one, saying it marked the first time that photography wasn't used to show beauty but to show ugliness.[16]

In the months that followed, Riis gave many more lectures, not just in New York City but also in Connecticut, New Jersey, and upstate New York. Several newspapers reported on the events. The *Long Island Democrat*, for example, praised Riis for giving an "exceedingly interesting" talk. The paper went on to say, "His lecture was well calculated to draw the attention of well disposed persons to the condition of the poor in our great cities."[17]

Among the most memorable of the images Riis showed was one of an elderly couple inside their tenement apartment in Hell's Kitchen—paint was peeling from the walls, and the squalid living space had no windows and no ventilation. Another photo was of the interior of a "two-cent restaurant" filled with homeless men; the caption explained that any patron who bought a round of drinks was allowed to spend the night sleeping in a chair or on a table. One exterior shot was of Bottle Alley; the scene showed a space strewn with bags of garbage, much of it spilling out onto the alleyway.[18]

Frequent subjects of Jacob Riis's photos included elderly men and women who were living their final days under inhumane conditions. Courtesy of the Library of Congress, LC-USZ62-25599.

REACHING A NATIONAL AUDIENCE

By the 1880s, magazines had emerged as America's first truly national journalistic genre, with a handful of monthlies circulating beyond individual cities. And so Riis decided he needed to write an article for one of these publications, thereby sending his message about the "dens of death" to a much larger audience than he was reaching through his *New York Tribune* articles or his lectures.[19]

He succeeded in late 1889 when *Scribner's*, one of the country's leading literary magazines, published his article titled "How the Other Half Lives: Studies Among the Tenements" in its Christmas issue. The piece ran for twenty pages and was illustrated with two dozen of Riis's photos.[20]

In the story, the author introduced his middle- and upper-class readers to a world strikingly different from the one they knew. He took them to the Mulberry Bend neighborhood that consisted of bars, back alleys, opium dens, and decrepit tenements. He also led his readers into the filthy slaughterhouses on Manhattan's Lower West Side and to the impoverished neighborhoods of Hell's Kitchen.[21]

As in the stories he was writing for the *Tribune*, Riis skillfully used his graceful prose style to paint a portrait of human pathos, while at the same time portraying his subjects as highly relatable human beings with feelings, worries, and hopes. Readers were made to see that these people weren't so different from them, except for the misfortunes they'd been dealt.[22]

One poignant section of the *Scribner's* article focused on a family living in what Riis labeled a typical tenement. "The man, his wife, and three small children shivered in one room, through the roof of which the pitiless winds of winter whistled," he wrote. "The room was almost barren of furniture, the parents slept on the floor, the elder children in boxes, and the baby was swung in an old shawl attached to the rafters by cords by way of a hammock. The father, a seaman, had been obliged to give up that calling because he suffered from consumption and was unable to provide either bread or heat for his little ones."[23]

It was critical, Riis argued, that the situation that he was describing be rectified. He said that if nothing were done, the slum conditions would spread and eventually undermine the very foundation of the country. "If New York's 1.6 million poor are not given help quickly," Riis insisted, "revolution and anarchy will spill over into the rest of society."[24]

Among the photos accompanying the article was one showing a woman holding her baby while surrounded by bags containing all her worldly possessions. Riis titled the image "Home of an Italian Ragpicker." Another photo was of a toddler standing in the hallway of a tenement; anyone who saw the image knew the run-down space wasn't somewhere a child should be living. A pair of images on one page showed groups of little boys huddled together on a sidewalk; all of them were homeless, according to the caption.[25]

TURNING TO LONG-FORM JOURNALISM

By early 1890, Riis had been trying for more than a dozen years to spur the public into improving the miserable conditions he'd been illuminating. A few charitable organizations had tried to help, but the need was too vast for them to handle. Riis was convinced that only officials of the New York City government had the power and resources to do the job properly.[26]

This powerful image shows a toddler standing alone in the hallway of a decrepit tenement building. Courtesy of the Library of Congress, LC-USZ62-25663.

The reporter was frustrated by the lack of substantial progress, but he didn't give up. Seeing that neither his news stories, nor his lectures, nor his article in a national magazine had accomplished what he'd hoped, he decided to try writing a book. He secured a contract with a publisher and wrote *How the Other Half Lives.*[27]

The book began with a dramatic manifesto designed to unite readers in a campaign to eliminate slum conditions throughout the country. Riis stated his case succinctly, identifying the causes of urban poverty, the extent of the problem, and how to alleviate it. "Today three-fourths of the urban population lives in the tenements," he wrote. Those overcrowded spaces "generate evil," he said, because they spawn health epidemics, crime, sin, and alcoholism. He contended that the primary cause of the slums was property speculation by greedy landlords, and he argued that the only way to curtail the inflated rents was through stricter legislation.[28]

The remainder of the book consisted mostly of material about tenement dwellers that he'd already published in the *New York Tribune*. These included the story of a young Irish day laborer, his lungs destroyed by poisonous fumes from the sewers where he worked, who went mad and would have killed his entire family if the police hadn't stopped him.[29]

How the Other Half Lives contained forty-four images, including all the photos that had appeared with the *Scribner's* article. Among the scenes highlighted in the book was one titled "Five Cents a Spot"; it showed the interior of a rickety lodging house where fifteen men and women and a week-old baby were spending the night, sleeping not in beds but on the floor. One exterior shot was of the court at 24 Baxter Street, an alleyway that was draped with laundry and that appeared forbidding because the buildings around it were so high that no light reached the area; several children were visible, but Riis said the youngsters were so tired and hungry that they rarely played.[30]

Jacob Riis's photos of the exteriors of tenement buildings illustrated how little light reached the children who spent many hours in the courtyards created by the multistory structures. Courtesy of the Library of Congress, LC-USZ62-19867.

Riis's book became a best seller and a widely praised journalistic work. *The Dial*, a political magazine, wrote, "such a study has never before been made with anything approaching the thoroughness and insight with which Mr. Riis has conducted his investigation." The *Silver Cross* literary magazine directed its subscribers to "read it, and do not omit a line; turn back to the beginning and read it over again."[31]

FINDING A CHAMPION IN TEDDY ROOSEVELT

The single most important of the book's admirers was a man, then in his early thirties, from one of New York's oldest and wealthiest families. Teddy Roosevelt found Riis's portrait of life on the Lower East Side so startling that he promised himself that he'd do whatever he could to improve the situation.[32]

In 1890 when he read *How the Other Half Lives*, Roosevelt didn't see how he could do anything about the suffering he learned about in Riis's book. But five years later when he was appointed police commissioner for the city of New York, the vivid images that the author had created were still firmly embedded in his mind.[33]

So, Roosevelt scheduled a meeting with the journalist on his very first day in office. He assured Riis that he wanted to clean up the city's slums and then asked, "What'll we do?" The author was elated that he'd finally found someone in a position of authority who was willing to take on the formidable task, so he quickly developed a strategy to transform Roosevelt's commitment into concrete action.[34]

The two men's initial step was to take a series of late-night tours of the dark alleys and dilapidated tenements so the new police commissioner, hiding his identity by wearing dark glasses and a hat pulled down over his forehead, could see the problems firsthand. "One might hear of overcrowding in tenements for years," Riis later wrote, "and not grasp the subject as he could by a single midnight inspection."[35]

Roosevelt then saw to it that he was appointed to the Health Board, the city's legislative body that regulated housing and, therefore, had the power to demolish buildings that it found unsuitable for human habitation. Next, Riis created a list of what he considered to be the worst slum areas in New York, and Roosevelt presented that list—without making a single change—to the board, proposing that all the tenements in those neighborhoods be torn down.[36]

With Roosevelt leading the charge, the board voted to condemn and demolish more than twenty of the buildings that Riis had identified, which included many of the tenement houses he'd photographed. The razing process didn't happen quickly, as city officials worked with property owners to create decent housing where residents of the tenements could be relocated.[37]

By 1897, and after intense lobbying by Riis and Roosevelt, clean and well-ventilated apartments for the city's poor were available. The derelict tenement buildings were then leveled. "Directly or indirectly," Riis later wrote, "I had a hand in destroying seven whole blocks of them, as I count it up."[38]

The land that had once been home to the worst of the tenements was turned into a city park, complete with trees, bushes, a large expanse of grass, and a children's playground. On the day it was christened Mulberry Bend Park (today Columbus Park), the final official who spoke at the ceremony made special mention of the journalist who'd been instrumental in the demolition of the buildings. "Without Jacob Riis," the man said, "this park would not be here today."[39]

PROPELLING POSITIVE CHANGE

It hadn't taken Jacob Riis long, back in 1877 when he began reporting for the *New York Tribune*, to decide that he had a higher calling than merely chronicling the news of the day. For the next two decades, he struggled to fulfill his chosen mission to clean up the country's worst urban slums. His wasn't an easy journey, as he repeatedly failed to bring about the change he knew was so desperately needed.

His initial method of choice was newspaper stories that he infused with humanity. Next came public lectures that Riis built around photos that documented the suffering he was determined to end. After that, the reporter wrote a blockbuster article in *Scribner's* magazine. And then, finally, he published a work of long-form journalism that became a best-selling book.

The failures along the way ultimately were dwarfed by the triumphant success that Riis achieved once Teddy Roosevelt read the powerful words and saw the compelling images. After twenty years of effort, the reform-minded journalist succeeded in delivering a fatal body blow to the ramshackle tenement buildings that had destroyed the lives of so many destitute Americans—most of them recent immigrants.

Riis lived another two decades after seeing those "dens of death" come tumbling down, but that event in 1897 remained his most enduring legacy. When the *New York Times* reported Riis's death, the headline above his front-page obituary read "Jacob A. Riis, Reformer, Dead," and the subhead stated, point-blank, "Cleared Mulberry Bend." In the body of that piece, the *Times* described Riis as "a four-square man who worked hard and cheerfully, and fought for high ideals." The paper also quoted Roosevelt—who by that point had served two terms in the White House—as saying that Riis represented "the ideal American."[40]

GIVING VOICE TO YOUNG WORKERS

In March 1906, the *Saturday Evening Post* printed the first of eight articles under the heading "The Cry of the Children." The story detailed the role that youngsters played in producing the cotton and woolen items that Americans wore and used as linens in their homes.[3]

The series, which was highly sentimental in tone, was written by Bessie McGinnis Van Vorst—in keeping with her upper-class sensibilities, she used the byline Mrs. John Van Vorst. She provided a few statistics, such as the fact that one in every four southern mill workers was under the age of sixteen, but her primary goal was to allow the children to speak for themselves.[4]

Van Vorst typically introduced a particular youngster and then entered into a dialogue with him or her. The first story, which began on the magazine's front cover, included a passage about her visit to a mill in Anniston, Alabama:

> As I came along down over the hillside, I met a child holding in her arms another smaller child. Both were covered—their hair, their clothes, their very eyelashes even—with fine flakes of lint, wisps of cotton, fibers of the great web in which the factories imprison their victims.
>
> "Hello," I said, "do you work in the mill?"
>
> "Yes, meaum." The voice was gentle and the manner friendly. She hitched the baby, who had a tendency to slip from her tiny, motherly arms, and showed me one of her fingers done up in a loose, dirty bandage. "I cut my finger right smart," she drawled, "so I'm takin' a day off."
>
> "How old are you?"
>
> "Tweayulve."
>
> "Got any brothers or sisters?"
>
> "I've got *him*." She straightened the piece of lemon stick candy in the baby's mouth and continued, "And I've got one brother in the mill."
>
> "Hold old is he?"
>
> "Tweayulve."
>
> "Twins?" I asked.
>
> She smiled, and shook her head.
>
> "He's tweayulve in the mill, and he's teyun outside."

Van Vorst then explained that many textile mills required workers to be at least twelve years old, so parents often lied to plant managers about the ages of younger children.[5]

In another passage, Van Vorst interviewed a second Anniston youngster. This conversation took place inside a mill:

> His face was wan, his eyes blue. His mouth was full of tobacco which had caught in a dingy crust about his lips. He presented, in his attitude and his gestures, the appearance not of a child, but of a gaunt man shrunk to diminutive size.
>
> Hastily I put the question, "How old are you?"
>
> "Goin' on tweayulve," he responded. "I've been workin' abeaout four years. I come in here when I was seven."
>
> "How many hours do you work a day?"
>
> "From six until six."
>
> Observing also the miniature shoulders that seemed to have been oppressed by some iron hand, I said:
>
> "Don't you get very tired?"
>
> There was a pause which made more marked the honesty of his response.
>
> "Why, I don't never pay much attention whether I get tired or not."[6]

Although most of Van Vorst's sources were children, she also quoted some adults. A teacher had a strong presence in one article.

> Perceiving a crippled boy, I asked how he had lost his arm, and received from the teacher this amazing answer.
>
> "He lost it in the mill. We get lots of them maimed, with one finger, or a hand, or an arm gone. They go in so young to work that they don't know what machinery is, and they try just for fun to see how near they can come to it without 'touching.' It's rather a dangerous game."[7]

Van Vorst mixed the dialogue with a smattering of her personal observations. "Nobody could pass through such spinning-rooms as I have described and not cry out lustily against child labor," she wrote. "These little toilers bear no resemblance to healthy children."[8]

ILLUMINATING THE "NATION'S SHAME"

In July 1906, the *Chicago Tribune* began its nineteen-part series on the bleak realities of child labor. The articles were written in a straightforward news style, and the reporters who wrote them weren't identified.[9]

The *Tribune* didn't pull any punches with its initial story, which ran under the headline "Nation's Shame Is Child Labor." It began, "Two million children in the United States under the age of 16 years are hard at work from early in the morning till late at night when they ought to be at school. One out of every forty of the total youth population of the country is deprived not only of the joys, but also of the natural growing time, of the healthy child."[10]

Later in that opening piece, the paper argued that a major repercussion of child labor was that it denied the nation any chance that its victims could mature into men and women who could contribute to society in a meaningful way. "There are tens of thousands of poor, pitiful, hopeless, dried up little child slaves," the *Tribune* said, "who can by no possibility make otherwise than poor citizens of the republic."[11]

Each of the articles that followed that first one focused on a specific aspect of child labor. A few of the stories were based in Chicago, but most described circumstances in other parts of the country.

A piece out of New York City made it clear that the "health perils" of child labor threatened the general public. "It is women's and children's work, unfortunately, which one finds in the tenements," the article reported, "and they make the things above all others by which disease most readily can be spread." Number one among the products that little girls helped to make were doughnuts. After the dough was prepared from "suspicious materials" and then fried, the *Tribune* reported, the doughnuts were placed on "filthy racks" where they were "exposed to the dust laden breezes down in the most awful places." From there, the items were distributed to bakeries throughout the city.[12]

Another article talked about the physical development of teenagers. This information was directly relevant to the topic of child labor because it was widely believed that working for lengthy periods of time could stunt a child's growth. "Figures derived from the examination of school children," the paper stated, "show that girls and boys during the year between the age of 14 and 15 grow sometimes as much as six inches in height and eighteen pounds in weight." This information prompted the *Tribune* to take an editorial stance, stating that children shouldn't, under any circumstances, be allowed to work full-time until they'd turned fifteen. "They ought to have their growing time."[13]

Several stories focused on specific jobs, such as boys working in glass factories. The main task of the youngsters was to carry white-hot molten glass from a furnace to the area where it was shaped into an object, such as a bowl or pitcher. The boys had to run at breakneck speed—to make sure the glass didn't harden before it could be shaped—while balancing the molten glass on long forks. "The work itself is not flagrant," the *Tribune* pointed out. "It is the pace which kills."[14]

The situation described in another story was even worse. "If there is a dirtier, darker, more unhealthy, more terrible means of employment for boys than the breaker of a coal mine," the piece began, "I have yet to discover it." The little boys' job was to break large chunks of coal into small pieces while also separating the coal from impurities, such as slate and rock. One hazard of the task was that the youngsters weren't allowed to wear gloves because their fingers were more nimble if bare than if covered; this inevitably led to the boys cutting their fingers so often that their hands were covered in blood. The *Tribune* noted that the setting itself was also a hazard: "Working in a cloud of coal dust, breathing it, laboring incessantly for a period of nine hours a day, these boys have about as unpleasant a lot as ever was heard of on this earth."[15]

Several of the *Tribune* pieces reported on the wages children were paid. The top earners were the boys who worked in the glass factories. "They are paid far better than children in other employment," according to the article. Specifically, the children earned $1 for working nine hours a day. Because they worked Monday through Saturday, their weekly salary totaled $6—comparable to $2.83 per hour in today's dollars. Among the most poorly paid workers were the boys who broke up pieces of coal. These youngsters earned only forty cents for a nine-hour day, which meant that for a six-day week they received $2.40—comparable to $1.13 per hour in today's dollars.[16]

CONDEMNING CHILD LABOR AS "EARLY SLAVERY"

The third series began in September 1906 in *Cosmopolitan*, a general-circulation magazine. Edwin Markham, who wrote the articles, was already well known for his 1899 poem "The Man with the Hoe," which depicted the American worker struggling to survive with "the burden of the world" on his back. In the two-part series titled "The Hoe-Man in the Making," Markham wrote about the children of that same careworn laborer.[17]

Cosmopolitan's articles, which were accompanied by woodcuts, were distinguished by the author's poetic prose style. In one of his pieces, for example, Markham called child labor a "cruel and wasteful fungus that destroys the present and threatens the future."[18]

Among his specific targets was the greed that drove employers to "suck the marrow" out of the nation's youth. "Since the era of machinery has added child-labor to the evils of civilization, it has been synonymous with child-robbery," he wrote. "Joy, health, education—the present and the future—are all staked on this iniquity, in the game where Greed plays with loaded dice and the little player loses all." On some occasions, Markham's voice grew fiery, such as when he screamed, "O Dollars, how diabolical are the crimes committed in thy name!"[19]

This tirade against greed led into a section that detailed how child workers were denied the schooling that could have lifted them out of their misery. "Education is vaunted as the supporting granite of our national life," Markham said, followed by the rhetorical question, "Should we not, in merest fair play of assassins, give the child command of the tools of schooling that will give him at least a fighting-chance in the fortunes of the world?" And yet, he continued, child laborers couldn't go to school during the day because they were working and couldn't take classes at night because they were too tired.[20]

One of the poet-turned-journalist's most powerful indictments of child labor was that it turned boys into alcoholics. It wasn't surprising, he wrote, that after long days in the factory, young men were desperate to find some way to relax. "What wonder, then, that utter exhaustion makes boy and man turn to stimulants! Very often the glass-worker degenerates into the confirmed sot, as does many a worker at the other frightful trades of civilization which race him at demonic pressure for a few hours, only to leave him limp and lifeless, so that he turns blindly to the false and futile revival at the ever-convenient corner groggery." Markham supported his accusation with statistics. Of the 185 boys working at an Indiana factory, he reported, all but 10 of them were addicted to alcohol.[21]

Child labor also turned many young workers into criminals, Markham argued. In this instance, the writer described the circumstances experienced by a particular boy. The lad had been sent to work in a factory at the age of ten, but after three years he refused to continue. He was then arrested and sent to jail on charges of vagrancy. "At the end of his term of detention, the little prisoner was sent back to this factory once more. He again refused to work, was turned out of his home, and again arrested for vagrancy." Markham then asked his readers, "Can anyone blame this poor, dulled, duped effigy of a boy for dumbly demanding the rest and play stolen from him at the early slavery?"[22]

Finally, Markham pointed out that child labor was having an intolerable impact on the physical health of youngsters. "Mothers of boys who go into the devouring work of the factory complain that the children are nearly always suffering from colds," he wrote. Among the other ailments that routinely "dog the steps" of child laborers, he said, were tuberculosis, pneumonia, and rheumatism. "The step is short," he wrote, "from the crimson purr of the glass-factory furnace to the chilly walls of the grave."[23]

CAMPAIGNING FOR CHILD LABOR LAWS

The three sets of articles concentrated mainly on reporting details about child labor, but each of them also called for laws to protect the nation's youngsters.

Bessie Van Vorst saved her appeal for protective legislation until her final *Saturday Evening Post* piece. She began her plea by citing statistics that identified precisely when children were injured while working in textile mills. In the previous year, she said, 110 accidents had occurred during the first hour of the workday (from 6 to 7 A.M.), compared to 750 during the last hour (from 5 to 6 P.M.). She followed the numbers with a rhetorical question, "What could be more convincing than the testimony of such figures?" She then added, "We must lift this burden of fatigue from frail young shoulders with laws to shorten their daily labor."[24]

Edwin Markham also placed his call for child labor laws in the last of his *Cosmopolitan* installments. After listing the various diseases that inflicted young factory workers, he challenged his readers by asking, "Is this the 'Christian civilization' we compute in our census returns and brag of in our Bible classes?" Markham then articulated the two specific restrictions that he believed should be the top legislative priorities. First on his list was "No child under fourteen shall be employed in any factory," and second was "No child under sixteen shall be allowed to work at night."[25]

The *Chicago Tribune* was adamant that certain jobs absolutely had to be eliminated. "There are some kinds of child labor which are unpardonable from any point of view," the paper insisted. "This applies particularly to the 'breaker' boys at the coal mines." This work was unacceptable, the paper continued, both because of the brutal nature of the labor and because of the health concerns, including that the boys suffered from bleeding fingers and constantly inhaled coal dust.[26]

As for specific legislation, the *Tribune* offered a three-pronged proposal. "The law should say," the paper stated, "that no child shall be permitted to work unless he is physically fitted for it, unless he has sufficient mental equipment to give him a fair start in life, and unless he has reached the age at which his growing days are comparatively over."[27]

PROPELLING POSITIVE CHANGE

Numerous scholars have credited journalism with playing a decisive role in the enacting of state child labor laws in the immediate wake of the three published series. One major event that made 1907 a banner year for social reformers was the U.S. Congress chartering the National Child Labor Committee. That group then set out, in earnest, to shape legislation tailored to the particular type of work that was prevalent in specific states, such as producing textiles in Alabama and mining coal in Pennsylvania.[28]

Then followed a string of laws enacted in states across the country. In concert with the recommendations the publications had campaigned for, the legislation restricted the ages at which children could be employed—fourteen was generally the agreed-upon minimum for full-time work, and sixteen was widely accepted as the earliest that youths could be assigned to night shifts. Workdays for youngsters also were shortened—ten hours generally established as the maximum, and eight hours the upper limit for unusually dangerous jobs, such as carrying molten glass hot out of furnaces. With regard to breaker boys, some mine owners created safety training programs, while others began replacing the young human workers with machines.[29]

By the end of 1907, fully two-thirds of the states had passed child labor legislation. Most of the holdouts were midwestern states where it was common practice for children to help their parents on family farms. This type of work generally wasn't controversial since it lasted only for short periods of time, such as when crops had to be harvested, and it didn't prevent boys and girls from continuing their educations.[30]

Numerous historians have applauded the role that news outlets played in enacting laws to protect the nation's children. One scholar has stated, "They helped to create a changed attitude toward child labor, and their studies gave impetus to child labor legislation," while another has praised the "strong and effective articles" as having "resulted in new reforms."[31]

Khara Lukanic

Creating a Better Life
for African Americans

In the early years of the twentieth century, 90 percent of African Americans lived in the South, suffering under conditions much like those of a feudal system. Adults weren't allowed to vote or hold public office, and the vast majority of men and women worked from dawn to dusk as field hands. Children weren't given decent educations, many women were forced to have sex with their white overlords, and men were kept in a constant state of fear that they would be lynched.

This despicable situation changed dramatically between 1916 and 1919 when an estimated 500,000 African Americans—out of a total U.S. black population of 10 million—left the South and moved to the much more hospitable North. Primary among the forces propelling what became known as the Great Migration were the opportunities brought about by World War I. But another key factor that historians have identified as having been instrumental in bringing about this historic mass movement was a relentless editorial campaign by the Chicago Defender *newspaper.*

The story of the *Defender* is synonymous with the story of Robert S. Abbott. He was born in Georgia in 1868 to former slaves. An excellent student, he earned a bachelor's degree from Hampton Institute in Virginia and a law degree from Kent College in Chicago. The ambitious man's dream of practicing law ended, however, when Chicago's leading African-American attorney told him his skin was "a little too dark" for him to succeed in the country's white-dominated courtrooms. Abbott then decided to go into journalism.[1]

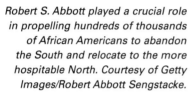

Robert S. Abbott played a crucial role in propelling hundreds of thousands of African Americans to abandon the South and relocate to the more hospitable North. Courtesy of Getty Images/Robert Abbott Sengstacke.

When he founded the *Defender* in 1905, Abbott didn't have enough money to hire anyone to help him, so he became the sole writer, editor, printer, ad salesman, and delivery boy. For the next several years, he struggled to keep the paper afloat, failing to increase his weekly circulation beyond a scant 1,000 copies.[2]

In 1910 and on the brink of abandoning the news business, Abbott changed his tactics. He stopped filling his pages with the sermons and announcements of local births, weddings, and deaths that were the staple of black journalism during the period and replaced them with much spicier fare.[3]

The new *Defender* contained shrill editorials denouncing black oppression and provocative political cartoons ridiculing white leaders. Most noteworthy of all were the front-page banner headlines—many of them printed in bright red ink—such as "White Man Rapes Colored Girl" and "Southern White Gentlemen Burn Race Boy at Stake."[4]

Many people derided Abbott's sensational approach to journalism, but the changes brought the success he'd been hoping for. By 1916, the *Defender* had a circulation of 20,000, and Abbott had several employees working for him.[5]

DEVELOPING AN INNOVATIVE STRATEGY

Buoyed by this success, Abbott set his sights on creating an African-American newspaper that lived up to the motto he placed at the top of page one—"The World's Greatest Weekly."

He focused on two goals. First, he wanted to expand below the Mason-Dixon Line, the area of the country that was home to most African Americans. Second, he set out to show his readers that the *Chicago Defender* was the preeminent voice fighting for Black America.

To circulate in the South, Abbott came up with an idea that was both simple and brilliant—he gave bundles of the hot-off-the-press *Defender* to porters just before they left Chicago, asking the men to deliver the papers to local agents in the hundreds of towns and cities the trains passed through as they headed south. Abbott's paper was soon being distributed in large southern cities, such as Atlanta and New Orleans, as well as in tiny communities, such as Yoakum, Texas, and Palatka, Florida.[6]

To show African Americans that the *Defender* was speaking up for them, Abbott adopted an editorial stance of unapologetic black pride and dignity. He was better able to lambast the white power structure than any other editor in the country because of his unique distribution. If a black editor located in the South had spoken so militantly, racist whites would have killed him. But because Abbott was located in the less racially charged North, he enjoyed a buffer zone of the 1,000 miles that separated Chicago from the Deep South.[7]

So the *Defender* positioned itself as the black publishing voice that wouldn't cower. After a white mob killed a black man in North Carolina, for example, the *Defender* told readers they were fools if they didn't respond to such white injustice with an equal dose of black violence—the headline on the story demanded "Eye for an Eye, Tooth for a Tooth." Other stories carried the same message of defiance, with headlines such as "When the Mob Comes and You Must Die, Take at Least One with You" and "Call the White Fiends to the Door and Shoot Them Down."[8]

The *Defender*'s strident news content convinced southern black readers not only that the World's Greatest Weekly truly was the *defender* of the race but also that the North must be a great place to live if an editor was allowed to print such statements.[9]

BECOMING AN INFLUENTIAL VOICE

By 1918, the *Chicago Defender* was the largest black paper in the country, boasting a circulation of 230,000. Two-thirds of the copies were going outside of Chicago, most of them to the South.[10]

These statistics, though impressive in their own right, don't tell the full story of the paper's influence. That is, illiterate African Americans gathered in southern churches and barbershops to hear the paper read out loud. Because of this communal sharing, historians estimate the *Defender*'s editorial content reached at least 1 million people.[11]

In many southern towns, the *Defender*'s arrival became a weekly community event. A Louisiana woman wrote that the paper was "a God sent blessing to the Race" and that she'd "rather read it than to eat when Saturday comes, it is my hearts [sic] delight," and another reader marveled that "Negroes grab the *Defender* like a hungry mule grabs fodder." In short, the paper achieved a mass appeal far beyond anything Black America had ever known before. "With the exception of the *Bible*," one historian observed, "no publication was more influential among the Negro masses."[12]

And the primary message the paper delivered week after week in thousands of articles and editorials was "Come North!"

VILIFYING THE SOUTH

Racial violence against African Americans was rampant in the South early in the twentieth century. But before the *Chicago Defender* achieved mass circulation, blacks knew about the abuse only through personal observation or word of mouth. Most African Americans didn't know how widespread the injustice was because white southern editors opted not to report on it and southern black editors couldn't report it—if they had, they'd have been killed.[13]

Not so Robert S. Abbott.

He was committed both to documenting the abuse and to showing that this violence was the South's way of ensuring that African Americans remained docile. So he recruited the 2,400 railroad porters who distributed the *Defender* to serve as correspondents, making sure that racist acts taking place throughout the South would find their way into his paper.[14]

For example, a story out of Winona, Texas, reported that a white girl walking near the railroad tracks was so startled when she saw a black boy coming out of the nearby woods that she screamed, and even though the boy didn't

touch or threaten the girl in any way, white townsmen lynched him. Another story reported that a white police officer in Memphis told an African-
American woman walking on the street to stop, but she refused, so the officer
shot her and then left her to bleed to death rather than take her to a hospital,
saying her blood would have ruined the upholstery in his brand-new car. A
third article told of a white mob in Paducah, Kentucky, that first lynched a
young black man accused of raping a white woman—he was never tried—and
then killed a second black youth who spoke in defense of the accused. In none
of the cases was anyone arrested for the deaths.[15]

Abbott also published uncompromising editorials. Typical was one that
began by pointing out that sixteen black men had been lynched in Georgia
during the previous month, the editor calling this "a record even for this state
of backward civilization where violence triumphs over law." Abbott ended the
piece with a statement and a question: "We have this same hideous story every year. Are we ever going to do anything about it?" In another editorial, he
insisted, "Anywhere in God's country is far better than the southland. Come
join the ranks of the free. Cast the yoke from around your neck. See the light.
When you have crossed the Ohio River, breathe the fresh air and say, 'Why
didn't I come before?'"[16]

GLORIFYING THE NORTH

Abbott's depiction of the appalling realities of life in the South stood in glar-
ing contrast to his praise of life in the North. The *Chicago Defender* painted
a vivid portrait of the fulfillment of the black American Dream awaiting
African Americans in Chicago, where the railroad tracks ended. Abbott also
negotiated with the Illinois Central Railroad for reduced fares for groups of
people traveling together, and he printed train schedules free of charge—one-
way from the South to the North.[17]

If any single word captured the reason, according to Abbott, that African
Americans should abandon the South and move to what he referred to as the
"Promised Land," that word was spelled J-O-B-S. "On account of the war
demands, economic conditions in our industrial life afford us an opportunity
to better our condition by leaving the South," Abbott said in one editorial.
In another, he wrote, "The bars are being let down in the industrial world as
never before. We have talked and argued and sat up late at night planning
what we would do if we only had an opportunity. Now that time is here."[18]

He reinforced such editorial statements by publishing thousands of employment ads. Most of them specifically mentioned that "Negroes" were urged to apply, and many said specific skills weren't required—only a willingness to work. The wages included in the ads were highly attractive, too, as farm laborers in the South were paid an average of seventy-five cents a day, but factory workers in the North typically earned between $4 and $10 a day.[19]

In addition to glorifying Chicago as offering plenty of jobs, Abbott also portrayed the city as a wonderland of leisure-time activities. The *Defender* was the first African-American newspaper to publish an entertainment section, which Abbott created so he could dazzle his readers with page after page of articles highlighting the city's social activities. For a southern fieldworker who spent his days looking at the rear end of a mule, opening the *Defender* was like visiting a whole new planet.[20]

Trooper of Company K was praised as one of the first films ever produced by an African-American studio, complete with an "all colored cast" of 350 and featuring heartthrob Noble Johnson as a courageous military hero. "Don't fail to attend the Washington Theater during the run of this wonderful picture," the *Defender* told readers. The film was only one of forty available to African Americans living in Chicago in 1916—forty more than were available anywhere in the South.[21]

Articles also promoted a variety of amenities that African Americans could enjoy during the day, including well-equipped playgrounds and sandy beaches along Lake Michigan. Meanwhile, the "Clubs and Societies" column highlighted "weekly gossip from social, religious, fraternal and other organizations," such as the Royal Art Club and Poinsettia Embroidery Club.[22]

Sports fans could read about the triumphs of black Chicago's "internationally admired" boxing champion, Jack Johnson. They also were repeatedly reminded of games between African-American baseball teams and of the Chicago-based American Giants, the "greatest black sluggers" in the country.[23]

By 1918, a Mississippi man spoke for thousands of African Americans when he wrote that, after reading the *Defender*, he knew Chicago was nothing short of "heaven itself."[24]

CREATING "MIGRATION FEVER"

Abbott believed that southern blacks were more likely to leave their homes if they saw themselves not as isolated individuals but as members of a mass movement. So he told his readers that a widespread exodus was under way. As one scholar put it, Abbott constructed "an atmosphere of hysteria. The more people who left, inspired by the *Defender*, the more who wanted to go, so the migration fed on itself"—all orchestrated by Abbott.[25]

The visionary publisher launched his crusade in the fall of 1916 by spreading a photo across his front page and labeling it, in huge letters, "The Exodus." The image showed the railroad tracks in Savannah, Georgia, covered with hundreds of African Americans waiting to board the next northern-bound train. The caption told readers that "men, tired of being kicked and cursed, are leaving by the thousands."[26]

After that beginning, Abbott kept up the migration mania by blanketing his pages with dozens of stories carrying headlines such as "300 Leave for North," "Farewell, Dixie Land," and "200 Leave for the North." He also published news items crafted to inspire more departures, such as one from Selma, Alabama, that read, "Over 200 left here on the railroad for the north," and another from Waycross, Georgia, that reported, "There are so many leaving here that Waycross will be desolate soon."[27]

The editor also tied specific acts of violence to the escalating pace of the movement. After Eli Persons was burned to death in Memphis, Abbott highlighted the incident with a page-one story that called the murder the "last straw" and told readers that "thousands are leaving Memphis" in the wake of the unjust crime. Abbott used the same technique after an angry mob in Abbeville, South Carolina, killed Anthony Crawford. The headline read, "Lynching of Crawford Causes Thousands to Leave the South," and the story raged, "Respectable people are leaving daily. The cry now is—Go North! where there is some humanity."[28]

RESISTING THE BACKLASH

Abbott was pleased that thousands of African Americans were relocating to the North, but many people in the South weren't happy. In particular, the mass movement angered southern white employers who relied on cheap black labor. Alabama's *Montgomery Advertiser* spoke for many of them when it protested, "Our very solvency is being sucked out from underneath us."[29]

Unwilling to allow the advancement of blacks to disrupt their lives and livelihoods, white southerners fought back. The state of Georgia began requiring anyone who recruited southern laborers to buy a license for the hefty sum of $25,000, and Alabama officials passed a law against "enticing Negroes" to leave the state. Illegal means were also used—northern-bound trains were sidetracked, and African Americans who talked of moving to the North were threatened, beaten, and arrested as vagrants.[30]

The *Chicago Defender* didn't allow the backlash to go unnoticed. A banner headline on page one announced, "Emigration Worries South; Arrests Made to Keep Labor from Going North." The Georgia-based story said, "The whites here are up in arms against the members of the Race leaving the south." The article went on to report that the "bully police" in Savannah were refusing to allow African Americans to enter the local railroad station. "They used their clubs to beat some people bodily," while arresting others merely for carrying suitcases in the vicinity of the station.[31]

Much of the white response was aimed at the *Defender*. A Tennessee law made it illegal to read "any black newspaper from Chicago," and an Arkansas judge issued an injunction making it a crime to distribute the paper. Two black men in Georgia were jailed for thirty days merely for having articles from the *Defender* in their pockets, and at least a dozen African-American men were run out of their respective hometowns for trying to sell copies of the paper. In the most serious incident, a white mob killed two Alabama men who were selling subscriptions to the *Defender*.[32]

Abbott received hundreds of threatening letters, including one from an Arkansas racist who wrote, "You are agitating a proposition through your paper which is causing some of your Burr heads to be killed. You could be of assistance to your people if you would advise them to be real niggers instead of fools."[33]

Unflinching, Abbott countered the backlash with more editorials, including many that appealed to the manhood of his male readers. Typical was one that read, "Every black man, for the sake of his wife and daughters especially, should leave the south where his worth is not appreciated enough to give him the standing of a man."[34]

ENDING THE "COME NORTH!" CAMPAIGN

Abbott and the *Chicago Defender* successfully overcame the anti-migration backlash mounted by the South, and the number of African Americans moving north eventually reached the half million mark.[35]

In 1919, however, Abbott ended his campaign. Two major factors led to this change. First, as the influx of African Americans swelled the population of Chicago and other northern cities, those urban metropolises began to strain at the seams. The rapid increase in population created enormous problems, especially with respect to crime, health, housing, and education.[36]

The even bigger problem came, ironically, with the U.S. victory in World War I. That success meant that millions of white soldiers returned home to find that the jobs they'd left behind had been filled by African Americans. The ebullient young white men were anxious to reaffirm the old caste system; the newly empowered blacks weren't keen on being pushed around.[37]

Racial tension exploded for four days in July 1919. The paper told the story with headlines such as "Riot Sweeps Chicago" and "Gun Battles and Fighting in Streets Keep the City in an Uproar." When the dust settled, fifteen whites and twenty-three blacks lay dead, while 500 others were wounded.[38]

After that tragedy, Abbott stopped portraying Chicago in such positive terms. He continued publishing his paper until his death in 1940, but he wasn't as defiant as he'd been during the height of the Great Migration.[39]

PROPELLING POSITIVE CHANGE

The journalistic crusade the *Chicago Defender* undertook from 1916 to 1919 permanently altered the face of the United States. During a time when African Americans were forced to endure lives of misery, the *Defender* offered readers an alternative. The country's largest black paper inspired hundreds of thousands of men and women to take advantage of a unique opportunity, thereby launching the first major migration in the history of Black America.

And a glorious event it was. The flight out of the South didn't merely mark a demographic shift but also signaled the end of the feudal existence that most African Americans had suffered under, thereby giving them a window on a modern and civilized way of life that was defined by personal and racial freedom.

For three remarkable years, the "World's Greatest Weekly" committed itself to advancing the exodus. The paper provided dramatic evidence of the inhumane treatment southern blacks were experiencing and showcased the employment and leisure-time activities awaiting African Americans in Chicago. In addition, the paper created an infectious "migration fever" that spread through virtually every city, town, and farming community in the South. The men and women who heeded Abbott's call created new urban communities in the North that have remained firmly in place—and have continued to grow both in size and impact—since that time.[40]

Historian Carl Sandburg was among the many cultural observers who credited the paper with sparking the migration, writing, "The *Defender*, more than any other one agency, was the big cause of the 'northern fever' and the big exodus from the South." Other scholars echoed Sandburg's assessment. One wrote that "Chicago's image as a northern mecca can be attributed mainly to the *Chicago Defender*," and another said, "The *Defender* became one of the most potent factors in changing the character and pattern of race relations in the United States."[41]

Closing Down the Original Ponzi Scheme

In December 1919, a Boston businessman named Charles Ponzi founded a company that guaranteed clients they'd double their financial investments in ninety days. Ponzi then proceeded, during the next six months, to take $15 million—comparable to $175 million today—from thousands of men and women who fell for his get-rich-quick promises.

In July 1920, the Boston Post *accused Ponzi of multiple counts of fraud. The newspaper's exposé caused throngs of the errant financier's victims to realize they'd thrown their money away. It's not known exactly how many other people the paper kept from being bilked, but there's no question that the number was substantial.*

Carlo Ponzi was born in Lugo, Italy, in 1882. The only son of a mailman, he was an excellent student and, after completing public education, enrolled at the University of Rome. He soon grew restless with the slow pace of academic life, however, so he dropped out of school and moved to the United States to make his fortune. He arrived in Boston in 1903 with $2.50 in his pocket.[1]

After learning English, Ponzi spent the next four years working as a dishwasher, grocery clerk, and waiter in various cities. He got a big boost in Montreal, where he landed a job as a bank teller and then advanced, in short order, to the position of manager. By this point, he'd Americanized his first name to Charles.[2]

Life took a downward turn for Ponzi in 1908. He'd grown impatient that he wasn't yet wealthy, so he forged the signature of a businessman on a check he wrote to himself. Ponzi was caught, convicted of fraud, and spent two and a half years in prison.[3]

He next moved to Atlanta and broke the law for a second time. In this instance, he tried to make money by illegally smuggling Italian immigrants across the border without proper documents. He was again convicted of fraud and jailed for two more years.[4]

After serving his time, Ponzi returned to Boston and worked as a clerk for a company that dealt in international trade. His personal life improved markedly when he fell in love with Rose Gnecco, the daughter of a success-ful merchant. Soon after the couple married in 1918, Ponzi quit his job and founded his own import-export business.[5]

His new enterprise didn't attract many clients, though, so Ponzi came up with another one. This time, his plan was to launch a publication focused on foreign trade. He had in mind that *Trader's Guide* would provide informa-tion to people hoping to start international businesses, but his initiative again failed to take off. So he had to close shop.[6]

Among the accessories that helped create Charles Ponzi's dapper appearance were a diamond stickpin and silver-topped walking stick. Copyright Bettmann/Corbis/AP Images.

Soon after *Trader's Guide* folded in 1919, Ponzi received a letter from a man in Madrid who asked to be sent a copy of the publication—he didn't know it had gone out of business. To pay the postage, the Spaniard enclosed something called an international reply coupon, which functioned much like today's stamped, self-addressed envelope.[7]

CHARLES PONZI HAS A CREATIVE IDEA

Ponzi had always been an unusually curious fellow, and at this point the topic that piqued his interest was the reply coupon. The item was part of an obscure process that sixty countries had created a dozen years earlier. Specifically, the coupon was created to help authors who were trying to have their work published in a foreign country.[8]

If a writer living in Spain, for example, wanted to submit a manuscript to a publishing house in the United States and was asked, when sending the material, to enclose return postage, the author bought an international reply coupon. He paid for the coupon in Spanish pesetas and sent it with the manuscript. When the coupon arrived in America, the publishing house exchanged the coupon for stamps equal in value to those the author had bought, but in U.S. dollars.[9]

This process worked efficiently until World War I, when currencies in some European countries plummeted in value. By 1919, when Ponzi learned about the coupons, the various governments hadn't yet recalibrated their postal exchange regulations to reflect the new worth of their currencies.[10]

And so, the coupon that Ponzi received from the Spaniard had a much higher value when it arrived in Boston than when it had been purchased in Madrid. After Ponzi exchanged the coupon for U.S. stamps and then sold those stamps for cash, he made a profit of a little more than 10 percent.[11]

Ponzi saw this exchange process as offering the potential, if pursued on a large scale, of making a hefty profit. Specifically, he believed that if the coupons were bought in his native Italy, where the lira had suffered much more severely than the Spanish peseta, the profits would be enormous. By Ponzi's calculations, coupons that could be bought in Rome for $1 were worth $3.30 in Boston—creating a payoff of an astounding 230 percent.[12]

In December 1919, Ponzi established the Securities Exchange Company in hopes of finally making his fortune. For the capital he needed to start his business, he pawned three diamond rings that belonged to his wife. Rose Ponzi supported her husband's new venture, but she didn't fully understand it.[13]

CHARLES PONZI GETS RICH QUICK

Ponzi's next goal, now that he had an idea and a company, was to attract investors.

He wasn't handsome and didn't have an imposing physique—he stood a mere five feet two and weighed only 130 pounds. But he was very excited about his new business, speaking with so much energy that his fervor became infectious.[14]

Besides being a great salesman, Ponzi also had something great to sell—at least that's what he told people. That is, rather than providing potential clients with a detailed explanation of how the international reply coupons would reap a handsome profit, he synthesized the process down to the simple statement: invest in my company, and you'll double your money in ninety days.[15]

The first man to take Ponzi up on his offer was a grocer named Ettore Giberti, who became so passionate about the profits he saw in his future that, within a few days, he'd persuaded eighteen other people to pony up money of their own. And so, by the end of January 1920, investors had given Ponzi $1,770.[16]

February was even more successful, as word of the profits that Ponzi was promising spread like wildfire. In its second full month, his company recorded $5,290 in new revenue. March brought bigger profits still, with investments that month totaling almost $25,000.[17]

Because of the explosion in revenue coming his way, Ponzi didn't have any problem paying Giberti and the other early investors, at the end of ninety days, the payoffs he'd promised them. That is, the $1,770 that he received in January required an outlay of $3,540 to investors at the end of April, a figure that was more than covered by the $142,000 in new revenue that Ponzi took in that month.[18]

As the diminutive financier handed out the profits in those first months, however, the information he didn't share with his investors was that he'd run into two serious snags in the idea that was driving his company. One problem was that Ponzi hadn't been able to find anyone in Italy who was willing to buy international reply coupons for him in the quantities he wanted. The second big concern was that he'd learned there weren't enough coupons available to sustain the scale of the business he'd set into motion.[19]

But Ponzi was caught up in the excitement of finding so many investors and receiving so much revenue. So instead of putting the brakes on his business, he devoted his time to recruiting more clients and spending the extraordinary profits that came his way after he paid out the promised returns on the initial investments.[20]

For a thirty-eight-year-old man who'd struggled for years to succeed, the exhilaration of finally having hit the jackpot was too intoxicating for Ponzi to resist. And the money just kept rolling in—$440,000 in May, $2.5 million in June.[21]

THE *BOSTON POST* GIVES CHARLES PONZI A BOOST

In the summer of 1920, the publisher of Boston's largest newspaper overheard some of his pressmen talking excitedly about investing in a new business. Richard Grozier thought the story was an interesting one, so he assigned a reporter to write an article about it. When the story was finished, an editor plastered the piece across the *Boston Post*'s front page.[22]

"Doubles the Money Within Three Months" screamed the headline. The article provided readers with lots of details, all of them complimentary. The first sentence read, "A proposition fathered by Charles Ponzi, as head of the Securities Exchange Company at 27 School Street, where one may get 100 per cent profit in 90 days, on any amount invested, is causing interest throughout Boston."[23]

Later sections of the piece chronicled the popularity of the company: "The proposition has been in operation for nine or ten months, rolling up great wealth for the man behind it and rolling up much money for the thousands of men and women who are tumbling over themselves to entrust him with their money." The story reported that Ponzi was now worth $8.5 million.[24]

Quotes from Ponzi about his humble beginnings were also included in the article, though he'd chosen not to tell the reporter about his criminal record.[25]

CHARLES PONZI GETS RICHER STILL

Being the subject of a highly flattering story on the front page of Boston's dominant newspaper transformed Ponzi—overnight—into a local celebrity.[26]

Two filmmakers arrived at Charles and Rose Ponzi's twelve-room mansion in the afternoon of the day that the article appeared. The men were sure the public would clamor to see newsreel footage of the "financial wizard" and his wife. The couple agreed to pose for the men, dressing up in their Sunday best and ambling back and forth in front of their gracious home.[27]

By the time Ponzi got to his office, the line of would-be investors waiting at the front door measured three blocks long. Indeed, many of the men waved wads of money they were eager to turn over to Ponzi.[28]

The prosperous financier arrived in a custom-built limousine. When his chauffeur opened the door, the boss stepped out of the luxury vehicle wearing one of the natty outfits that had become his signature—white flannel trousers and a bright blue suit jacket, with his trademark diamond stickpin glinting from the center of his necktie and a silver-topped walking stick tucked under his arm. The crowd greeted him with exuberant cheers and applause.[29]

The *Boston Post* had published its story on July 24, which meant new investors only had seven days before the end of the month to add their names to the list of Ponzi's clients, and yet the surge still resulted in a huge jump in the money coming into the business. That total soared to $6.5 million for July—more than twice the figure for June.[30]

Telephone calls and telegrams flooded into Ponzi's office from men begging to work with him. He took several of the admirers up on their offers and had them set up offices in numerous cities along the East Coast. By the end of July, Ponzi was boasting of branches in New York City and throughout New England.[31]

THE *BOSTON POST* EXPOSES THE "PONZI SCHEME"

The publisher who'd directed his reporter to write "Doubles the Money Within Three Months" had misgivings about the story once he saw it in print. For Richard Grozier, after reading the article in his paper, sensed that Ponzi's business was too good to be true. He then ordered his reporting staff to look deeper into Ponzi's financial goings-on.[32]

And so, a week after that first article had portrayed Ponzi as a genius, another one on the *Boston Post*'s front page accused him of being a criminal who was swindling unsuspecting investors out of their money. "Declares Ponzi Is Now Hopelessly Insolvent," screeched the headline.[33]

"After this edition of the Boston Post is on the street," the story began, "there will be no further mystery about Charles Ponzi. He is unbalanced on one subject—his financial operations. He thinks he is worth millions. He is, in fact, hopelessly insolvent. Nobody will deny it after reading this story."[34]

Grozier had paid William McMasters, a public relations expert hired by Ponzi, $5,000 to write the exposé that laid out in blunt terms exactly what the fast-talking financier was doing. "If any money is paid out today at Ponzi's office," the story said, "that money will be paid out at the expense of those who are foolish enough to hold Ponzi's notes."[35]

McMasters's article went on to say that Ponzi wasn't earning any money whatsoever from redeeming international reply coupons but was relying solely on the money from recent investors to pay the profits owed to early ones. The writer further explained that this system would work only as long as the number of investors continued to mushroom and, therefore, it was impossible for the "Ponzi scheme" to be sustained in the long run.[36]

The next day's paper reported that several thousand recent investors, after reading what McMasters had to say, had gone to the Securities Exchange Company's office and asked for their money back, forgoing the profits they'd hoped to make. The paper said Ponzi had met the demands by refunding $3 million.[37]

Up to this point, the *Post* had been the only paper reporting on Ponzi. But the McMasters accusations combined with the throngs of people lining up for refunds now propelled the financier's name into the headlines of the city's other papers. A page-one story in the *Boston Globe* announced, "All Demands Met by Ponzi," and a similar one in the *Boston American* reported, "Hundreds Paid by Ponzi."[38]

THE *BOSTON POST* REVEALS CHARLES PONZI'S CRIMINAL PAST

Even after the *Boston Post* reported that Ponzi's moneymaking scheme was fatally flawed, the errant financier continued to attract throngs of followers. These admirers included the small number of people who'd received big payoffs from their investments, but most were would-be investors who still believed Ponzi's promises would make them rich.[39]

After Richard Grozier printed the McMasters exposé, the publisher received dozens of letters from readers who railed against the *Post*'s article.

Many of the critics accused the paper of being either too conservative or too shortsighted to embrace a visionary plan as clever as Ponzi's. Grozier published several of these letters in the *Post*.[40]

Ponzi also pushed back against the paper. He hired a New York–based legal firm to represent him. These attorneys then went to Grozier's office and threatened to sue him for libel and character assassination.[41]

Grozier also benefited from the exposé, however, when a reader who was familiar with Ponzi's activities before coming to Boston contacted the publisher and told him that the charismatic charlatan had spent time in a Montreal prison some years earlier. Grozier then sent a reporter to Canada to investigate those charges.[42]

Nine days after delivering its first body blow to the swindler, the *Post* hit him again. "Canadian 'Ponsi' Served Jail Term" was the headline that appeared above the resulting story. The first paragraph read, "Charles Ponzi, Boston's financial wizard, and Charles Ponsi, a convicted forger who spent two and a half years behind bars of a Canadian jail, were pronounced one in the same today."[43]

The public now knew, thanks to the *Post*, that Ponzi wasn't new to criminal activity but had been convicted of fraud a dozen years earlier. This knowledge prompted thousands more of the investors to demand their money back. The stories also had made federal and state officials aware of Ponzi's past life, prompting them to look more closely at his financial activity.[44]

CHARLES PONZI IS DISGRACED

By the middle of August 1920, the Ponzi scandal had grown from a local story to a national one, because newspapers all over the country were now reporting on the wayward businessman's meteoric rise and fall.

Both the *Philadelphia Inquirer* and *San Francisco Chronicle*, for example, put stories on their front pages when federal authorities arrested Ponzi on multiple counts of fraud. Likewise, the *Wall Street Journal* reported it when experts announced that people who'd entrusted their money to Ponzi would get back only thirty cents for every dollar they'd invested.[45]

Papers continued to publish stories about Ponzi's trial, which ended when he was found guilty on federal fraud charges and sentenced to five years in prison. He was still front-page news after he was released and then convicted on state fraud charges, earning him another seven years behind bars. Ponzi returned to page one yet again in 1934 when U.S. officials had him deported back to Italy.[46]

The country's leading newspapers also thought their readers would be interested in how life turned out for Rose Ponzi. Her name appeared in the headlines when her personal car was confiscated, again when she was evicted from the Ponzi mansion because it was sold at auction, and finally when— once her husband was deported—she divorced him.[47]

When Charles Ponzi died in a hospital charity ward in 1949, of a blood clot on his brain, the *New York Times* relegated the news to a story on page 56.[48]

THE *BOSTON POST* WINS ACCOLADES

Anyone who'd followed the events that had unfolded in Boston during the second half of 1920 knew the *Boston Post* had been instrumental in closing down the Ponzi scheme.[49]

Those observers also recognized that the paper's exposé had kept would-be investors from losing millions of dollars. While it's impossible to calculate exactly how many people benefited from the *Post*'s warning, there's no question that the figure was large. Ponzi's clients had catapulted from 110 in March to 20,000 in July, and the number clearly would have continued to rise if the *Post* hadn't reported on the impostor's previous criminal activity.[50]

The *Boston Post*'s achievements were recognized in May 1921 when the paper received the highest honor in American journalism: the Pulitzer Prize gold medal for public service.[51]

News coverage of the award publicly revealed, for the first time, some of the behind-the-scenes obstacles that Richard Grozier had faced in pursuing the Ponzi story. It was reported that the publisher had been besieged, when the *Post* first began reporting on Ponzi's wrongdoing, with hundreds of letters from the financier's defenders. Stories about the award also told how Ponzi's lawyers had repeatedly threatened to sue Grozier. The publisher had stood firm, the articles stated, and had made sure that the truth was reported, thereby serving his readers and doing public good.[52]

Assuring Citizens That "G-Men" Were Keeping Them Safe

In the late 1920s and early 1930s, many citizens of the United States were trembling with fear. Armed robberies of banks and businesses were out of control, and both kidnappings and killings were rampant. A sizeable number of Americans viewed the streets of their towns and cities as no safer than wartime battlefields.

But then, during the mid-1930s, the front pages of the nation's leading newspapers provided readers with reassuring words. Journalistic voices from coast to coast reported that law-abiding citizens no longer had to be afraid to leave their homes, as notorious criminals—one by one—were being either captured or killed by an army of fearless, clean-living, and professionally trained federal agents known as "G-men."

Historians point to 1920s crime figures from various American cities to support their observation that breaking the law had risen to epidemic proportions. During the decade, those scholars note, crimes such as bank and drugstore holdups had jumped from seventeen to 965 a year in Dallas and from nine to 836 in Saginaw, Michigan.[1]

One factor that contributed to the rise in crime was that local law enforcement officials weren't keeping up with the advancing technology. Faster and more powerful weapons, such as the Thompson submachine gun, which fired 800 bullets a minute, allowed bank robbers to outgun small-town police officers armed with nothing but pistols and single-shot rifles. Likewise, gangsters driving late-model vehicles with powerful V-8 engines escaped from the crime scene while the county sheriff was still hand-cranking his Model A.[2]

By 1931, residents of New York City were so frustrated by the failure of law enforcement officials to provide adequate protection that 20,000 of them gathered in Madison Square Garden to organize private citizen groups charged with reducing crime. A year later, crime had become so pervasive nationwide that the Boys Scouts of America stepped forward with a plan to replace police officers with Eagle Scouts. An exasperated national scout leader announced, "We are determined to break the grip that manifold types of lawlessness seem to have taken on our nation."[3]

When the national crime wave was at its peak, headlines that proliferated on the front pages of American newspapers seemed chillingly similar, whether the crimes were being reported in Florida's *Miami Herald*—"Two Women Are Shot in Front of Home"—or across the country in California's *Sacramento Union*—"Bank Robbers Shoot Woman, Kidnap Mate."[4]

The papers didn't, however, support all actions. In 1932 when gangster Al Capone was convicted of income tax evasion and sentenced to ten years in prison, many papers weren't impressed. The *Washington Star* wrote, "No matter how satisfactory will be the eventual incarceration of Capone in a federal prison for the failure to make an income tax return as a technical means to the end of getting him in jail, there will remain the sense that the law has failed."[5]

"MACHINE GUN" KELLY CREATES THE "G-MAN"

The event that marked the turning point in what American newspapers reported about crime came in the fall of 1933.

After George "Machine Gun" Kelly robbed a number of midwestern banks, he moved into the national spotlight when he kidnapped Charles F. Urschel, a wealthy Oklahoma City oilman in July 1933. The millionaire's family paid the $200,000 ransom that Kelly demanded, and Urschel was released unharmed.[6]

Agents from the U.S. Department of Justice's Bureau of Investigation—the word "Federal" would be added to the name in 1935—then conducted a series of interviews with Urschel, who'd been blindfolded throughout his ordeal. Questions from agents included minutiae such as what Urschel had heard, smelled, and tasted during the nine days he'd been held prisoner.[7]

In response to the intense questioning, Urschel told the agents how long his kidnappers had driven after taking him from his home. He also recalled that each day, at exactly 9:45 A.M. and 5:45 P.M., he'd heard an airplane flying over the house where he'd been held. The agents used the information to estimate that the criminals' hideout was about 600 miles from Oklahoma City. They then checked airline flight schedules and pinpointed the exact location of the house in Tennessee where the kidnappers had kept Urschel.[8]

The agents soon surrounded and raided that residence, capturing Kelly and several of his accomplices. A few days after that, the agents recovered most of the ransom money. Newspapers around the country turned Kelly's arrest into page-one banner headlines. The *Atlanta Constitution* screamed, "Gunman Kelly Trapped in Hideaway," and the *Los Angeles Times* went with "Raid Traps Desperado."[9]

The papers also told their readers exactly how the agents had found Kelly and his fellow criminals, as well as how they'd captured him. Among the quotes the papers printed were the words the gangster had yelled when he first saw the men, "Don't shoot, G-men! Don't shoot!" After those stories appeared on front pages throughout the country, the term "G-men" that previously had applied to all "government men" became synonymous with agents working for the Bureau of Investigation.[10]

More headlines followed when Kelly and his wife were convicted and sentenced to life in prison. Several of the men who'd worked with the gangster were also placed behind bars.[11]

G-MEN TRACK DOWN "BONNIE AND CLYDE"

The next major milestone in American journalism's campaign to tell the public that federal agents were making the country a safer place to live came in May 1934.

Clyde Barrow had committed his first crime at age sixteen when he stole a car in his native Texas. His lawless behavior increased after he hooked up with Bonnie Parker in 1930. She catapulted the couple into celebrity status because photos of the beautiful young woman wielding a pistol while smoking a cigar were so novel that newspapers placed them on page one.[12]

The nature of the couple's crimes added to the story. "Bonnie and Clyde," as they became known, focused mostly on robbing small banks and businesses. But in 1932 they added murder to their list of crimes when they killed a gas station attendant who refused to hand over the money they demanded. More notoriety came when they gunned down a sheriff, a prison guard, and two highway patrolmen. By early 1934, the outlaw couple and their gang were wanted for the murders of more than twenty people.[13]

Federal agents started tracking them because of the geographic scope of Barrow and Parker's crimes. Their initial robberies and murders were in Texas, but law enforcement officials from that state weren't, at the time, allowed to pursue criminals who crossed state lines. So when the couple raced their car into Oklahoma or Arkansas, local officers had to give up the chase.[14]

Not so G-men. Federal agents began following "Bonnie and Clyde" in late 1932 when the couple stole a car in Oklahoma and later abandoned it in Michigan.[15]

The agents again used their attention to detail—as they had in tracking down "Machine Gun" Kelly—to their advantage. Among the items the G-men recovered from the abandoned car was a prescription bottle that Barrow had left in the vehicle. The agents used the information on the bottle's label to locate the drugstore where the outlaw had gotten the medicine, hoping he'd return to the same pharmacist when he needed a refill.[16]

When the nation's papers reported the couple's fiery death on a gravel road in rural Louisiana, they described exactly how agents in Washington, D.C., had located the outlaws. There wasn't any question that those details would become widely known, as the eye-popping headlines above the stories guaranteed the public would read every word—"Clyde Barrow and Bonnie Parker Trapped and Killed" in the *Dallas Morning News*, "Texas Bad Man and His Gun Girl Slain by Posse" in the *Chicago Tribune*.[17]

JOHN DILLINGER GUNNED DOWN ON A CITY STREET

Less than two months after reporting that Barrow and Parker had been killed, the titans of American journalism told the public about another notorious criminal who'd been gunned down by G-men—this time on a street in downtown Chicago.

John Dillinger had robbed his first bank in 1933 and soon after that had killed a sheriff. For the next year, he and his gang terrorized the Midwest by robbing two dozen banks and stealing hundreds of firearms from local police stations.[18]

In March 1934, Dillinger made the mistake that ultimately cost him his life when he stole a police car in Indiana and headed for Chicago. By driving the vehicle across the Illinois state line, the outlaw violated a federal law, thereby prompting the G-men to begin pursing him.[19]

Because the gangster was, by this point, wanted for murdering ten men, Bureau of Investigation director J. Edgar Hoover designated him "America's Public Enemy No. 1." Hoover also persuaded Congress to offer a $25,000 reward—equal to $437,000 today—to anyone who provided information leading to Dillinger's arrest.[20]

Hoover took both of these actions because of their potential to generate publicity. That is, he knew the unique label and hefty reward would prompt the country's papers to place stories about the hunt for Dillinger on their front pages. And he was absolutely right—papers all over the country did exactly what he'd hoped, with editors crafting attention-grabbing headlines such as "New Dillinger Hunt On" in the *Chicago Tribune* and "20,000 Police on Dillinger's Trail" in the *Washington Post*.[21]

The lawman's tactics paid off in July 1934 when a prostitute contacted federal agents and volunteered to help capture Dillinger. Ana Cumpanas, a native of Romania, agreed to work with the G-men in exchange for the reward and a promise that she wouldn't be deported.[22]

In this 1935 photo, J. Edgar Hoover demonstrates how to fire a machine gun while Detroit Tigers manager Mickey Cochrane looks on. AP Photo.

Cumpanas then persuaded Dillinger to take her to see the film *Manhattan Melodrama* on a particular night. The gangster often had eluded police by wearing disguises, so Cumpanas told the agents they'd be able to spot him this time because she'd be walking beside him wearing a bright red dress. When she and Dillinger exited the Biograph Theater, three agents confronted him and, after he pulled out a pistol, gunned him down.[23]

The next morning, every major paper in the country exploded with banner headlines, such as "Dillinger Killed by U.S. Agents" in the *Minneapolis Tribune* and "John Dillinger Shot to Death by Federal Marksmen" in the *New Orleans Times-Picayune*. The stories gave the G-men full credit for ending the gangster's crime spree, with the *Times-Picayune* story, for example, beginning, "The government got John Dillinger tonight, just as it promised to do."[24]

J. EDGAR HOOVER GLORIFIED AS AMERICA'S NO. 1 G-MAN

Several news outlets, after Dillinger's death, took a giant step beyond reporting on individual criminals being captured or killed by publishing lengthy profiles of the director of the Bureau of Investigation. All the stories were highly flattering, highlighting their subject's single-minded devotion to waging a war against crime.

The *Washington Post* was Hoover's hometown paper, so its story focused on his personal life. "At night, John Edgar Hoover goes home to the little frame house on Seward Square where he was born 39 years ago and where he still lives with his aged mother," the *Post* wrote. "It is furnished largely with antiques collected in nearby Virginia and Maryland, for collecting antique furniture is his hobby."[25]

Other details in the *Post*'s Sunday magazine story told how Hoover had earned a law degree and then had taken a job with the Justice Department. The article continued by saying how "America's No. 1 criminal catcher" had such a strong work ethic that he was promoted, at the age of twenty-four, to director of the department's Bureau of Investigation.[26]

"Mr. Hoover rose from a government clerk to become the nemesis of the nation's criminals," the *Post* wrote, and now as the "super-investigator" in charge of 500 agents was "drawing the strings that trap criminals from coast to coast."[27]

The *New York Times*, in its profile, concentrated on how both the bureau's director and the agents working under him were all men of the highest character. Before Hoover took charge, the *Times* reported, G-men had been given their jobs as payoffs for working on the campaigns of politicians they'd helped get elected.[28]

"He learned that some of his men had shady records," the paper said. "The clean sweep he made of questionable personnel brought a storm of protest from persons in high places, but he stood by his guns and continued to blast away until only agents of unassailable integrity and demonstrated ability remained."[29]

The *Times* praised Hoover not only for being honest, hardworking, and imaginative but also for advocating effectively for more money for the agency. He'd used the bureau's successes against criminals, the paper reported, to persuade Congress to increase his budget substantially, allowing him to buy advanced weapons and late-model cars.[30]

Among the Hoover profiles published in national magazines was one that appeared in *Time* in 1935. The country's largest-circulation news weekly splashed a photo of the director across its cover and devoted five pages inside to praising him as a role model without peer. "Hoover has built in the past decades one of the finest, most efficient law enforcement agencies the world has ever known," the article stated.[31]

Time didn't stop with superlatives, however, as it backed up its laudatory comments about Hoover with plenty of statistics documenting the effectiveness of the operation he headed. "Last year, the Bureau obtained convictions in 94% of all cases it took to court," the magazine reported. "Since the Bureau entered the national bank robbery field, robberies have declined from 16 per month to four per month."[32]

J. EDGAR HOOVER BECOMES THE FBI'S NO. 1 PR MAN

Although it wasn't widely known at the time, the Bureau of Investigation's director played an active role in the public's positive feelings about his agency—and about Hoover himself. In his book titled *G-Men: Hoover's FBI in the American Popular Culture*, Richard Powers said, "Hoover worked to make sure news stories reflected the bureau's public relations line."[33]

America's No. 1 G-man was, from as early as 1929, conscious of the importance of his agency being portrayed in a favorable light. So whenever a journalist requested information about the bureau, the director met face-to-face with the reporter and then personally put together whatever documents and photos were needed. He also voluntarily provided a narrative of any relevant cases that had been solved, hoping this would lead to the bureau coming across as effective.[34]

By 1934, Hoover's public relations efforts were leading some reporters to cross the line into unethical behavior, as they were taking the director up on his offer to help them write their stories. The *New York Times* profile that portrayed Hoover as a man of the highest possible character was an example of such a source-reporter partnership. Similar stories that were written either partially or entirely by Hoover appeared in the *Washington Star* and *Milwaukee Journal*.[35]

Another way Hoover ensured that reporters published flattering stories about the bureau was by playing favorites. As a government employee, he was obligated to provide all journalists with information about his tax-supported agency and its work. In fact, though, Hoover saw to it that only the reporters who wrote positive articles were given the concrete details about a case that made their stories come to life. In addition, according to one scholar, "Hoover learned which reporters could be trusted, and he gave these friends of the bureau the inside track on breaking news, a priceless asset for Washington reporters."[36]

MORE CRIMINALS GUNNED DOWN

More high-profile outlaws continued to fall victim to the Bureau of Investigation's efforts. Newspapers spotlighted each of the successes, consistently placing the words "Federal Agents" or "U.S. Agents" in their front-page headlines.

In October 1934, the papers told of Charles Arthur "Pretty Boy" Floyd's death. The tall, handsome man's crimes included robbing a dozen banks, killing six police officers, and collecting hefty ransoms after kidnapping two wealthy men. The *Cleveland Plain Dealer*'s story about his death ran under the headline "Floyd, No. 1 Outlaw, Slain by Federal Agents."[37]

A month later, G-men killed George "Baby Face" Nelson. Like other outlaws of the era, Nelson had robbed a number of banks and killed several people. The *Atlanta Constitution*'s headline above its story reporting his death read, "'Baby Face' Nelson Found Dead in Roadside Ditch, Victim of Bullets Fired by U.S. Agents."[38]

Another widely reported killing was that of "Ma" Barker and her son Fred in January 1935. Beginning in the late 1920s, Kate Barker and her four sons had created a gang that killed a dozen people during a series of bank robberies and kidnappings. G-men eventually either killed or sent all of the outlaws to jail. The headline above the *Philadelphia Inquirer* story reporting the deaths of the Barkers read, "U.S. Agents Slay 'Ma' and Fred Barker."[39]

PROPELLING POSITIVE CHANGE

Historians who have studied what is now considered the worst crime wave in American history agree that it ended in 1935. In the succinct words of a book about the phenomenon, "An era had passed." The number of crimes in the country rapidly declined in the second half of the decade, and no new high-profile gangsters emerged to replace the ones the federal agents had either killed or sent to prison.[40]

With regard to what caused the criminal activity and the widespread public anxiety to subside, scholars point to the fact that the Justice Department's Bureau of Investigation—which was renamed the Federal Bureau of Investigation the same year the crime wave ended—had been given the funds to purchase powerful weapons and fast cars equal to those the gangsters had used.[41]

Congress appropriated those funds to the agency, scholars say, because the public and the elected representatives in Washington had developed great respect and admiration for the G-men. And, as for exactly why the agents were held in such high regard, scholars consistently credit two factors: their impressive record of success and the news media's relentlessly positive portrayal of them.[42]

A clear sign that the federal agents had risen to heroic stature within American culture came in April 1935 when Hollywood released a film titled *G-Men*. Warner Brothers promoted the movie with the tagline "The First Great Story of the Men Who Waged America's War on Crime!" The plot featured one of the top stars of the day, Jimmy Cagney, as a young federal agent struggling to bring a band of kidnappers to justice.[43]

Anyone who'd been keeping up with the news for the previous several years—which was virtually everyone in the country—knew the Cagney character was based on J. Edgar Hoover. It wasn't a shock, therefore, when the nation's leading papers raved about the film. The *Kansas City Star*, for example, lauded it as "the action epic of the year." The paper went on to say, "It's the story of the men who have made it safe for you to put your money in the neighborhood bank and to send your child to school without a bodyguard." After the film drew huge audiences, Hollywood released half a dozen more FBI-themed movies before the end of the year.[44]

Stopping Smokers from Killing Themselves

During the early decades of the twentieth century, the American news media had a fervent love affair with cigarettes. Newspapers across the country consistently highlighted what they saw as the benefits of using tobacco, lauding the activity as having a highly desirable calming influence on smokers.

That love affair ended in 1938. When a research biologist released the results of a study showing that smokers died at an earlier age than nonsmokers, newspapers turned those findings into front-page news. More headlines followed two years later when a respected doctor suggested there was a link between cigarettes and lung cancer. A third defining moment came in 1952 when papers showcased a large-scale scientific study confirming that smoking often leads to lung cancer and death. These three milestones show the news media were committed to stopping smokers from killing themselves. What wasn't clear is if the public would listen.

Typical of the relentlessly positive stories about tobacco use that appeared in the early twentieth century was one in 1904 in the *Milwaukee Sentinel* that applauded cigarette smoking for reducing a potential criminal's desire to break the law. "Alcohol is an excitant and moves to violence and hence crime," the paper wrote. "The cigarette, on the contrary, is a known soother and sedative, and as such the antithesis of alcohol in its results." To support its argument, the *Sentinel* piece quoted a prosperous businessman as saying, "I am always glad to see the poor man or the poor child smoking. For not only is he preparing for himself a happy old age, but he is not likely to swell the list of the criminal classes. When he is carried away by his passions, instead of avenging himself on someone, he simply smokes a cigarette and it all goes off. It is almost like reading the Bible."[1]

World War I brought more praise for tobacco. The country's newspapers reported that smoking had enormous benefits for American soldiers fighting on European battlefields. "The cigarette is one of the easiest and most harmless of indulgences," the *Philadelphia Public-Ledger* wrote in 1917. "It relieves the tedium of the trench life and gives a soothing effect through the smoke, and the casual occupation of getting mental distraction and a physical stimulus in critical situations is not to be disputed." The end of the *Public-Ledger* story—which ran under the headline "My Lady Nicotine"—stated, "Under the profound psychosis of war, the testimony of all is that to smoke is a real relief that may well be put at the command of all through affection or charity."[2]

The country's leading papers kept showing their love for cigarettes after peacetime returned. "The man who smokes is likely to be a more dependable and steadier worker—more dependable than the non-smoker," the *San Francisco Chronicle* told its readers in 1926. In this instance, the paper drew its conclusion from the findings of a physician. "Tobacco is a sedative," the *Chronicle* quoted Dr. Knight Dunlap as saying. "The man who smokes is more likely to go along in his work with production larger in amount and quality than is the man who does not." Dr. Dunlap acknowledged that smoking may cause a person's blood pressure to increase slightly, but he pooh-poohed this potential concern, saying, "So does the telling of a good joke."[3]

INFORMING READERS THAT SMOKING SHORTENS LIFE

The nation's newspapers changed their tune when an eminent biologist on the faculty at Johns Hopkins University released the findings of a study he'd conducted. His 1938 examination of the factors that shorten the lives of American men identified smoking cigarettes as one of those negative influences. And so, the news outlets that previously had presented cigarettes in a positive light now were highly critical of them.

Among the many papers that turned the findings into front-page news was the *Des Moines Register*. "Dr. Raymond Pearl reported the first 'life table' on tobacco," the Iowa paper wrote. "It showed that all smoking, even in moderation, shortens life."[4]

Dr. Pearl included 6,813 men in his study. The participants were, the *Register* said, divided into three categories: heavy smokers, moderate smokers, and nonsmokers. "The study's findings showed that smoking definitely impaired longevity," the paper quoted the doctor as saying. "This impairment is proportional to the habitual amount of tobacco usage in smoking, being great for heavy smokers and less for moderate smokers."[5]

As for data to support his conclusion, Dr. Pearl provided two contrasting numbers. He said that among every 100,000 heavy smokers in the United States, the number dying before the age of sixty was 53,774, but the comparable number of nonsmokers dying before that age was only 43,436.[6]

Exactly how many newspapers published articles about the study isn't known, but there's no question that the number was substantial. Dr. Pearl later said, "The matter has been printed in every crossroads newspaper in the country, and the clippings have been delivered to me by the pailful." Among the many high-circulation newspapers that had stories in that pail were the *New York Times*, *Washington Post*, *Baltimore Sun*, *Cleveland Plain Dealer*, and *Los Angeles Times*.[7]

REPORTING A POSSIBLE LINK BETWEEN CIGARETTES AND LUNG CANCER

Cigarette smoking jumped into the headlines again in 1940 when the nation's papers trumpeted the findings of another medical expert. This time the articles connected tobacco use to a specific—and deadly—disease.

Among the news outlets that reported the story was the most influential paper in the country, the *New York Times*. Editors crafted a headline reading, "Lung Cancer Rise Laid to Cigarettes." After that phrasing grabbed the readers' attention, the first paragraph stated, "An assertion that the increase in the smoking of cigarettes was a cause of the rise in recent years of cancer of the lung, which now ranks with cancer of the stomach as a dominant form of cancer in the United States, was made today."[8]

In its second paragraph, the *Times* provided a direct quote from the accusing physician, Dr. Alton Ochsner. He said, "My contention is that smoking cigarettes is a cause of cancer of the lung, because we know that chronic irritation is a factor in the incidence of cancer and we know that smoking causes chronic irritation."[9]

According to the article, Dr. Ochsner had reached his conclusion after observing men and women who had died of cancer, during the previous twenty years, at the New Orleans hospital where he practiced.[10]

The *Times* also stated, "The lung cancers, Dr. Ochsner reported, were most prevalent between the ages of 50 and 60, adding further support to the view that chronic irritation over a period of years plays a part in the causation of cancer of the organ irritated by the inhalation of smoke."[11]

As had been the case two years earlier about heavy smoking shortening a person's life, the exact number of newspapers that printed articles about the 1940 revelation of cancer findings isn't known. The news definitely rated headlines in many leading papers across the country, however, with their geographic span stretching as far north as Minnesota and as far south as Florida, as the *Minneapolis Tribune* and *Miami Herald* were among the dozens—if not hundreds—of news outlets that warned their readers about the apparent dangers of smoking.[12]

WARNING READERS THAT CIGARETTES KILL

One of the biggest breakthroughs in research on the effects of using tobacco came in 1952. And when the scientists released their findings from the large-scale study, American journalism pulled out all the stops to inform the public.

Headlines told the story quickly and succinctly. The *Atlanta Constitution* opted for "Study Links Lung Deaths to Smoking," the *Baltimore Sun* went with "Smoking Tied to Cancer Rise," and the *Los Angeles Times* labeled its story "Cancer of Lungs Linked to Smoking."[13]

Dozens of papers chose to highlight the same pair of quotes they found in the report that summarized the results of the four-year study. The first of those statements read: "It is concluded that the association between smoking and carcinoma (cancer) of the lung is real." The second read: "Our estimates indicate that the risk of dying of lung carcinoma increases with age and in approximately simple arithmetical proportion with the amount smoked."[14]

After showcasing those two quotes, the papers provided readers with the specific details of the study that had just been published in a fifteen-page article in the *British Medical Journal*. The *Chicago Tribune*, for example, reported that the findings were based on the medical histories of 5,000 patients in more than twenty London hospitals and that the study was conducted by Dr. Richard Doll and Dr. A. Bradford Hill.[15]

Reporters and editors knew that numbers don't make for easy reading, but they also realized that at least some statistics were essential to ensure that the public found the study—and the articles—credible. In its story, the *St. Louis Post-Dispatch* stated, "Among men of ages 45–64, the death rate in nonsmokers is negligible, while in the heavier-smoking categories, it is estimated to reach three to five deaths per annum per 1,000 living."[16]

Something else the journalists knew was that readers who were also smokers would have some very specific questions about the latest findings. The *Post-Dispatch* answered two of those questions in a pair of sentences when it reported, referring to the doctors who'd conducted the research, "They said the study showed little difference in cancer rates between smokers who inhale and those who don't. But they added there are 'appreciably lower risks for pipe smokers compared with cigarette smokers.'"[17]

The *New York Times* added more detail still. The paper's lengthy story told readers that researchers conducted "exhaustive" interviews with study participants to eliminate other circumstances that could have led to a cancer diagnosis. By the end of those sessions, the *Times* reported, there was no question that the disease was a result of the victims smoking cigarettes rather than factors such as other medical problems or "their proximity to gas works."[18]

REINFORCING THE DANGERS OF CIGARETTE SMOKING

There's no question that American newspapers sent their strongest message regarding the dangers of smoking through their prominent coverage of the trio of announcements that doctors and medical researchers made in 1938, 1940, and 1952. During this same period, though, the various journalistic voices also reinforced that message with any number of other articles that appeared in their pages.

Many of these items were published in health advice columns that hundreds of papers routinely ran, often on a weekly basis. Typical was a 1938 piece in the *Chicago Tribune*'s "How to Keep Well" column written by a local physician. "Everyone with a peptic ulcer wants to bring about recovery as speedily as possible," Dr. Irving Cutter began. "One of the things that must be overcome is too much hydrochloric acid in the stomach, which is likely to hinder healing." The doctor, who also served as the *Tribune*'s health editor, then went on to say, "Physicians advise these victims not to smoke, on the ground that the use of tobacco is inclined to stimulate the secretion of acid."

Later in the column, Dr. Cutter summarized a recent experiment that had found that smoking cigarettes "brought about a considerable rise" in the acid among patients included in the study.[19]

Other articles warning readers about the dangers of smoking appeared when papers reported on the activities of a national organization called the Anti-Cigarette Alliance. The *Washington Post* was among the papers that published numerous stories about the activities of the group's local chapter. In 1940, for example, the *Post* ran an article, under the headline "Anti-Smokers Meet," that summarized the content of a presentation by Dr. Daniel H. Kress, who'd written a book critical of cigarette smoking. "England's young men are stunted and unfit for war service," the article quoted Dr. Kress as having said, "because of the use of tobacco."[20]

Still other papers reminded their readers of the health dangers inherent in smoking by informing readers when a widely known public figure said that people shouldn't use tobacco. The *Los Angeles Times* was particularly fond of this category of story. For instance, the paper reported a comment made by Lady Nancy Witcher Langhorne Astor, an American-born socialite who married British nobleman Waldorf Astor; the article quoted her as saying, "Smoking is one of the crimes of the age." The *Times* also published an article when a Methodist bishop living in the South denounced smoking; in this case, the clerical leader stated that he believed it was far more damaging to a person's health to smoke cigarettes than to drink an excessive amount of alcohol. Another *Times* story of this type highlighted a statement by Daniel J. Tobin, president of the American Federation of Labor's Teamsters Union; "Tobin said the younger generation is smoking much too much," the paper reported. "And, he added, so are middle-aged people."[21]

READER'S DIGEST CRUSADING AGAINST CIGARETTES

At the same time that American newspapers were warning their readers about the health risks of smoking, the country's largest-circulation magazine was also waging a campaign to inform the public about the topic. Most journalists and media scholars don't consider the monthly *Reader's Digest* to be a news outlet. On this particular subject, however, the magazine—which has, throughout its history, published many stories related to health and medical issues—had information to impart and advice to share.[22]

The crusade began in 1924 with an article titled "Does Tobacco Injure the Human Body?" To answer that question, the *Reader's Digest* turned to a variety of experts. One of those sources was the president of the New England Life Insurance Company, who said he refused to issue policies to heavy smokers. Another source for the article was the manager of the Philadelphia Athletics professional baseball team, who said, "I make it a rule not to sign up players who smoke." A third expert was a physician who, after examining heavy smokers, found they were 27 percent more likely than nonsmokers to suffer from inflamed gums and decaying teeth.[23]

After quoting these various experts on the topic, the article's author concluded, "The truth is, tobacco lowers the whole tone of the body and decreases its vital power and resistance." If readers still weren't sure where the magazine stood on the issue, they definitely knew after reading the final sentence in the piece: "From every indication, it behooves the man who wishes to remain fit to omit tobacco from his daily schedule."[24]

Another important article appeared in 1938. Like the stories that made headlines in major papers that year, the *Reader's Digest* piece summarized the results of the study that documented smokers died at an earlier age than nonsmokers. The magazine took a broader look at the issue, however, and expressed alarm at the dramatic increase in tobacco consumption. "From the way we Americans smoke cigarettes—162 billion a year, nine times as many as in 1915—one might assume we thought them harmless," the article stated. It then went on to list some of the ways that smoking contributed to health problems: "Cigarettes clearly aggravate certain unhealthy conditions of the throat, heart and lungs. Tobacco smoke has been accused of impairing breathing, of causing stomach disorders, of dulling mental powers and lowering muscular strength." After naming these various concerns, the article synthesized the material by then saying, "Nicotine does us harm."[25]

One of the ways the *Reader's Digest* differs from traditional news organizations is that it publishes more first-person pieces. An example of this technique during its antismoking campaign came in 1941 when the magazine enlisted former heavyweight boxing champion Gene Tunney to write an article that it titled "Nicotine Knockout, or the Slow Count" and that carried the subtitle "A Great Athlete Indicts Tobacco for Poison and Fraud." Among the boxer's statements were "With every puff, heavy smokers shorten their lives" and "I can bluntly say that few things could be worse for physical fitness than the cigarette habit." Tunney ended his piece by speaking directly to readers, telling them, "If you smoke as much as you can, you will have many diseases and will die young."[26]

Some media historians say the single most important article the *Reader's Digest* published about smoking cigarettes ran under the headline "Cancer by the Carton." It appeared in 1952, the same year the country's newspapers showcased the large-scale study confirming a link between cigarettes and lung cancer. The magazine version of the story differed in that it included a frightening quote from the United Nations World Health Organization: "Above the age of 45, the risk of developing the disease increases in simple proportion to the amount smoked, and may be 50 times as great among those who smoke 25 or more cigarettes daily as among non-smokers." The landmark article also challenged readers to do something about the health crisis, saying, "Cancer of the lung presents one of the most striking opportunities for preventive measures."[27]

One scholar has described the "Cancer by the Carton" piece as "extremely powerful" as well as one that meant "millions of American smokers could avoid the issue no more."[28]

FAILING TO PROPEL POSITIVE CHANGE

Even though the love affair between newspapers and cigarettes had screeched to a halt in 1938 and the *Reader's Digest* had begun campaigning against smoking in 1924, the American public's use of tobacco continued to increase as the decades passed. In 1938, the per capita annual consumption of cigarettes by adults stood at 1,830; by 1952, that figure had soared to 3,886. That consumption figure kept rising higher and higher over the next three decades, showing no sign of declining until 1982.[29]

It's clear that the news media's effort to stop smokers from killing themselves was ineffective. The stories simply didn't cause readers to change their habits.

This lack of effectiveness begs the question: Why did journalism fail?

Part of the answer is simply that a large portion of the American public enjoyed smoking cigarettes. News outlets can't force people to change their behavior, even if it's clearly in their best interest to do so. The United States places great value on freedom, and that includes allowing men and women to do harm to their health.

A second relevant factor is that although news organizations published articles about the dangers of cigarette smoking, that didn't mean they refused to accept advertising from tobacco companies. For example, in 1938 when the *Des Moines Register* reported on its front page that a scientific study had found conclusive evidence that smoking tobacco shortens a person's life, the paper ran an ad for Camel cigarettes four pages later. Likewise, in 1952 when the *St. Louis Post-Dispatch* was among the plethora of papers that reported that researchers had found a link between smoking cigarettes and suffering from lung cancer, the same issue that carried the story also carried an ad for Parliament cigarettes—the tagline highlighted the brand's logo at the time: "You're So Smart to Smoke Parliaments." (The *Reader's Digest* didn't publish ads for products of any kind between 1924 and 1952 when its most notable articles about cigarette smoking appeared, as the magazine depended entirely on subscription fees for its revenue.)[30]

The third and most important force that played a role in people continuing to smoke cigarettes was the tobacco industry. In the words of one scholar of American marketing, "Cigarette smoking is not a natural but an acquired habit, and getting people to acquire and maintain that habit has been an exercise in which the tobacco industry has poured many billions of dollars."[31]

One advertising initiative began in 1920 soon after American women won the right to vote. Seeing the potential for millions of new smokers, the American Tobacco Company hired public relations pioneer Edward Bernays to transform this opportunity into a reality. Bernays, in turn, decided to capitalize on many American women's yearning for independence and equality. In 1929, he hired a gaggle of debutantes to march down Fifth Avenue in New York City's annual Easter Parade while smoking cigarettes. The fashionably dressed young women waved the cigarettes in the air and called them "torches of liberty." Photos of this novel activity were published on newspaper front pages across the country, kicking off a campaign that enjoyed enormous success—in 1924, women accounted for only 5 percent of smokers; by 1931, that figure had jumped to 14 percent.[32]

A second remarkably effective publicity effort involved soldiers who fought in World War II. Tobacco companies volunteered to provide free cigarettes to the various branches of the U.S. military to include in the packets of food rations that every soldier received. The long-term benefits of this plan manifested themselves in two ways. First, millions of young men and their families had positive feelings toward the generous tobacco companies. Second, by the end of the war, many of the soldiers were addicted to tobacco.[33]

A final example among the countless campaigns the tobacco industry undertook was one that began in 1946. Creative staff members at R. J. Reynolds came up with the advertising slogan "More doctors smoke Camels than any other cigarette." The copy for the ads told readers, "Every doctor in private practice was asked." For their images, the ads showed doctors in white coats smiling as they puffed away on Camels. Advertising scholars have identified the ads as among the most effective in the history of the field.[34]

There's no question that news organizations have, throughout American history, represented a highly influential force in the American culture. For much of the twentieth century, however, the tobacco industry was clearly even more persuasive than journalism was.

This ad was part of a highly successful campaign that the creative team at R. J. Reynolds came up with to promote Camel cigarettes. Courtesy of the Advertising Archives.

8

Celebrating a Jewish Miss America

Anti-Semitism was rampant in the United States during the 1930s and 1940s. Social clubs barred Jews from becoming members, oceanside resorts posted signs reading, "No Dogs or Jews Allowed," and employers routinely rejected job applicants with Jewish-sounding names. Nazi sympathizers organized massive parades that featured flags emblazoned with swastikas. During race riots in Detroit in 1943, dozens of Jewish-owned businesses were looted and burned.

But in the fall of 1945, the country's leading newspapers saw an opportunity to send a very different message. The story at hand involved a twenty-one-year-old woman who strolled gracefully into the public eye. When the papers recognized that Bess Myerson—the first Jewish contestant to compete in the Miss America pageant—wasn't merely strikingly beautiful but also talented, articulate, and whip-smart, they presented her to their readers in an unremittingly flattering light.

Bess Myerson was born in the Bronx in 1924. Both her parents had been born in Russia and had immigrated to the United States as children. When Bess was growing up, her father worked as a house painter, and her mother cared for the couple's three daughters. The Myerson family, which spoke Yiddish at home, lived in a one-bedroom apartment in the Sholom Aleichem housing development.[1]

Bess began piano lessons when she was nine years old. She quickly proved to be so musically gifted that she was accepted, at age thirteen, into the High School of Music and Art, a public institution for select New York City students.[2]

After high school, Bess enrolled at the tuition-free Hunter College where she majored in music and earned excellent grades. By this point she was also playing the flute and giving private piano lessons to a number of youngsters.[3]

Bess developed, while in college, into a beautiful young woman—perfect teeth, flawless skin, and a smile so brilliant it lit up a room. Because she was so attractive, her older sister decided Bess should be a model, so Sylvia Myerson sent photos of Bess to a modeling agency. That effort didn't go far, though, because the company's owner responded that he preferred the "all-American type." The Myerson girls knew exactly what that phrase meant: he wanted models with blond hair, blue eyes, and a non-Jewish last name.[4]

BECOMING A BEAUTY QUEEN

Sylvia Myerson took a proactive role in her sister's life for a second time in the summer of 1945 by entering Bess, who'd just earned her college degree, in the Miss New York City competition. Applications only needed to include photos and basic biographical information about the contestant. So Sylvia sent in the material without telling Bess, hoping to spare her sister more rejection if her Jewish background again worked against her.[5]

But that didn't happen with the beauty contest, as the judges invited Bess to be a finalist and compete in the live pageant. After walking across the stage in a swimsuit and playing the piano and flute as her talent, she won the title.[6]

Myerson's victory brought her a degree of celebrity, as the *New York Post*, *New York World-Telegram*, and *Washington Post* all ran stories about her victory. Each item was accompanied by a photo of her wearing a swimsuit.[7]

But the newly minted beauty queen didn't have much time to bask in the media attention—she had to prepare for the Miss America pageant that began a month later. Myerson also faced a major personal decision during this period.

Lenora Slaughter, the director of the Miss America Pageant, recognized that Myerson had the potential to win the national contest. She thought the young woman's chances would be dramatically reduced, though, because her last name identified her as Jewish. So Slaughter urged Myerson to change her name, suggesting she become Betty Meredith.[8]

Myerson later recalled Slaughter's precise words: "Bess Myerson is just not an attractive name." When Myerson said she wasn't sure she understood that statement, Slaughter said point-blank that anyone who heard the name instantly recognized it as being Jewish and this could be a problem with the judges. Slaughter also pointed out that many Jewish celebrities had Anglicized their names, such as Betty Joan Perske becoming Lauren Bacall and Archie Leach becoming Cary Grant.[9]

And yet, Myerson rejected Slaughter's advice, deciding that if she couldn't win the Miss America title with her Jewish identity intact, she didn't want to win at all. "I knew I had to keep my name," Myerson wrote in the 1980s. "To have given up my name would have been like masquerading in someone else's skin."[10]

WINNING THE MISS AMERICA CROWN

When Myerson arrived in Atlantic City for pageant week in September 1945, people were already talking about her being the only Jewish contestant among the forty beauties representing either their home state or home city. Those familiar with the high-profile event knew that, since its founding in 1921, neither a Jewish woman nor a woman of color had ever competed for the national title.[11]

Myerson wore a size twelve white suit for the swimsuit contest and a light green dress for the evening gown competition. As her talent, she played Edvard Grieg's Concerto in A Minor on the piano and George Gershwin's "Summertime" on the flute.[12]

Several newspapers covered the pageant throughout the week, and they soon identified Myerson as the front-runner. "In the clockers' opinion," the *Philadelphia Bulletin* reported, "Miss New York City, Bess Myerson, is an odds-on choice." When U.S. Army veterans attending a formal dance with the contestants voted Myerson their choice to win the title, the *Los Angeles Times* and *Philadelphia Inquirer* were among the papers that ran a photo of her.[13]

It was a reporter who warned Myerson that some people associated with the pageant were working to block her from winning. The journalist pulled her aside, midway through the week, and whispered, "Watch yourself, Bess. There are people involved here who don't want a Jewish winner. Something may happen to ruin your chances." Myerson took the cautionary words to heart and made sure she followed the pageant rules, which included never being alone with a man, to the letter.[14]

Neither Myerson nor the reporters covering the pageant were aware of another activity that her ethnicity triggered. Indeed, it wasn't until after the competition had ended that five of the judges compared notes and realized that they'd all received threatening phone calls just before leaving the hotel for the pageant finale. In each instance, the anonymous caller had told the judge that if he voted for Myerson, he'd regret it.[15]

Later that night, in front of a crowd of 6,000 people, Myerson won the competition. Her smile seemed even more dazzling than usual as she stood tall and proud when the sparkling crown was placed on her head and an ermine-trimmed red velvet cloak was placed around her shoulders. Bess Myerson was now officially the epitome of American womanhood.[16]

"At the moment I won," she later wrote, "I looked out at the crowd and saw all the Jewish people hugging each other, congratulating each other. They all felt like they had won." Many of those gleeful fans shouted "Mazel Tov!" at the top of their lungs.[17]

MAKING MISS AMERICA 1945 A MAJOR NEWS STORY

The next morning, newspapers across the country began their love affair with the first Jewish Miss America. None of the papers—either on that morning or anytime during her reign—specifically identified Myerson as being Jewish, allowing her last name to make that point for them.[18]

Newspapers across the country gave prominent play to this 1945 photo of Bess Myerson, the first Jewish beauty to wear the Miss America crown. Copyright Bettmann/Corbis/AP Images.

Many of the papers showed their enthusiasm for Myerson by treating her victory as major news, even though they hadn't done that with the previous winner. A year earlier, when Venus Ramey had won the title, for example, the *Miami Herald* hadn't published a story of any sort. But now that a non-Gentile was wearing the crown, the Florida daily placed the breakthrough on its front page.[19]

Other papers made the same decision. The *Minneapolis Tribune* splashed a story and photo of Myerson across page one, even though it hadn't run a story about Ramey. The *Seattle Post-Intelligencer* did also, turning Myerson's triumph into front-page news after having ignored Ramey's success a year earlier.[20]

American journalism's infatuation with Bess Myerson didn't end on the morning after she won her title, as papers kept her in the spotlight. The *Los Angeles Times* published eight stories about Myerson during her yearlong reign; the *Times* had run only two stories about Ramey. Likewise, the *Chicago Tribune* ran nine articles about Myerson but only two about Ramey, and the *New York Times* ran seven stories about Myerson but none about Ramey.[21]

Even more important than the quantity of coverage was the specific messages the papers sent about the first Jewish Miss America.

BESS MYERSON BEING BEAUTIFUL

Because the pageant was primarily a beauty contest, the papers placed a high priority on reporting Myerson's physical attributes.

The fact that she stood a towering five feet ten inches tall clearly contributed to many of the papers, such as the *Los Angeles Times*, selecting the adjective "statuesque" when telling readers what she looked like. Other papers opted for different terms. The *Seattle Post-Intelligencer* chose "gorgeous," the *Atlanta Constitution* went with "beauteous," and the *New York Post* called Myerson an "Amazonian lovely."[22]

Papers offered plenty of other details about Myerson's looks, too. The *Cleveland Plain Dealer* reported that she possessed "ravishing brunette hair and radiant skin," the *Pittsburgh Post-Gazette* told its readers that she was "olive-skinned" and had "dark brown tresses," and the *New York Daily News* added that she was "hazel-eyed" and "weighs 136 pounds."[23]

The *Philadelphia Inquirer* took the top prize when it came to documenting the beauty queen's figure. After giving her height and weight, the *In-*

quirer reported, "Her other measurements are bust, 35½ inches; waist, 25 inches; hips, 35 inches; thigh, 20 inches; calf, 14½ inches; ankle, 8½ inches; and neck, 13½ inches."[24]

BESS MYERSON HAVING SIMPLE TASTES

Many of the papers also sent the message that Myerson was a down-to-earth young woman who possessed the simplest of tastes.

Some papers were straightforward on this point. The *New York Post* said, "Bess is unaffected by her Cinderella experience," and the *Pittsburgh Post-Gazette* wrote, "Miss Myerson is modest and unassuming."[25]

Other papers were more subtle. The *Atlanta Constitution* reported that although she played a classical piano piece in the pageant, "Her musical tastes include good boogie woogie"—an African-American style of blues that was popular in the 1940s. The *Philadelphia Daily News* sent the message that Myerson wasn't pretentious when it quoted her self-effacing response when asked how well she played tennis—"Well, I can get the ball over the net."[26]

The blue ribbon in the effort to depict Myerson as having simple tastes went to a syndicated columnist whose words appeared in 175 papers across the country. Earl Wilson phoned the woman he called "the Bronx Bombshell" and then summarized their conversation in his column, using a question-and-answer format.

Wilson: "What's your favorite cocktail?"

Myerson: "Milk."

Wilson: "Do you ever say 'damn' or 'hell'?"

Myerson: "I say 'Gee whiz.'"

Wilson: "Did anything surprising happen at the contest?"

Myerson: "Yes, I won!"[27]

BESS MYERSON CHOOSING MUSIC OVER STARDOM

Two major prizes that prompted thousands of young women to enter the Miss America competition in 1945 were a $5,000 scholarship and a Hollywood screen test. And so, when Myerson told reporters that she'd use the money to pursue a master's degree in music but wouldn't take the screen test, the country's papers transformed her response into big news.[28]

Several editors were so startled by Myerson's rejection of the screen test that they turned her decision into headlines. The words above a *Los Angeles Times* story read "Miss America of 1945 Shuns Career in Films," and those in the *Atlanta Constitution* stated "Miss America to Study; Declines Hollywood Offer."[29]

The pieces that ran under the headlines reported that the only reason Myerson had agreed to remain in the Miss New York City contest, after her sister had entered her, was that she wanted to pursue a graduate degree but couldn't afford the tuition. "I want to study music," the *New York Journal-American* quoted her as saying. "I've studied it for 12 years and I want lots more of it." As for why she was turning down the Hollywood screen test, Myerson told the paper, simply but firmly, "I don't want the movies."[30]

BESS MYERSON BEING PATRIOTIC

Another route the papers followed to portray the country's first non-Gentile Miss America in a flattering light was to showcase her patriotism. This was a significant point at the time because many Jewish Americans weren't happy with the United States in 1945, disappointed that their country hadn't intervened to stop Nazi Germany from killing 6 million European Jews during the Holocaust.

The earliest instance of news outlets communicating that Myerson was staunchly loyal to the United States came in the explosion of stories reporting that she'd won the title. That is, many papers went out of their way to include in those articles that her first public activity after being crowned was to visit wounded soldiers who were recuperating in Atlantic City. "She bestowed her first kisses as Miss America," the *Baltimore Sun* wrote, "on four GIs—amputees at the Thomas M. England Hospital."[31]

A month after Myerson won the title, papers covered her public appearances in support of a campaign by Bronx residents to raise $1.2 million for returning World War II veterans. A *New York Times* story about her effort reported that the crowd at one event was so excited that she was a speaker that the scheduled program had to be delayed for several minutes after her speech "because of the distraction caused when autograph-seekers besieged Miss Myerson with requests."[32]

The *Washington Post* told its readers that Myerson was patriotic by reporting on her appearances at events that raised money to help former soldiers transition back into civilian life. "Miss America Comes to D.C. to Aid Victory Bond Drive" read a typical headline, with *Post* editors placing the article on page one.[33]

BESS MYERSON PROMOTING TOLERANCE

Several months into her reign, "the Bronx Bombshell" began devoting time and energy to another initiative. She did this after officials from the Anti-Defamation League of B'nai B'rith, a Jewish service organization, asked her to give speeches encouraging the public to be more tolerant toward members of racial and ethnic minority groups.[34]

When Myerson took up this new cause, America's newspapers threw their editorial might behind supporting her efforts. She made her first speeches in Chicago in February 1946, and the city's papers made sure her words reached an audience much larger than the few dozen people who came to hear her in person.[35]

Myerson titled her speeches "You Can't Be Beautiful and Hate" and began each one with a statement on the order of, as reported on the front page of the *Chicago Daily News*, "Hate is a corroding disease that affects the way you look. Prejudice shows in your eyes and warps your expression. It damages your character." She continued this theme throughout her talks. "Some girls and fellows are born handsome," the *Chicago Herald-American* quoted her as telling 1,000 high school students. "But their personalities and features are distorted because they question a person's color and religion before they decide to like him."[36]

The thirty speeches Myerson gave in Chicago were so well received, often prompting a standing ovation, that the league sent her on to Milwaukee and then to Boston, Hartford, and Buffalo. In each city, papers reported on her appearances, drawing attention to the stories by running photos with them. "I have visited dozens of veterans' hospitals where white and Negro, Jew and Gentile, Yank and Dixie share the same ward," the *Buffalo News* quoted Myerson as saying. "They will all tell you that if you have prejudice against any race or religion, it will do nothing but harm you and make you ugly as a person."[37]

Miss America 1945 kept making speeches throughout her reign, and the crowds remained large. After an appearance in New York City in June 1946, she told the *Brooklyn Eagle*, "If I'm supposed to be representative of the American girl, I want to make constructive use of that fact. In the tolerance talks I've been making, it's a great draw. Last week in a Brooklyn school, I got 100 percent attendance—6,000 girls, all on time."[38]

PROPELLING POSITIVE CHANGE

During Bess Myerson's reign, her name appeared in the country's papers thousands of times, and those references were consistently flattering. Although it's impossible to know how many of the articles were published because she was the first Jewish woman to win the Miss America title, her ethnicity seemed to be a factor. When Marilyn Buferd won the competition in 1946, many major papers chose to ignore that event, just as they'd done with Venus Ramey's victory in 1944. Among the papers that placed Myerson's victory on page one but didn't report either Ramey's or Buferd's were the *Des Moines Register, Miami Herald, Minneapolis Tribune, Philadelphia Daily News*, and *Seattle Post-Intelligencer*.[39]

It's also difficult to gauge the degree to which the positive coverage of Myerson contributed to the fading of anti-Semitism that occurred in the United States in the second half of the 1940s. And yet, again, there's evidence that the abundance of articles made a difference—particularly in the lives of young Jewish girls. "In the Jewish community, she was the most famous pretty girl since Queen Esther in ancient Persia," wrote the author of one Myerson biography. "Girls from Brooklyn put her picture on the bathroom mirror and tried to do their hair the way she did hers." That same author quoted a Jewish girl, who grew up to be a doctor, as saying, "If you were in high school at the time of her victory, Bess Myerson was the most important female image in your life."[40]

Breaking the Color Barrier in Major League Baseball

In 1945, Branch Rickey decided that he just might be in a position, as general manager of the Brooklyn Dodgers, to help reduce racial discrimination. And so, Rickey signed an African-American man to play for his team. Rickey didn't know if his effort to integrate major league baseball would work, recognizing that it all depended on how the young athlete was received by the American public.

For the next two years, a handful of the country's leading newspapers used their positions as shapers of public opinion to make sure Rickey's grand experiment was a grand success. The papers—located in the North, Midwest, and West—began by praising Jackie Robinson's athletic prowess. Beyond that, however, they also portrayed the ballplayer as a man who possessed the personal traits that enabled him to deliver a body blow to racial segregation.

Jack Roosevelt Robinson was born into a family of Georgia sharecroppers in 1919. When Jackie was a year old, his father abandoned the family. His mother then packed up her five kids and moved to Pasadena, California, to be near relatives. Mallie Robinson supported her family, as best she could, by working as a domestic.[1]

By the time he reached his teens, Jackie was excelling as an athlete. In high school, he played quarterback on the football team and shortstop on the baseball team, and he broke the school record in the broad jump. His success continued when he won a football scholarship to the University of California at Los Angeles, where he earned varsity letters in four sports—baseball, basketball, football, and track.[2]

It was also while in college that Robinson met his future wife, Rachel Isum, another UCLA student. Robinson left college after two years to play semiprofessional football with the racially integrated Los Angeles Bulldogs.[3]

A year later, he was drafted by the U.S. Army and accepted into officer candidate school. He was commissioned a second lieutenant and served much of his time in uniform as a coach for army athletes.[4]

After being discharged in early 1945, Robinson joined the Kansas City Monarchs of the Negro American Baseball League. He performed well for the Monarchs. At the end of the season, his batting average was an impressive .387, and he'd hit five home runs and had thirteen stolen bases.[5]

BRANCH RICKEY UNDERTAKES A "NOBLE EXPERIMENT"

Sitting in the bleachers for many of those games were men sent by the general manager of the Brooklyn Dodgers. Branch Rickey was determined to find talented African-American players who could help him—in an effort that scholars call his "noble experiment"—integrate his team, and the Monarchs were one of the clubs he had his scouts check out.[6]

In August 1945, Rickey brought Robinson to New York City for a talk. During that session, the general manager said he was looking for a man to become the first African American to play in major league baseball. The key moment in the conversation came when Rickey asked Robinson if he'd be able to keep from reacting angrily when he faced racial hatred. Robinson was stunned by the question, responding, "Are you looking for a Negro who is afraid to fight back?" Rickey looked firmly into Robinson's eyes and said, "I'm looking for a player with the guts *not* to fight back."[7]

Robinson took some time to consider Rickey's question, but the twenty-six-year-old eventually accepted the challenge. And so, in October 1945, Rickey publicly announced that he was signing Robinson to play for the Montreal Royals, a Brooklyn Dodgers farm team.[8]

EMBRACING A "REALLY GREAT PROSPECT"

Several of the newspapers that reported on the signing provided a taste of how they'd treat Jackie Robinson in their coverage.

Among the papers that put the story on page one were the *Baltimore Sun*, which described Robinson as a "one-time UCLA ace," and the *Chicago Tribune*, which subtly portrayed the player as earnest and articulate by quoting

By the time Jackie Robinson put on his Brooklyn Dodgers uniform for the first time in 1947, American newspapers had already spent two years portraying him as a role model. Courtesy of Getty Images/ Transcendental Graphics.

him as saying, "I can't begin to tell you how happy I am that I'm the first member of my race in organized ball" and "I realize how much it means to me, to my race, and to baseball. I can only say I'll do my very best to come thru in every manner."[9]

The most extensive coverage came in the *Los Angeles Times*, which ran three separate articles, one of them calling Robinson "one of the greatest athletes ever developed in Southern California, if not the nation." That story went on to describe the player's performance in high school as "spectacular," and the writer of another *Times* story said, "Robby is a really great prospect."[10]

In addition to lauding Robinson, the papers also spoke to the larger sig-nificance of the signing. The *Baltimore Sun* reported that Branch Rickey's historic step had its roots in an incident that had taken place decades earlier when he was coaching football at Ohio Wesleyan. "The West Virginia team refused to play us if our Negro backfield star, Charlie Thomas, was in the lineup," the *Sun* quoted Rickey as saying. "Later we went to South Bend for a game with Notre Dame, and Charlie was refused a room in a hotel. I finally prevailed upon the manager to put a cot for him in my room."[11]

PRAISING AN AFRICAN-AMERICAN MONTREAL ROYAL

When Robinson played his first game for Montreal in April 1946, the papers again filled their columns with accolades.

"For the first time in the modern history of organized baseball," the *New York Times* began, "a Negro player received a chance to make good today—and Jackie Robinson converted his opportunity into a brilliant personal triumph." The story then summarized Robinson's successes of the day, which included a home run, three other hits, and two stolen bases. "This would have been a big day for any man," the paper gushed. "Under the special circumstances that prevailed for Robinson, it was a tremendous feat."[12]

Other papers joined the *Times* in praising Robinson after that first game. The *Baltimore Sun* called his performance "dazzling," and the *Washington Post* wrote, "Robinson completely stole the fancy of the sellout crowd." The *Chicago Tribune* communicated its enthusiastic support for Robinson by running a photo of him and a story with the headline "Smash Hit!"[13]

As the 1946 season unfolded, the various papers continued to lace their accounts of games with praise for Robinson. The *Washington Post* reported that observers were "impressed with his speed afoot and his fielding," as well as his "art of pivoting on the double play." Several other dailies joined the *Post* in September to report that Robinson finished his year with a batting average of .349—the highest in the farm league. The *Los Angeles Times* dubbed Robinson a "sensation" for leading his team to a victory in the league's version of the World Series.[14]

After all those complimentary stories, it seemed almost anticlimactic when Rickey announced that he'd bring Robinson up to the Brooklyn Dodgers for the 1947 season.[15]

CHEERING FOR AN AFRICAN-AMERICAN BROOKLYN DODGER

The papers ran into a problem when covering Robinson's first game in the majors because he failed to get a hit. Nevertheless, the publications rose to the challenge and found creative ways to put a positive spin on their stories.

For the *Washington Post*, that meant running a photo that showed Robinson smiling and waving his glove as he opened a door labeled "Dodgers Club House." The *Post* story quoted the team manager as saying the less-than-stellar performance was fully understandable. "Playing in the big leagues for the first time," Clyde Sukeforth said, "the boy was bound to be nervous."[16]

The *Los Angeles Times* opted to deflect attention away from the rookie's poor performance by reminding readers of how well he'd played in previous games. The paper labeled Robinson a "brilliant Negro infielder" and then said, "He had a great season with Montreal last year. He led all second basemen in fielding with a percentage of .985." The *Times* went on to note that Robinson had been "flawless" in his fielding in his first game with the Dodgers, catching all fourteen balls that came his way.[17]

Coverage in the *New York Times* included calling Robinson's record during the 1946 season "extraordinary" and pointing out that Ebbets Field was filled to capacity on opening day. "Several thousand Negroes were in the stands at yesterday's game," the *Times* reported. "When Robinson appeared for batting practice, he drew a warm and pleasant reception."[18]

The *Times* also published an editorial about the nation's first African American to join a major league team. "If Robinson had been a white man," the *Times* asserted, "the name would have been there long before this." The editorial then praised Branch Rickey for having the "moral courage" to sign Robinson. "For that action, Mr. Rickey is to be congratulated."[19]

PORTRAYING JACKIE ROBINSON AS HUMBLE

A close reading of the various stories that appeared between 1945 and 1947 reveals that the papers' relentlessly positive coverage of Robinson stressed his personal attributes. Topping that list was his humility.

Among the earliest stories that depicted Robinson as humble was one the *New York Times* ran immediately after he'd been signed to play for Montreal. The piece said of Robinson, "He modestly asserted that he realized his entry into organized baseball was a great responsibility." To support that characterization, the *Times* quoted the ballplayer as saying, "I hope to make good and to open the way for others of my race to do likewise. I sincerely hope that I am able and lucky enough to make the grade."[20]

Such words coming out of Robinson's mouth must have stunned many readers, as most pro athletes were boastful men who displayed their machismo proudly, taking every opportunity to brag about their physical prowess and invincibility. Rarely did the public hear a player say he hoped "to open the way for others" or that being "lucky" had anything to do with his success.

The papers continued to communicate that Robinson was humble. After he amassed the highest batting average of any player on any farm team, the

Los Angeles Times highlighted his quote that read, "The good Lord was on my side last year. I hope He's with me again this year." Likewise, the *New York Times* quoted Robinson as saying, "I don't know whether I can make it—I just hope I can."[21]

Robinson's humble nature remained a theme in stories published after he arrived in Brooklyn. The front-page story the *Washington Post* ran after Robinson signed to play in the majors reported, "As he posed for pictures in his Dodgers uniform and the Montreal players with whom he played last year rushed up to congratulate him and wish him luck, Robinson replied: 'Thanks, I'll need it.'"[22]

Player No. 42's humility was reinforced when the papers quoted him as repeatedly attributing his success not to himself but to other people. For example, in the fall of 1947 after having an excellent season with the Dodgers, Robinson said of Branch Rickey, "He coached me on conduct and baseball all season, and I wouldn't trade anything for his advice. He has great foresight, and I'm deeply indebted to him."[23]

PORTRAYING JACKIE ROBINSON AS CONGENIAL

A second of the racial pioneer's personal traits the papers showcased was one that combined his amiable personality with his willingness to cooperate.

One example came in 1946 when Robinson arrived in Florida for spring training with Montreal. He weighed in at 195 pounds, which was fifteen pounds more than he'd weighed while playing for UCLA. When an observer remarked that the extra weight didn't show, the *New York Times* noted that Robinson grinned and said, "It's in my feet."[24]

Other papers also depicted Robinson as congenial. After he played his year for the farm club and it was announced he'd be moving up to the Dodgers, a *Los Angeles Times* reporter asked him how he expected to be received by his white teammates. His response was remarkably empathetic, so the *Times* made sure to quote it verbatim. "I read that some of the boys, especially some of those from the South, had said some things about me," the paper quoted Robinson as saying. "I don't know whether they really said them, but, if they did, I understand how they feel, because they're from the South. That's the way they were raised, and I understand it."[25]

Robinson's willingness to cooperate was severely tested when he joined Brooklyn because of the position he was assigned. The team already had strong players at shortstop and second base, the positions Robinson had previously played, so Rickey put him at first base. Sportswriters knew that shifting to this position would challenge the rookie, so they again played up his response when they asked him about the change. "I want to play any position," Robinson was quoted as saying, "where the manager believes I can help the team."[26]

The *Baltimore Sun* communicated that No. 42's agreeable nature extended to how he interacted with the fans. "A crowd of over 25,000 almost pulled the shirt off Robinson's back as the game ended," the *Sun* reported in one instance, "and the young player was kept busy for several minutes shaking hands and autographing score cards." The paper went out of its way to make clear that Robinson didn't mind the crowd being a bit unruly. "The clubhouse was a mad scene after the final out, with well wishers fighting to get in to congratulate Robinson," the *Sun* reported. "He was so excited he had to tie his necktie three or four times, but he was as happy as a kid on Christmas morning."[27]

PORTRAYING JACKIE ROBINSON AS WHOLESOME

When Rickey was searching for an athlete to break the color barrier, he knew the player couldn't merely perform well on the field but also had to have an exemplary personal life. He found that candidate in Robinson, and the papers that supported the racial pioneer consistently told their readers what a fine man he was.

The *New York Times* set the pace after Rickey signed his new recruit, describing Robinson as "a church-going Methodist" and "a high-class citizen in every respect." Other papers soon sang his praises as well, the *Los Angeles Times* reporting that major league baseball's first African-American player "neither drinks nor smokes," and the *Baltimore Sun* observing that "Robinson represents the cream of colored ball players."[28]

After Robinson married his college sweetheart—Rachel Isum first earned her nursing degree—in early 1946, the papers had more fodder to use in portraying him as unequivocally wholesome. When a *Los Angeles Times* reporter asked him how the couple celebrated their first wedding anniversary, the paper wrote that "he laughed" and then said, "My wife and I couldn't figure out what to do. We don't drink and we don't like night clubs. So we just went to the movies—two of 'em in one night."[29]

That same story described Robinson's home as "unpretentious" and his wife as "trim" and "attractive." Later in the piece, the writer reported the ballplayer's response when asked to give advice to "young Negroes who aspire" to become professional athletes. "My advice to young Negroes is the same as to young whites," Robinson said. "The one thing which is most important is to be a gentleman."[30]

Jackie and Rachel Robinson had their first child in late 1946, and the arrival of Jackie Jr. offered the papers still more ways to portray the ballplayer as a man to be admired. The *Chicago Tribune*, for example, ran a photo of the proud father, dressed in a Dodgers jacket and cap, holding his son in his arms as the baby played with his daddy's fingers.[31]

The *Washington Post* did its part to contribute to the image of the athlete as a role model when it reported, in the fall of 1947, that he was receiving "about 400 letters a week from kids, most of them colored, who aspire

Thanks to extensive newspaper coverage, the American public became familiar not only with Jackie Robinson but also with his wife, Rachel, and his son, Jackie Jr. Courtesy of Getty Images/PhotoQuest.

to be baseball players." The *Post* went on to say that Robinson "answers all the letters personally."[32]

DOWNPLAYING NEGATIVE STORIES

While the papers kept Robinson's career milestones and admirable personal traits in the spotlight, they gave only minimal coverage to the problems he encountered. The papers clearly wanted to portray his progress positively, which meant downplaying the obstacles that racists put in his way.

One example came in early 1946 while Robinson and the other members of the Montreal farm club were in Florida for spring training. The Royals were scheduled to play a game in Jacksonville, but when city officials learned that Robinson had joined the team, they said he couldn't play because of his color. Royals management then canceled the game rather than play without Robinson. The *Chicago Tribune* compressed the unpleasant incident into a two-paragraph story.[33]

Another instance of discrimination against Robinson received similar treatment a year later. This time, a *Los Angeles Times* reporter learned that some St. Louis Cardinals—at the time, St. Louis was the southernmost city with a major league team—were planning to go on strike because they didn't want to play Brooklyn now that Robinson was on the roster. The *Times* boiled the controversy down to a three-paragraph piece that wasn't published until after league officials had talked to the St. Louis players and averted the strike.[34]

On one occasion, the *Washington Post* chose not to publish even a brief article about a negative incident, relegating the details to a single paragraph buried deep inside a column consisting of sports trivia. "The Phillies thus far are the only club to give Jackie Robinson of the Dodgers a fierce riding from the bench," the item stated. In this case, the *Post* also decided the Philadelphia player's exact statement—"Hey, you black nigger! Why don't you go back where you came from?"—was too ugly to quote verbatim.[35]

The *Los Angeles Times* minimized another fact it could have made into a major story. Specifically, the paper knew that some white players had attempted to physically harm Robinson by digging the spikes of their shoes into his leg or foot whenever they had the chance and by hitting him with pitches—the seven times he was struck in his first year was the highest of any player in the majors. The *Times* buried these details at the bottom of a resolutely positive story about Robinson's thoughts on his experience in pro baseball. "Jackie brushed off questions about spikings he received and balls that were thrown at him," the *Times* reported, "saying those incidents were just part of the game."[36]

One negative incident received prominent play in the papers because Branch Rickey insisted it was too serious to ignore. In May 1947, the Dodgers general manager told reporters that Robinson had received a number of threatening letters. "Two of them were so vicious," the *Chicago Tribune* quoted Rickey as saying, "that I felt they should be investigated." The paper then ran a story that included the fact that police weren't able to identify who sent the letters. A story about the threats also appeared in other papers, including the *New York Times*.[37]

PROPELLING POSITIVE CHANGE

By the end of 1947, Rickey's effort to break the color barrier had succeeded. One measure of that victory came when *Sporting News* magazine named Robinson major league baseball's rookie of the year. But the more conclusive proof that professional baseball had been integrated was that other teams began adding African Americans to their rosters. That breakthrough was soon followed by similar action in other professional sports—most notably football and basketball.[38]

Robinson deserved the lion's share of the credit for having triumphed over segregation because for two years he'd repeatedly proven himself, both on and off the field. Rickey merited praise, too, as he'd used his position to set the process in motion by finding and signing Robinson. Anyone who looks closely at the content in several leading newspapers between 1945 and 1947 must acknowledge that those journalistic voices also contributed to this important breakthrough. Indeed, No. 42 himself praised the papers for giving him a boost; when a reporter asked him in 1947 to summarize how news outlets in the North, Midwest, and West had treated him, Robinson said, "The papers, in my opinion, have been for me all the way."[39]

The impact of breaking the color barrier wasn't confined to the baseball diamond. Robinson's victory over segregation in a highly visible American institution offered a compelling example of a peaceful transition from an all-white system to one in which African Americans worked alongside whites to achieve the common goal of winning ball games. In the words of the author of one book about the phenomenon, "The integration of baseball represented both a symbol of imminent racial challenge and a direct agent of social change." That scholar and others like him have drawn a direct connection between professional baseball adding an African-American player in 1947 and the U.S. Supreme Court outlawing segregated public schools in the *Brown v. Board of Education* case a mere five years later.[40]

Giving Average Citizens More Say in Choosing Their President

Beginning in the 1830s, the presidential nominees for this country's major po-litical parties were chosen by the delegates attending national conventions. For the next century after that, a small number of political insiders decided which two names would appear at the top of the ballot on Election Day, with minimal input from the country's rank-and-file voters.

That situation changed dramatically in 1952. In that year, the growth and power of TV news made it possible, for the first time, for millions of men and women from around the country to see what was happening as events unfolded at the conventions and on the campaign trail. A critical mass of those viewers took advantage of that opportunity by reacting to what they saw on their TV screens and then playing an active and decisive role in choosing the nominees.

When the national political conventions were in their infancy, the delegates who selected the nominees numbered only a few hundred. A total of 320 Democrats chose Andrew Jackson to be their party's nominee in 1832, and a mere 175 delegates decided that Henry Clay was the right man to lead the National Republican Party ticket that same year.[1]

The number of delegates gradually grew as the decades passed. By 1948, a total of 1,592 Democrats gathered at their national convention to choose Harry S. Truman, and 1,094 Republicans did the same to nominate Thomas E. Dewey. Even with this substantial expansion of the numbers, though, it was still a small group that was coming together every four years to decide which names would be on the ballot—and which wouldn't.[2]

Television made its debut at the presidential conventions in the 1940s, but its influence was negligible during that first decade. When Truman and Dewey became the nominees, for instance, only a handful of television viewers in the Northeast were able to see images from the conventions. A mere nine cities could receive signals on network lines that year, and only 400,000 American homes had TV sets. The impact of the limited coverage provided by the networks, therefore, was minimal.[3]

Not so in 1952.

That was the first year TV news had a large enough audience to matter. The *New York Times* spoke to this new reality in late June, predicting, "Television is going to wield a major and perhaps determining influence this year over both the conventions and the campaign to follow." The *Times* went on to say that the presence of TV cameras "will turn the nation into a gigantic town meeting." It soon became clear that the paper had it right, with the cameras and correspondents going on to have a major impact on the delegates and the events themselves.[4]

Men and women attending the conventions, which both took place in Chicago, were warned in advance that the cameras would capture every movement they made while sitting in their seats. An image so seemingly innocuous as a delegate reading a book rather than listening to a speech, party leaders cautioned, could send the message that the convention was boring. Delegates also were told to be careful about the words they spoke, even if there wasn't a microphone nearby, because attentive TV viewers could be reading their lips.[5]

Female delegates had even more to worry about than their male counterparts because they had to be mindful of how they dressed. Leaders of both parties said women shouldn't wear expensive jewelry; diamonds or pearls could offend working-class viewers—perhaps even make them switch to the opposing party. Female delegates also were warned to steer clear of clothing that would be distracting on the TV screen; the *New York Herald Tribune* reported, "The ladies are being asked to abandon, for God's sake, large flowered print dresses."[6]

One of the most consequential changes in the conventions had to do with how long speakers talked. At previous conventions, nominating speeches often lasted more than an hour as politicians droned on at length about a candidate's background and qualities. TV producers at the 1952 conventions, however, told party leaders that viewers at home would lose interest if a speaker went on for too long. So the leaders of both the Democrats and the Republicans limited nominating speeches to no more than fifteen minutes and seconding speeches to no more than five. Likewise, the floor demonstrations that followed each candidate's name being put into nomination weren't allowed to continue longer than twenty minutes.[7]

Another change was that TV producers rather than party officials decided exactly what aspects of the conventions American viewers saw while sitting in their living rooms. That is, whenever activities at the rostrum became dull, the networks—ABC, CBS, and NBC all provided gavel-to-gavel coverage—diverted their cameras away from the scripted main event and switched to one of their roving correspondents interviewing a nationally known governor or member of Congress from the convention floor.[8]

Far more important than these influences on the delegates and the conventions was that TV news also was instrumental in choosing the presidential nominees for both parties.

TV VIEWERS HELP SELECT THE DEMOCRATIC NOMINEE

By 1952, the Democrats had been in control of the White House for twenty years. Franklin D. Roosevelt had first been elected in 1932 and then had been reelected three times, holding onto the job until he died in 1945. Vice President Harry S. Truman finished out FDR's last term and then was elected to one of his own.

When the Democratic delegates arrived in Chicago for the 1952 convention, however, it wasn't clear who would take home the nomination. President Truman had at one point indicated that his preference was Illinois governor Adlai Stevenson, but he'd later backed away from that position. So Stevenson became only one of five serious contenders for the nomination.[9]

Then TV entered the picture.

It was customary for the governor of the state where the convention was being held to make a welcoming speech to open the five-day event. So Stevenson was given fifteen minutes in the spotlight—with a national TV audience of 60 million people watching him—and the chance either to dazzle the American public or to fizzle into obscurity. He dazzled.[10]

Stevenson's most important decision when writing his speech was that he wouldn't merely welcome the 1,250 delegates to his home state but would also seize the moment to lash out at the Republicans, in shimmering eloquence, for having derided Truman and other Democratic leaders who'd led the nation for two decades.[11]

"Intemperate criticism is not a policy for the nation," Stevenson said in his stirring address. "Denunciation is not a program for our salvation." The governor also spoke for all Democrats when he said, "We will never appease. We will never apologize for our leadership in the great events of this critical century from Woodrow Wilson to Harry Truman."[12]

Near the end of his address, Stevenson laid down a principle so compelling that it would soon become a standard in American political rhetoric. "*Who* leads us is less important than *what* leads us—what convictions, what courage, what faith—win or lose," the governor bellowed, while placing dramatic emphasis on key words. "A *man* doesn't save a century or a civilization, but a *militant party* wedded to a principle can."[13]

The crowd of Democratic stalwarts interrupted Stevenson's rousing speech a stunning twenty-seven times. On some occasions, the governor had to stop speaking because the thunderous applause was so loud that he knew his voice couldn't be heard above it, and other times he had to pause and wait for the spontaneous chants of "We want Stevenson!" to subside.[14]

After Stevenson finished speaking, thousands of Democrats from around the country who'd watched his speech on TV either telephoned or sent telegrams to the delegates attending the convention. Those viewers had found Stevenson's speech electrifying, and so they wanted to give him an enthusiastic thumbs-up to become their party's nominee.[15]

Suddenly, the Illinois governor broke from the pack of contenders to become the front-runner. Headlines in the nation's newspapers reflected that momentum—"Stevenson Speech Sends Him to Fore" in the *New York Times*, "Big Swing to Stevenson" in the *San Francisco Chronicle*, "Rush to Get Ride on Adlai's Kite" in the *Chicago Sun-Times*.[16]

The endorsement from those throngs of viewers—which wouldn't have happened if TV hadn't broadcast Stevenson's address—propelled Truman to support the Illinois governor. With the TV audience and the sitting president now in his camp, Stevenson went on to win the nomination over his four rivals.[17]

Anyone who'd been keeping up with the politics at the convention knew that TV viewers had, for the first time in history, played a pivotal role in choosing a major party's standard-bearer.[18]

TV VIEWERS HELP SELECT THE REPUBLICAN NOMINEE

TV's impact on deciding who would top the Republican ticket was more complicated but equally decisive.

When the 1,206 delegates gathered in the Windy City, Senator Robert A. Taft of Ohio was the clear front-runner. "Mr. Republican," as the son of former president William Howard Taft was widely known, was the top choice of most people who came to the convention, as he had more delegates committed to him, on paper, than did former five-star general Dwight D. Eisenhower. In addition, Taft's supporters also controlled the Republican Party machinery.[19]

One controversy going into the convention was whether pro-Taft or pro-Eisenhower delegates from Georgia, Louisiana, and Texas would be seated. Precinct conventions in the three states had elected the pro-Eisenhower delegates, but the GOP committees in each of the states argued that those outcomes weren't valid because Democrats and independents had been allowed to vote. So the state committees had selected alternative delegates, all of them pro-Taft. As the national convention got under way, the question of which delegates would be seated was unresolved.[20]

Eisenhower supporters, with their candidate coming into the convention as the underdog, were looking for an issue that would allow them to gain momentum. So they grabbed onto the dispute over the delegates from the three southern states. The general's advocates used TV to tell the American people that Eisenhower was the victim of political operatives who were rejecting fair play in an effort to help their candidate win. Just before the convention, Eisenhower made a radio address in which he accused the Taft camp of "chicanery" and "crookedness" in blocking the rightly elected delegates from being seated.[21]

Taft supporters fought to keep the issue out of the glare of the TV cameras. That is, they wanted the credentials committee to hold a closed-door meeting to decide which set of delegates would be seated. TV correspondents got wind of the controversy, however, and reported that Eisenhower's people sided with broadcasters in demanding that cameras be allowed inside the credentials committee's hearing room.[22]

Eisenhower's supporters generally favored TV coverage of more unscripted activities, and they knew that airing this particular hearing would definitely work to their advantage. They were confident, in other words, that if people saw and heard the debate with their own eyes and ears, they'd side with Eisenhower's position that the elected delegates should be seated. Further, the pro-Eisenhower camp hoped that if its man won this battle, he'd get the boost he needed to defeat Taft and secure the Republican nomination.[23]

So the Eisenhower folks talked to TV correspondents whenever and wherever they could, taking special care to place plenty of "I Like Ike" banners in the background so viewers at home could repeatedly read the words. The reporters were happy to provide the airtime, as they wanted the cameras in the hearing room, too. Persistence by the Eisenhower camp eventually paid off, with the Taft folks finally agreeing—mainly to end the divisive interviews appearing on the TV screen—to allow the committee hearing to be televised.[24]

Eisenhower's leading biographer later wrote of the hearing, "It made for spectacular TV." Within a matter of minutes after the live coverage began, thousands of Republican viewers at home started phoning their delegates in Chicago, saying the Taft supporters were coming across as arrogant and mean-spirited bullies who were trying to deny the delegates the seats they'd been duly elected to fill. Leaders of the pro-Taft camp were soon scrambling to figure out what to do, eventually deciding it would be better for the Republican Party, in the long run, if the hearing ended so voters wouldn't continue to witness the GOP delegates behaving badly.[25]

The committee then awarded the seats for the three states to Eisenhower, and that victory gave him the attention and the positive energy he needed to secure the nomination. Viewers who'd been watching the convention from home, in short, had taken the nomination away from the candidate the Republican old guard had wanted and gave it to the underdog whose supporters understood the power of television.[26]

As the *Washington Post* reported the day after Eisenhower's triumph in the delegate battle, "Television is dominating the convention and is leaving a mark that will be discussed for a great many years."[27]

DWIGHT EISENHOWER EMBRACES TV TECHNIQUES

Staff members working for Eisenhower were so buoyed by television's central role in securing their candidate's nomination that they were soon catering to the needs of what was fast becoming the most powerful medium in the history of communication. As stated by the authors of the book *Unsilent Revolution:*

Television News and American Public Life, "it was the Eisenhower campaign that grasped the new techniques of the television age."[28]

One highly consequential decision those staff members made came near the end of the convention. At the Democratic gathering, Stevenson's acceptance speech on the final night of the convention didn't begin until 1:45 A.M. That meant that the vast majority of TV viewers had already gone to bed, and therefore the newly nominated candidate had squandered an opportunity to draw a large audience for the speech that would launch his campaign. It was a very different story at the Republican gathering, where Eisenhower's staff members made sure their man gave his acceptance speech early enough in the evening that millions of TV viewers heard what he had to say at this triumphant moment.[29]

That was merely prelude to what was to come. After the convention ended, Eisenhower's staff created the first presidential campaign ever designed to appeal specifically to television viewers. In cities across the country, the general rolled into one auditorium after another, all of them bathed in the glare of TV camera spotlights that allowed Eisenhower's million-watt smile to light up the room. Each time he stepped onstage, he raised his arms over his head to create the famous V-for-victory sign that reminded people that he'd been in charge of the Allied forces in Europe that had defeated the Nazis and Adolf Hitler in World War II.[30]

The military man trusted his political advisers, and so he dutifully followed their orders. He kept his speeches to no more than twenty minutes, punctuating them with pauses to allow for the applause that GOP operatives orchestrated. On the campaign trail that fall, Eisenhower also cut a handsome figure in a classic double-breasted camel's hair coat and brown fedora.[31]

Mamie Eisenhower, after spending the previous three and a half decades as a military wife, also did what the TV-savvy political advisers told her to do. That meant appearing with her husband at public events, standing by his side with a broad smile on her face. The somewhat dowdy candidate's wife waved at the crowds but didn't speak—and the public loved her for it.[32]

Democratic nominee Adlai Stevenson, in contrast to Eisenhower, rejected advice from his political advisers that he adapt to the needs of television. Stevenson, who was one of the most intellectual presidential nominees in history, insisted that voters should choose the leaders of their country

The TV networks broadcast hundreds of images of Republican candidate Dwight Eisenhower and his wife, Mamie, during the 1952 presidential campaign. AP Photo.

on the basis of substance, not superficial factors. Indeed, the Democratic nominee tried to turn his opponent's TV-friendly campaign style into a political issue, charging that Eisenhower had become nothing more than another consumer product being sold by the advertising world. "I don't think the American people want politics and the presidency to become the plaything of the high-pressure men," Stevenson said. "This isn't Ivory soap versus Palmolive soap."[33]

Stevenson also suffered because he was divorced. That meant he didn't have an adoring wife for the TV cameras to put on the screen to balance out their images of Mamie Eisenhower.

DWIGHT EISENHOWER USES TV TO HELP WIN THE WHITE HOUSE

Eisenhower's campaign staff members ignored Stevenson's charges that the Republican was turning himself into a commercial product and pushed their candidate to learn the skills that transformed him into an effective TV performer.[34]

During televised rallies at airports and on the rear platforms of trains, the candidate frequently used one of two props to make his points. Sometimes he pulled an egg out of his pocket and asked the crowd, "Do you know how many taxes there are on this single egg?" He then recited a long list of levies that caused shudders to run down the spine of the stalwart Republicans—the vast majority of them favoring limited government—who packed his audiences.[35]

Eisenhower's other prop was a thin, two-foot-long piece of wood that a campaign staff member had scored down the center so it would break easily. An aide handed the stick to the general as the words coming out of his mouth denounced the alleged shrinking value of the American dollar under the previous twenty years of Democratic rule. "This is what is happening to your hard-earned dollar," Eisenhower told his audience. He then snapped the piece of wood in two, a dramatic gesture that looked terrific on the TV screen.[36]

The Eisenhower camp's embracing of made-for-TV techniques didn't stop with using visual images, as the candidate's staff also crafted the words that came out of his mouth. One of Eisenhower's political advisers consulted the George Gallup polling organization—something that hadn't been done before—and learned that the biggest concern for millions of voters was rising inflation.[37]

So the adviser read Eisenhower's earlier speeches and extracted any reference to the topic he'd previously made. The aide next drafted scripts on the subject, drawing his inspiration from what Eisenhower had said in the past, and presented them to the candidate. The political adviser also wrote the exact words on cue cards that he had the nominee read out loud numerous times before a speech.[38]

After this preparation, the phrasing was embedded in Eisenhower's mind. So whenever anyone at a campaign event mentioned rising prices at the grocery store, the candidate automatically responded with a statement such as "Yes, my Mamie gets after me about the high cost of living. It's another reason why I say that it's time for a change—time to get back to an honest dollar and an honest dollar's work." Another scripted response Eisenhower repeatedly gave in that same situation was "A few years ago, the same groceries cost you $10, but now they cost $24, next year $30—that's what will happen unless we have a change."[39]

TV PLACES THE POWER IN THE HANDS OF AVERAGE AMERICANS

It's impossible to know exactly how much impact Eisenhower playing to the TV cameras had on the country's voters, but some scholars argue that it ultimately was a key factor in his victory in the November election. Eisenhower won 442 electoral votes; Stevenson won 89.[40]

There's absolutely no question, however, that TV's coverage of the 1952 national political conventions the previous summer was decisive in Stevenson and Eisenhower becoming the presidential nominees for their respective parties. For the first time in the nation's history, the most important decision made at those events had been placed in the hands of the American people—or at least those who were watching TV.[41]

Improving the Lives of Migrant Farmworkers

In the mid-twentieth century, between 2 million and 3 million Americans who picked the fruits and vegetables that made their way onto the country's richly laden dinner tables were enduring lives defined by despair, degradation, and crushing poverty. Any socially conscious observer who knew about these shameful circumstances couldn't help but see these migrant farmworkers—many of them either African American or Mexican—as modern-day slaves.

On the day after Thanksgiving in 1960, the CBS television network aired an hour-long documentary that brought the disgraceful situation into the nation's living rooms. Leading newspapers praised Harvest of Shame *as a poignant and powerful piece of broadcast journalism. Thousands of Americans who saw the program called or wrote their members of Congress, urging the lawmakers to create new policies designed to improve the lives of migrant workers.*

Harvest of Shame was narrated by Edward R. Murrow, the most revered figure in the history of broadcast news. He'd risen to prominence while working for CBS radio during World War II and had earned more acclaim in 1954 for his reporting that helped end the anticommunist witch hunts of Senator Joe McCarthy.[1]

The man who came up with the idea for *Harvest of Shame* was Murrow's longtime producer Fred Friendly. During the 1950s, Murrow and Friendly created documentaries that aired every few weeks on a primetime series titled *CBS Reports*. Friendly had heard about the difficulties that migrant workers faced, but he didn't think these largely uneducated men and women would be willing to be interviewed—at least not on film.[2]

CBS newsman Edward R. Murrow narrated 1960's Harvest of Shame, *which is now remembered as one of the finest documentaries in television history. Courtesy of Getty Images/CBS Photo Archive.*

And then, in early 1960, an eager job applicant named David Lowe approached Friendly, pleading to be hired as a producer. Friendly gave Lowe $1,000 and sent him and a cameraman to Florida for a month to talk with migrant workers. If Lowe could get them to speak in front of the camera, Friendly promised, he'd have a permanent job with CBS.[3]

For the next eight months, Lowe and the cameraman traveled with the workers as they picked tomatoes in Florida, beans in the Carolinas, corn in New Jersey, and apples in New York. Lowe also went to California and conducted interviews with laborers there.[4]

OPENING A WINDOW ONTO A SHOCKING WORLD

Viewers who tuned into the November 25, 1960, broadcast immediately found themselves witnessing a chaotic scene, as *Harvest of Shame* began with images of what was known as a "shape-up." This was the process during which workers milled around a dusty parking lot where crew leaders yelled out the wage that the farmers they worked for would pay people to pick produce on that particular day.

"This scene is not taking place in the Congo," listeners heard Murrow say. "It has nothing to do with Johannesburg or Cape Town. It is not Nyasaland or Nigeria." Then he paused for a moment before saying, "This is Florida. These are citizens of the United States, 1960. This is 'shape-up' for the migrant workers."

The narrator added that the wages these crew leaders promised during the degrading bidding wars invariably turned out to be higher than the workers ultimately were paid. Perhaps the most memorable statement Murrow made during this opening sequence was "One farmer looked at this scene and said, 'We used to own our slaves. Now we just rent them.'"[5]

Harvest of Shame then shifted to another scene every bit as appalling as that first one, though much more personal. It showed David Lowe interviewing an African-American youngster named Jerome. The nine-year-old boy was inside a dilapidated shack with three little girls. Lowe explained that

One of the most powerful scenes in Harvest of Shame *came when nine-year-old Jerome was interviewed by producer David Lowe. Courtesy of Getty Images/CBS Photo Archive.*

Jerome had recently been injured, so he was caring for his younger sisters—Lois, Beulah, and Kathy—while their mother and the other ten children in the family worked in the fields picking beans.

The camera zooms in on the underside of Jerome's foot, focusing on a nasty-looking open wound. A fly can be seen buzzing nearby.

"What happened to your foot, Jerome?" Lowe asks the boy.
    "I drove a nail in it—out there by the washhouse," Jerome responds.
    "What did your mother do for that?"
    "Put some alcohol on it."

The camera next focuses on the bed where Jerome and his sisters sleep. Up where a pillow ought to be is a large hole, about a foot in diameter, with wads of cotton stuffing pulled out from inside the mattress casing. Lowe asks, "How did you get that hole in that bed there, Jerome?" The boy answers matter-of-factly, as if such an occurrence isn't anything out of the ordinary, "Rats."

Mixed in with these early scenes were various facts that Murrow added. Among them was that the average annual earnings for a migrant worker was $900—equal to $7,117 today.

GIVING VOICE TO THE DOWNTRODDEN

As viewers watched the documentary, they came to see Lowe not only as a sensitive interviewer but also as a man who was respectful of his subjects. No matter how dire a family's circumstances were, Lowe didn't give any indication that he was judging the workers.[6]

Such was the case when he talked with Mrs. Blakely, a middle-aged African-American woman wearing a freshly laundered white dress. She was living in a migrant worker camp in North Carolina.

"Mrs. Blakely," Lowe asks, "how many years have you been working in agriculture—in the fields?"
    "Practically all my life," she replies. "I raised all my kids working in the field."
    The camera moves from Blakely to a pile of loose straw that's strewn a few feet away from her.
    "I noticed that there's some straw laying over there. What is that for?"
    "Well, that's the straw they brought for the people to sleep on."

"Weren't mattresses supplied here?"

"They used to be, but they ain't now."

Lowe stays silent for a few seconds and then asks, "Mrs. Blakely, how many bathrooms are there here?"

She shakes her head and smiles with amusement.

"But where do you—where do you use the bathroom?" Lowe asks, a trace of confusion in his voice. "Where—where are the facilities?"

Blakely laughs heartily and says, "Don't have none."

PORTRAYING WORKERS AS STRUGGLING TO SURVIVE

One of the most somber of Lowe's interviews was with a white man named Roach, his face deeply wrinkled from his long days in the sun. The interview took place in a wooded area in northern Florida. Mrs. Roach and the couple's four sons, dressed in overalls, stood silently next to the head of the family as he told Lowe that he'd driven 1,600 miles in search of work.

"Mr. Roach," Lowe asks, "where did you spend the night last night, with your family?"

"Over in the woods," Roach says. "Pulled off on the side of the road—on a little dirt road—and slept in the woods outside the car."

"May I ask you, sir, what did you and your family have for dinner last night?"

"Well, we had bologna sausage and a loaf of bread."

"That isn't very good for a growing family, is it?"

"Well, we made do on it."

"How much money do you have in the world right at this moment?"

"Oh, I have about $1.40."

"Well, what do you intend to do about food for your family today?"

"Well, I've always worked and I always figured I could get work. I have never been where I couldn't get a little something to do."

Lowe didn't interview any Mexican workers because he didn't think they spoke English well enough for viewers to understand what they said. He did, however, talk with a Mexican-American minister who'd spent time with the migrant workers.

"They are treated like slaves," the minister told Lowe. "Only in their name are they not slaves. Someone is making thousands of dollars off of their sweat. Is that a slave or not?"

This same minister also talked about how crew leaders took advantage of Mexican as well as American migrant workers. "The grower pays them forty-five cents to pick a crate of tomatoes," he said. "And then they turn around and pay the laborer twelve cents—at the most."

EXPOSING A CYCLE OF POVERTY

One section of *Harvest of Shame* was devoted to the topic of education. It began with Murrow saying, "Everyone who knows anything about this situation agrees that the best hope for the future of the migrants lies in the education of their children. But for the children of migrants, education is not easy to come by."[7]

He supported that pessimistic observation by pointing out that most labor laws ignored farm children. Murrow also reported that statistics from the U.S. Office of Education showed that migrant workers had the highest illiteracy rate in the country.

Murrow's next series of statements were equally depressing. "Approximately one out of every 500 children whose parents are migrant laborers will finish grade school," he said. "Approximately one out of every 5,000 ever finishes high school. And there is no case on record of the child of a migrant laborer ever receiving a college diploma."

The documentary next took viewers to an elementary school in New Jersey where David Lowe interviewed an African-American girl named Laura Weeks, her hair in pigtails.

"Laura," Lowe asks, "what grade are you in?"
  "In the sixth grade," Laura says.
  "Do you intend to go to high school?"
  "Yes."
  "What would you like to be, Laura?"
  "I would like to be a teacher."
  "And what would you like to teach?"
  "I would like to teach fifth grade."

Next to speak was the children's teacher, an attractive African-American woman wearing a black sheath dress and a pearl necklace. Lowe tells Christine Shank that he's talked with Laura, and then he asks the teacher, "Will she really have a chance to continue her education?"

Shanks is an articulate woman who pronounces her words precisely. "Laura is from an exceedingly large family. In fact, I believe there are eight or nine girls—all girls—in the family." The teacher takes a breath, and her expression suggests she regrets what she now has to say. "Because of the family's financial condition, she probably will get no further, with luck, than upper junior high school."

Murrow appeared on the screen to conclude the section on education by making a pair of one-sentence statements. As he said, "The federal government spends $6.5 million annually protecting migratory *wildlife*," an image of a flock of birds—perhaps geese flying toward Canada—was shown. "This year, Congress failed to appropriate $3.5 million to educate migratory *children*." That second statement referred to legislation that had been introduced in 1960 but had been defeated.[8]

ADVOCATING FOR CHANGE

Putting those two statements back-to-back wasn't the only place in *Harvest of Shame* that the documentary veered into subjectivity. Murrow and his producers clearly thought the government should enact new policies to improve the lives of migrant workers, and they wanted their TV audience to come to that same conclusion.[9]

Another example of juxtaposition was designed to tell viewers that the housing where migrant workers lived was inadequate. Murrow made his first statement—"A family of six will move into this room"—while the TV screen showed a filthy, ten-foot-by-twelve-foot space furnished with a crude table consisting of boards that had been nailed together. He made his second statement—"Nearby, a trotting raceway has new stables for horses. They cost $500,000"—while the screen was filled with images of a modern, spotlessly clean building where men were meticulously bathing and grooming handsome thoroughbred racehorses.

How the migrants were transported was highlighted in a similar manner. First came words and images about produce and farm animals. "The vegetables the migrants picked yesterday move north swiftly on rails," Murrow stated. "Produce on route to the tables of America by trailers is refrigerated and carefully packed to prevent bruising. By federal regulation, cattle carried to market must be watered, fed, and rested for five out of every twenty-eight hours." As the journalist made these statements, viewers saw streamlined train cars racing down tracks and sleek trucks—vented to give the animals fresh air—moving swiftly along superhighways.

Then came words and images about the migrants. "People—men, women, and children—are carried to the fields in the North in journeys as long as four days and three nights," Murrow said. "They often ride ten hours without stopping for food or facilities." While the newsman spoke these words, the TV screen showed a rickety truck rumbling down a country road. The back end of the vehicle was open, and several dozen men and women were packed tightly together—standing and pressed body to body with no space between them.

As *Harvest of Shame* neared its end, the documentary went beyond using the juxtaposition of contrasting facts and images to suggest the need for reform. Specifically, Murrow listed new policies the U.S. Congress and state legislatures could enact if they wanted to improve the lives of migrant workers and their families.

First on his list was expanding child labor protections to cover the sons and daughters of migrant workers. Murrow also said lawmakers could create health clinics for the laborers and their children, could require farmers who employ temporary workers to provide them with sanitary housing, and could ensure that educational programs be developed so migrants could attend school at least until they were sixteen.

After articulating these suggested changes, Murrow said, "There will, of course, be opposition to these recommendations—too much government interference . . . too expensive . . . socialism."

The journalist then made a dramatic call to action. "The migrants have no lobby," Murrow said, a slight catch in his raspy voice. "Only enlightened, aroused, and perhaps angered public opinion can do anything about the migrants." He paused, looking sternly into the camera. "The people you have seen have the strength to harvest your fruit and vegetables. They do not have the strength to influence legislation. Maybe we do." The narrator finished his challenge to American TV viewers with his signature closing, "Good night, and good luck."

ALLOWING THE OTHER SIDE TO SPEAK

There's no question that the men who made *Harvest of Shame*—Murrow as narrator, Fred Friendly as executive producer, and David Lowe as producer—

expressed a strong point of view vis-à-vis the plight of migrant workers. At the same time, though, they gave the farmers who hired the workers the opportunity to defend their actions.

One statement came from a man named Jones, who was identified as a California farmer who employed hundreds of migrant workers. Lowe asked Jones if he thought the laborers were happy. As the screen showed an image of men and women stooping over in the field behind where the producer and farmer talked, Jones said, "Well, I guess they got a little gypsy in their blood." Jones then snickered slightly as he continued, "They love to go from place to place. They don't have a worry in the world. They're happier than we are. They're the happiest race of people on Earth."

The most articulate comments on behalf of the farmers came from Charles Shuman. He was president of the country's largest farm lobby, the American Farm Bureau Federation, and Lowe interviewed him at the organization's headquarters in Washington, D.C. "We take the position," Shuman said, "that it's far better to have thousands of these folks—who are practically unemployable—earning some money, doing some productive work rather than doing nothing."

Shuman also defended the housing where laborers lived, pointing out that the farmers shown in the documentary were the only employers in the country who provided their workers with a place to live. "And we also furnish extra benefits—perquisites," Shuman said, apparently referring to the farmers transporting workers to the North and feeding them meals when they labored all day in the fields. "It's almost impossible to calculate the value of these added benefits."

WINNING PRAISE AND SUPPORT

The response to *Harvest of Shame* was overwhelmingly positive. More than 2,700 members of the public either telephoned CBS or sent letters to the network praising the program. Virtually all of those viewers specifically stated that they favored the government enacting the policies Murrow had listed as having the potential to improve the lives of the migrant workers.[10]

Elected officials were soon hearing from the public. In a letter to Murrow, Senator William Proxmire of Wisconsin wrote, "Rarely have I received such an outpouring of mail expressing concern about a social issue."[11]

TV critics quickly applauded the documentary. "Harvest of Shame," the *New York Times* stated in its review, "was uncompromising in its exposure of the filth, despair and grinding poverty that are the lot of the migratory work-ers." The *Times* was particularly complimentary of the film's close-up images, saying, "The faces of the migratory workers were their own eloquent editorial on a national disgrace."[12]

The *Times* was so impressed by the documentary that it published a lengthy feature story about it, a week after the review had appeared, that was filled with more praise. "The film was a challenging and tremendously disturbing study of the migratory workers who pick the fruit and vegetable crops that adorn the nation's tables," the story read. "The contrasting scenes of humans jammed vertically into dangerous trucks while cattle rode in spa-cious freight cars required no elaboration." The paper went on to commend Murrow for being "at his crusading best" and CBS for "putting the influence of TV behind the elimination of a national sore."[13]

Numerous other papers heaped on more praise. The *Miami Herald* wrote that *Harvest of Shame* was "a model of pictorial reporting," the *Washington Evening Star* called it "an important social documentary," and the *Los Ange-les Times* gave the program an enthusiastic thumbs-up by saying it had been "produced with distinction and honesty."[14]

More words of approval came from *Time* magazine. The country's largest-circulation news weekly labeled the documentary "a moving muck-raking masterpiece" and praised Murrow for having gone beyond illumi-nating the problems by also suggesting specific policy changes to remedy the situation. *Time* was highly critical, by contrast, of what Charles Shuman of the farm lobby had to say, writing that he "painfully elaborated his foot-dragging conservatism."[15]

FAILING TO PROPEL POSITIVE CHANGE

The only member of Congress who appeared in the documentary was Senator Harrison Williams, who chaired a subcommittee that oversaw migrant labor. Murrow interviewed him on camera, with Williams expressing his strongest concern about the deplorable living conditions migrant workers had to en-dure. "The migrant farmer is the most poorly housed member of our society," the New Jersey senator said.

After *Harvest of Shame* aired, Williams led the effort to enact federal legislation to improve the lives of the workers. He knew the CBS program told the story in a compelling fashion, so he hosted a screening on Capitol

Hill exclusively for members of Congress. He also scheduled congressional hearings so his subcommittee could hear from a long list of experts on the subject of migrant labor.[16]

But not everyone on Capitol Hill agreed with Williams—far from it. When he introduced bills to provide medical, educational, and housing aid to migrant workers, many senators opposed the legislation. Senator Spessard Holland of Florida railed against the bills and the documentary. Holland accused CBS of "misrepresentation" and "extravagant overstatement." The senator, whose constituents included some of the farmers who came across so negatively in the TV program, also lambasted the men who created the program, saying, "The producers must have sought far and wide to discover the most dilapidated housing they could find."[17]

In 1961, Williams succeeded in winning Senate approval for five bills, but opponents in the House of Representatives blocked them all. The same story unfolded in 1962 and again in 1963. These legislative failures came about even though newspaper editorials supported the efforts to improve the lives of the workers—the headlines above those pieces included "Justice for Migrants" in the *New York Times* and "An End to Farm Peonage" in the *Washington Post*.[18]

Journalism scholars have credited the American Farm Bureau Federation with defeating the legislation. One author has pointed out that statements made by the legislation's most vocal opponent in the House, Representative Robert Michel of Illinois, read "almost word for word" like those that federation officials wrote in denouncing the program. Among Michel's comments were that the program was a "strange type of reporting—the cub type."[19]

Despite the documentary's lack of success in prompting changes in the lives of migrant workers, *Harvest of Shame* soon achieved legendary status in the history of broadcast news. In the words of one scholar who has studied investigative reporting, the program was a "great example of television muckraking."[20]

Popularizing the
Birth Control Pill

In the late 1950s, American gynecologists began prescribing a new medication for the small number of their patients who suffered from certain obscure menstrual disorders. The physicians soon became aware that the tiny tablet also suppressed a woman's ovulation, but they considered this to be merely a minor side effect of the pill.

Then the news media heard about it. After the nation's leading newspapers and magazines began promoting the medication as a form of contraception, women started asking their doctors, in a phrase they picked up from the media, to "put me on the pill." Within half a dozen years, the national birthrate had plunged, as had the level of anxiety among sexually active women who weren't eager to become pregnant.

News articles about the medication that eventually became known as the birth control pill began appearing in numerous publications more than three years *before* the U.S. Food and Drug Administration licensed it as a contraceptive in May 1960.

Time was among the first journalistic outlets to report on the development. In early 1957, the news weekly wrote, "Last week, after months of rumors, president John Searle of the Chicago-based drug manufacturer G. D. Searle & Co. guardedly told stockholders that the company hopes to introduce this year an item for a variety of menstrual disorders. There has been speculation that the drug may have a use in the field of physiological birth control." If a woman wasn't menstruating, the piece said, she could take the pill for ten to fifteen days and then would begin a regular cycle.[1]

The country's largest-circulation news magazine clearly recognized, however, that the synthetic hormone's potential as a contraceptive was the bigger story, as it devoted more space to that aspect of the pill than to its effect on menstruation. "The possibility of 'fertility control' arises from the fact that the drug, when taken on certain schedules, apparently prevents ovulation," *Time* reported.[2]

Particularly significant about the *Time* article—in the context of the news media promoting the birth control pill—was the statement the magazine placed immediately after the one about the new medication's "fertility control" potential. That is, *Time* editors knew that many of their readers would object to a pill if it was seen as a form of *artificial* birth control. So they did what they could to quash that would-be controversy by adding this sentence: "Since no ovum is released, there is technically no destruction of life."[3]

Other early stories also went out of their way to portray the pill in a positive light. In a 1957 piece headlined "Birth Control Pills on Way," for example, the *Washington Post* reported that "the oral contraceptive has proven successful in various tests at leading hospitals throughout the United States." Likewise, a 1958 story in the *New York Times* reassured readers that a pair of two-year studies, one in Puerto Rico and the other in Los Angeles, hadn't just proven the pill to be "100 percent effective" but also had shown there were "no lasting side-effects" if the medication was taken continuously.[4]

The *New York Times* also showed its support for the pill, though the medication still hadn't been approved by federal health authorities, in 1959 with an editorial titled "Progress on Birth Control Pill." In the piece, the *Times* articulated seven important pluses of the tablet. Heading the list was its effectiveness, followed by factors such as "does not cause any significant abnormalities in the menstrual cycle" and "does not impair fertility upon cessation."[5]

BECOMING NATIONAL NEWS

During the late 1950s, the fact that drug manufacturers had developed a medication with the potential to prevent pregnancy led to this trickle of news stories in several publications. And then, in mid-1960, the number of articles on the topic increased exponentially.

That flood of stories came after federal drug officials gave their approval for American women to begin taking the tablet every day—but a doctor's prescription was still required. Now that government authorities had sanctioned the pill to prevent pregnancy, every major daily news outlet in the country showcased the news.

Among the headlines: "U.S. Clears Pill for Contraceptive Use" in the *San Francisco Chronicle*, "Birth Control Pill O.K.'d by Drug Administration" in the *Boston Globe*, and "Birth Control Pill Wins U.S. Approval for Safety" in the *Atlanta Constitution*.[6]

The texts of the stories filled in the various details. "For the first time, the Food and Drug Administration has approved a pill as being safe for contraceptive or birth control use," read the first paragraph of the *Minneapolis Tribune*'s version of the news, which ran on the paper's front page. A later paragraph told readers that the new pill, when taken daily, cost a woman about $10 a month—comparable to $79 today.[7]

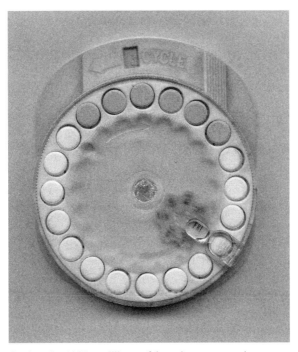

During the 1960s, millions of American women became familiar with the dispensers that contained a month's supply of birth control pills. Courtesy of the Division of Medicine & Science, National Museum of American History, Smithsonian Institution.

Each news article included the brand name of the medication, Enovid, and a statement telling readers that research studies had found the pill to be safe for women to use. The *Boston Globe*, for example, reported, "The FDA said it was authorizing use of the drug over long periods of time on the basis of tests that had showed there were no harmful side effects."[8]

The papers also made sure readers knew that gynecologists would oversee the pill's use. "Under the clearance granted by the agency," wrote the *Pittsburgh Post-Gazette*, "it may be used only on a doctor's prescription."[9]

Along with supplying the straightforward information, news outlets also found room to sing the pill's praises—and exuberantly so. Editors at *Newsweek* magazine, for example, called it "the remarkable pill," and their counterparts at *Reader's Digest* labeled it "one of the outstanding research accomplishments of our day." These weren't the only instances of influential publications going beyond mere reporting and moving into the realm of promoting the pill. *Time* magazine—in a cover story—dubbed it "a miraculous tablet," and the *New York Times*—in a story on page one—described it as "a scientific dream-come-true."[10]

Very few stories about the birth control pill aired on TV news programs, as this was an era when the major networks steered clear of content related to sexual activities for fear of offending their viewers.

DOWNPLAYING THE DOWNSIDE

From the earliest stages of the development of an oral contraceptive, researchers and potential users were understandably concerned about the new medication's side effects. The various news outlets that reported on the pill dutifully listed these factors, but then—in the next breath—characterized them as nothing more than minor inconveniences.

Coverage by the *Chicago Tribune* was typical. "Because Enovid imitates the action of hormones normally occurring during pregnancy, some women experience reactions similar to those of early pregnancy when they first begin to take the pills," the paper reported. "The most common of these are nausea and sometimes tenderness of the breast, some degree of fluid retention, and a marked sense of well-being." In the sentence that followed, the *Tribune* minimized the concerns by stating, "These reactions wear off rapidly, even faster than in pregnancy."[11]

Treatment of the topic was similar in other papers. "There may be undesirable effects when the pills are used," wrote the *Baltimore Sun*. "Women may become bloated or nauseated, and have fullness and soreness of the breasts." Once again, the list of side effects was accompanied by a statement discounting them as minor and temporary. "Fortunately, these complaints disappear within a couple months, as in pregnancy," the *Sun* reported.[12]

Despite the Food and Drug Administration's assurances that research studies had found the pill safe to use, rumors persisted that the medication might be harmful. Some critics, for example, blamed the pill for causing deadly blood clots. In response, the *Los Angeles Times* published a story containing unusually blunt phrasing. In the first sentence of the article, the *Times* said point-blank, "There is not a shred of medical evidence to connect the birth control pill with the deaths of American women."[13]

On other occasions, news outlets responded to concerns about the pill by mocking them. When scientists at the University of Oregon released a study showing that Enovid accelerated the growth of existing breast cancer in rats, *Newsweek* dismissed the issue by saying, "As one New York physician scoffed last week, 'All this proves is that if you're a rat and have breast cancer, you shouldn't take Enovid.'"[14]

LAUNCHING A REVOLUTION

The news about the birth control pill had, by mid-1961, grown even larger than chronicling a major medical breakthrough. For the repercussions of the tiny tablet were rippling through society, propelling a sizeable number of Americans to change their bedroom habits. That shift, in turn, prompted *Esquire* magazine to announce that the nation had entered a new phase in its cultural evolution, observing, "We appear to be living through a sexual revolution."[15]

Esquire's seminal piece on the topic was titled "Sex: The Quiet Revolution" and carried the subtitle "Among the Fallen Idols: Virginity, Chastity, and Repression." The trend story didn't leave any doubt that the birth control pill was the catalyst for transforming sex, at least among many Americans, from its function as a means of procreation to its new and vastly more popular role as a form of recreation. Sources for the article ranged from a theology professor who said, "The old repressiveness is gone—what we generally associate with the word *puritanism*," to a plethora of sexually active young women whose quotes included such candid comments as "I don't know any virgins" and "I used to think it was terrible if people had intercourse before marriage. Now I think each person should find his own values. Why not?"[16]

After *Esquire* attached a name to the radical changes taking place in American bedrooms, the floodgates opened and other news voices reported on the new sexual permissiveness. The *Washington Post* wrote, "Campus sex morals have been changing," and then quoted from a nationwide report on sexual activity among college students that concluded, "Sexual relations among undergraduates are markedly more frequent than they were a generation ago." The *Los Angeles Times* told a similar story. In a prominently displayed feature, the *Times* quoted a sexually promiscuous college student named Bev as saying, "I don't feel that I am rebelling or revolting or creating a new morality. I just feel that I am expressing myself the way I feel at the moment, in the most natural way."[17]

U.S. News & World Report, the most conservative of the three major national news weeklies, also took note of the sexual revolution that had swept the country. A lengthy piece titled "The Pill: How It Is Affecting U.S. Morals, Family Life" began by telling readers, "An era of vast change in sexual morality now is developing in America." Among the sources in the story was an official from Mills College in California, who said, "There is less talk than there used to be about right or wrong—the question today is more about whether the *individual* is making a wise decision for her future." The *U.S. News* article also reported that "sex clubs" were popping up not only at many colleges but also in a significant number of high schools.[18]

PORTRAYING USE OF THE PILL AS A FEMINIST ACT

Coverage of the birth control pill extended to stories chronicling profound changes in the lives of American women. Some of the articles discussing the tablet's central role in the Sexual Revolution had hinted at a shift toward women becoming more independent, but it took journalist and feminist icon Gloria Steinem to articulate the point clearly and directly. She did so in a second blockbuster article in *Esquire*, this one published in 1962 and titled "The Moral Disarmament of Betty Coed."[19]

In the piece, Steinem first asserted that "the development of the 'autonomous girl' is important," and then listed the defining characteristics of an independent woman. "She has work she wants to do and with which she feels

Legendary feminist Gloria Steinem's 1962 article in Esquire *articulated the extraordinary impact the birth control pill was having on the lives of American women. Courtesy of Getty Images/ Cynthia MacAdams.*

identified," Steinem wrote. "She can marry later than average and have affairs if she wishes, but she can also marry without giving up her work. She can lay aside her job during childbearing years and resume it full or part time afterward."[20]

The pill was an essential element in achieving female independence, Steinem continued, because it allowed a sexually active woman to delay childbirth until she completed her education and established her career. What's more, the author pointed out, a woman now had the ability to limit how many children she had and to space them in a timeframe that suited her plans. A woman with this level of autonomy and control "does not feel forced to choose between a career and marriage, and is therefore free to find fulfillment in a combination of the two," Steinem said. She then concluded, "Like men, they are free to take sex, education, work and even marriage when and how they like."[21]

Steinem's article that identified using birth control as a feminist act prompted other publications to follow suit. *Time*, for instance, communicated the same idea by running a profile of a teacher from Indiana—in an article titled "Contraception: Freedom from Fear"—who was the epitome of the independent woman. "When I got married I was still in college, and I wanted to be certain that I finished," the twenty-three-year-old said. "With the pill, I know I can keep earning money and not worry about an accident that would ruin everything." The *New York Times*, for its part, told readers that a growing number of young women were choosing "not to rush into marriage" but, at the same time, were seeing "no reason why they should not have a sex life during their early adult years."[22]

COMBATTING THE CATHOLIC CHURCH

In choosing to promote the birth control pill, the country's newspapers and magazines took a position in direct conflict with the Catholic Church. Clerical officials from the pope on down the ecclesiastical chain of command told women that if they prevented or even delayed childbirth, they were violating God's will and, therefore, were committing a sin.

Newsweek provided the most comprehensive treatment of the topic in a 1964 cover story labeled "Birth Control: The Pill and the Church." The article began by laying out the issue. "The traditional church view is that the 'primary' end of marriage—and therefore of sexual intercourse—is the procreation and rearing of children. Interference with the 'power to generate life' violates natural and divine law."[23]

The fact that *Newsweek* considered the pill to be beneficial to society, despite Church opposition, became apparent as the article continued. For the magazine soon abandoned all pretense of objectivity, with the cover story sounding like an editorial. Before the end of the first page, the piece already had pointed out that the Church's opposition to birth control had forced many Catholic families to live in poverty and that the Church was out of step with most of American society because "all major Protestant sects sanction birth control." At other points, the article praised the oral contraceptive as "ingenious," called it the "magic pill," and credited it with improving the marriages of millions of sexually active couples because "sex is more fun with oral contraceptives."[24]

In one direct affront to the world's most powerful religion, the story pointed out that, despite what officials said, "Moral theories about contraception are not always observed" by Catholic couples. Indeed not. *Newsweek* reported that "as many as 70 percent of U.S. Catholics use some form of contraception" and bolstered its point by quoting a New Jersey woman who defiantly stated, "I don't confess that I take the pill because I don't believe it is a sin."[25]

The article was so bold in its assault on the Church's anti-contraception stand that, at times, it adopted a tone of blatant ridicule. After reporting that the only form of birth control that Catholic officials sanctioned was the rhythm method and then explaining that the technique involved a woman avoiding intercourse during the time she was ovulating, the article derided the method by dubbing it "Vatican roulette."[26]

Newsweek's strongest pro-contraception stance came when it argued that the Catholic Church was wrong to oppose the pill because taking it wasn't, in fact, a form of *artificial* birth control. The oral contraceptive was altogether different from such "mechanical contrivances" as the diaphragm or intra-uterine device, the news weekly insisted, because it merely modified the time sequence in a woman's normal body functions by suppressing ovulation— much like the rhythm method. The article concluded by stating unequivocally, "The pill should be considered morally acceptable."[27]

Although the *Newsweek* cover story was the most high-profile journalistic questioning of the Catholic Church's opposition to the pill, that article certainly wasn't the only one that dealt with the topic. In 1965, for example, the *Baltimore Sun* gave prominent coverage to efforts by Dr. John J. Rock to pressure Catholic leaders to allow priests to condone the pill's use in individual cases, such as when a pregnancy would endanger a woman's health. When Dr. Rock, the Catholic physician who was credited with developing the pill, brought his campaign to Capitol Hill, the *Sun* highlighted his criticism of the Church. "Many clergymen realize," the paper quoted him as saying, "that independent expression is required in this situation." The *Sun* also quoted Dr. Rock as saying the Church was wrong in opposing the pill because using it merely "imitates nature."[28]

PROPELLING POSITIVE CHANGE

Scholars who have studied the history of the birth control pill have documented the news media's key role in advancing the groundbreaking medical and social phenomenon. In her book, *On the Pill: A Social History of Oral Contraceptives, 1950–1970*, Elizabeth Siegel Watkins wrote, "Popular periodicals contributed greatly to the dissemination of information about oral contraception." Watkins also observed, "The *New York Times* (and many other daily papers that took their cues from the *Times*) consistently reported news of the pill in particular and birth control in general."[29]

Consistent with that assessment, in 1966 the *Times* ran a front-page story headlined "The Pill: Revolution in Birth Control" that identified some of the changes that had taken place in American society since the Food and Drug Administration had approved the new medication half a dozen years earlier. One important fact the *Times* reported was that some 6 million American women—one-fifth of those considered to be of childbearing age—were using the pill. A second stunning statistic was that the national birthrate had plunged, in a mere six years, by an astonishing 24 percent. Perhaps even more dramatic evidence of the pill's effect on American life was that, as the birthrate had plunged, the frequency of sexual intercourse had soared, studies showed, by an even more extraordinary 40 percent.[30]

Although those two facts were definitely newsworthy, other statements in the high-profile *Times* story spoke to changes in society brought about by the pill that were equally important to individual Americans. "For most of its users," the paper noted, "the pill has revolutionized family planning and relieved a traditional source of family tension: the fear of having unwanted children." The *Times* may have summarized this dimension of the story most succinctly in the first direct quote that appeared in the piece. The statement came from a mother of three children who said, simply but eloquently, "With the pill, we don't have to worry anymore."[31]

13

Fueling the Space Race

In 1958 when Congress created the National Aeronautics and Space Administration, the American public had scant interest in exploring the world beyond the Earth. Few people believed that a man would ever walk on the moon, and anyone who suggested such a thing was ridiculed as being either certifiably insane or impossibly foolish.

Things began to change three years later when the country's TV networks aired live coverage of the first U.S. spaceflight. After viewers saw that event, huge numbers of them began to dream of the day that an American would step onto the lunar surface. TV news continued to showcase missions throughout the decade, fueling what became a national fixation about the United States winning the Space Race.

The best date to begin a summary of the American news media's involvement with outer space is April 12, 1961. That's the day the Soviet Union's Yuri Gagarin became the first man to travel beyond the Earth's atmosphere and into orbit.[1]

Many historians argue that the next relevant event in such a summary came a mere five days later. That's when John F. Kennedy suffered his first major defeat as president. He'd sent 1,400 Cuban exiles—trained, equipped, and transported by the U.S. Central Intelligence Agency—back to their homeland in hopes of overthrowing communist leader Fidel Castro. The Bay of Pigs attempted invasion of Cuba was an unmitigated disaster.[2]

These two events created a dark shadow of disappointment that hung over the United States. Both the president and the country as a whole needed a success story to boost their sagging morale.[3]

CAPTURING THE PUBLIC IMAGINATION

American leaders chose to place their hopes on the sturdy shoulders of the country's first astronaut to enter space. And so, less than a month after Gagarin's triumph, they sent Alan Shepard 116 miles above the Earth's surface.

"Astronaut Has a Perfect Flight," the *Washington Post* boasted the morning after Shepard's mission. The article under that headline was one of three about the flight that the *Post* ran on its front page that day. Other papers highlighted the event in similar fashion.[4]

The news coverage that had the most impact, however, was the combination of eye-popping images and exuberant commentary coming from the nation's TV sets. As one journalism critic put it at the time, with spaceflights, "the medium that counts is television."[5]

ABC, CBS, and NBC all aired live shots from Cape Canaveral as the rocket with Shepard inside was poised for takeoff. Correspondents reported that millions of Americans had stopped whatever they'd been doing and were now watching TV.[6]

The networks "united a nation," the *New York Times* later wrote, as viewers were transfixed by the images they saw. No one moved when the jet of yellow flames lifted the slender rocket and sent it soaring into the clear blue sky. The audience remained riveted for the next fifteen minutes while the mighty machine powered forward, creating a breathtaking scene like nothing Americans had ever witnessed before. "The missile, first rising and then arcing with a bird's grace," the *Times* wrote, "was unforgettable."[7]

Network correspondents stayed quiet for much of the flight, allowing the action on the screen to speak for itself. During these periods of silence, TV reporters could occasionally be heard saying, "Gosh" or "Wow." Once the rocket was out of sight, they grinned and became giddy—like six-year-olds who'd just won a baseball game.[8]

That lighthearted feeling continued as the journalists reported that the capsule containing Shepard had landed safely in the water off the Bahamas and that his first words after returning to Earth were, "Boy, what a ride!"[9]

TV cameras were on hand in May 1961 to capture images of Alan Shepard as the first American to be launched into space. Courtesy of NASA.

All three networks aired congratulatory specials that night, with legendary anchor Walter Cronkite hosting for CBS. "There is high drama in the risks a man takes in order to ride a rocket into space," the avuncular newsman said in his emotional closing remarks. "And there is high drama, too, in the risks a free nation takes in publicizing that effort." Cronkite paused and smiled proudly before concluding, "Today, America took the gamble—and America won."[10]

Soon after the flight, the A. C. Nielsen Company reported that the coverage had attracted a TV audience of an impressive 45 million viewers.[11]

Historians later pointed out that the networks had downplayed that Shepard's flight was, in fact, modest when compared to Yuri Gagarin's. That is, Shepard hadn't orbited the Earth and had traveled only about 1 percent of the distance the Soviet cosmonaut had. In the words of one scholar, "American television did not dwell on the fact it was a lesser feat. It was presented, instead, as the glorious beginning of the U.S. manned space flight program."[12]

CONTINUING TO PROMOTE THE SPACE RACE

Soon after its highly positive coverage of the Shepard flight, TV news took two more steps that further fueled America's efforts to catch up in the Space Race.

In late May 1961, the president gave a special address to Congress. It wasn't standard practice at the time for the networks to disrupt their regular programming to air such speeches. When TV executives learned that Kennedy would announce an ambitious initiative related to outer space, however, they decided to cover the event live.[13]

The youthful president began his address with a reference to Shepard's triumphant flight and then moved on to the single most important statement he made that day. "I believe that this nation should commit itself to achieving the goal, before this decade is out, of landing a man on the moon and returning him safely to Earth."[14]

He went on to acknowledge that putting an astronaut on the lunar surface would be expensive, but he insisted the goal was an important one. "In a very real sense, it will not be one man going to the moon," Kennedy said firmly. "It will be an entire nation. For all of us must work to put him there."[15]

The next instance of TV helping propel the Space Race forward came in July 1961, with the nonorbital flight of astronaut Gus Grissom. Network officials wanted to provide live coverage from inside the control center, but NASA wouldn't allow it. The executives then asked if their cameramen could at least film the control center during a rehearsal to be conducted several days before the real flight, and NASA said they could.[16]

Grissom's blastoff and flight went smoothly. To make the coverage more interesting, CBS and NBC mixed some of the rehearsal footage from the control room in with the live shots from the launchpad and the sky. Correspondents told their audience early in the coverage that some of the footage had been prerecorded, but viewers who missed those brief statements assumed the control-room shots were live.[17]

Things became more complicated during the splashdown. When the capsule hit the water, the escape hatch blew open and water began pouring in. Grissom got out and stayed afloat until he was rescued, but the capsule sank and was lost. During the time the astronaut's fate was uncertain, NBC aired stock footage of a helicopter—filmed thousands of miles away from the capsule—moving swiftly over water. This image gave viewers the impression that Grissom was on the verge of being rescued when, in fact, that didn't happen for another fourteen minutes.[18]

Some publications criticized CBS and NBC for using poor judgment in airing the footage. "The incident is all too typical of the type of thinking," scolded the *New York Times*, "wherein values are warped and compromised for greater drama and greater entertainment."[19]

GOING WHERE TV HADN'T GONE BEFORE

By the end of 1961, the Soviet Union had surged even further ahead in the Space Race by sending a second cosmonaut into orbit, this one circling the Earth seventeen times. All the United States had done, by contrast, was put a chimpanzee named Enos into space for various tests.[20]

And so, when America's TV networks learned that NASA planned to send astronaut John Glenn into orbit for three revolutions, they decided to portray the February 1962 event as their country's heroic comeback.[21]

NASA again refused to allow cameras in the control room, so the networks devised a whole new strategy. They sent teams of reporters and cameramen to multiple locations around the country, with all of them contributing to the live coverage. To reduce expenses, the networks would pool their coverage, meaning that a single team in each location would provide identical content for ABC, CBS, and NBC.[22]

The sights chosen included the home of Glenn's parents in Ohio and his own home in Virginia where his wife, Annie, would watch the flight on TV. More teams would report from the White House where President Kennedy would speak and from New York City where correspondents would interview average Americans on the street. Still more live coverage would come from people gathered in Cape Canaveral to watch the flight.[23]

Both the flight and the coverage were spectacular successes, with one scholar of the Space Race praising TV for creating "wonderful theater." The networks went live at 6:30 A.M. and continued nonstop for eleven and a half hours. Viewers were so eager to watch their TVs that thousands of stores across the country closed their doors for the day, knowing that so many people would be "glued to their sets" that sales would have been negligible.[24]

The networks were soon celebrating, as the Nielsen figures documented that more than 135 million viewers had watched the flight. That meant that the coverage had amassed the largest audience in television history.[25]

A week later, the networks aired what ultimately may have ranked as the most consequential event of their live coverage. The setting was a Senate meeting room, and the subject was NASA's budget request for the next year. After hearing Glenn speak, the senators voted to double the agency's allocation for 1963. A scholar of the era's news media later wrote, "Television was a major factor in enabling NASA and the Kennedy administration to garner the support needed to meet their goals in space."[26]

RACING TOWARD THE MOON

Now that the Soviet Union and the United States had both sent astronauts into orbit, the two countries focused, in earnest, on taking the steps necessary to achieve their ultimate goal of putting a man on the lunar surface.

The Soviets maintained their lead throughout the early 1960s. One of their major achievements was sending two and then three cosmonauts into space in the same vehicle, and another was having a man "walk" in space—that is, allowing him to move away from his spacecraft while tethered to it by only a single cable for breathing.[27]

Despite repeatedly being outdone by the Soviets, the U.S. space effort continued to have the unequivocal support of TV news. This happened even when the missions began to extend into multiple days, meaning it wasn't possible to provide live coverage of the lengthy flights. So the networks developed a new approach of interlacing periodic updates into their regular programming and then airing one- or two-hour summaries of the day's events in the evening.[28]

The tables in the U.S. versus Soviet rivalry turned by late 1965. That's when two American vehicles achieved the first rendezvous in space.[29]

EXPERIENCING A TRAGIC SETBACK

NASA officials were relieved that the next major event in the Space Race wasn't being televised live, as it ended in heartbreak. The disaster took place during a routine test maneuver on the launchpad at the Kennedy Space Center in January 1967 when the module burst into flames, killing the three

TV viewers became accustomed to images of U.S. spacecraft lifting off as part of the race to the moon. This rocket sent John Glenn into orbit in February 1962. Courtesy of NASA.

astronauts inside. The deaths of Roger Chaffee, Gus Grissom, and Ed White were attributed to faulty wiring.[30]

In response to that terrible incident, the *Columbia Journalism Review* published a scathing critique of the news media's previous coverage of the Space Race. "If there was one aspect of the space program in which it was incumbent on the press to serve as watchdog, it was in the matter of safety," the magazine stated. "Yet the record shows a superficial and incomplete performance."[31]

CJR chastised the nation's news organizations for not reporting on a series of lesser accidents and "evidence of shoddy workmanship" related to the module, choosing to ignore those details because they didn't want to cast NASA and the space program in a negative light. "Journalists were so caught up in the challenge, drama, and excitement of the race to beat the Russians to the moon that they came to regard themselves as part of the space 'team.'"[32]

RESUMING THE RACE TO THE MOON

Almost two years passed between the fatal incident and the next U.S. space mission. When that launch took place, TV aired the event live to a public that had again become anxious about spaceflights. Officials at NASA and the networks joined forces to send reassuring messages. Specifically, the three astronauts were given their own cameras, allowing them to film themselves floating weightlessly in the topsy-turvy world aboard the spacecraft. By the time the splashdown was aired live eleven days after liftoff, the American public had regained its confidence in the space program.[33]

Three more flights followed, all of them unfolding without any significant problems. Although the major goal of each undertaking was limited to testing equipment and procedures to prepare for the future moon landing, the networks continued to air the highlights live.[34]

Coverage of the missions provided evidence that major print publications had altered their reporting in light of the 1967 tragedy and now were addressing safety issues. In the March 1969 coverage of a spaceflight, for example, newspapers made sure to tell their readers that astronauts James McDivitt and Russell Schweickart could die while attempting to separate their module from the main spacecraft and then rendezvous and dock again.

A page-one *Chicago Tribune* story included the paragraph: "The risks lie in the possibility that the two spacecraft might collide during the rendezvous and the possibility of the lunar module being unable to find or return to the spacecraft. If the latter happens, McDivitt and Schweickart would be doomed because the lunar module is not capable of returning to Earth."[35]

Similar statements appeared in the stories published by other major papers—including the *Boston Globe, Philadelphia Inquirer,* and *Washington Post.* Such cautionary words didn't find their way into the stories aired on TV, however, as the networks continued to portray the space program in relentlessly positive tones.[36]

TAKING A GIANT LEAP FOR MANKIND

It's difficult to communicate how excited the American public was feeling on the eve of July 20, 1969, when a U.S. astronaut was to become the first man to place his foot on another celestial body. This was the moment NASA had been working toward since Congress had created the agency—and the one the country had spent $20 billion to make happen.[37]

TV's big disappointment came when NASA said the three astronauts wouldn't be given cameras to take live images of the lunar module touching down on the moon's surface, as they'd be too busy with other activities. A camera bolted to the module's exterior wouldn't be able to capture the landing either because the touchdown would stir up a huge cloud of dust, but it would transmit images, if all went well, of Neil Armstrong stepping onto the moon's surface.[38]

To compensate for the lack of live images of the module landing, each network chose to simulate that event. This entailed constructing life-size replicas of the lunar module to help viewers follow what was happening 250,000 miles above them.[39]

All three networks provided live coverage of the liftoff and then updated viewers on the mission's progress over the next four days. On the morning of the landing, they started reporting live at 6 A.M., and they told their audiences later that morning that the module carrying Armstrong and Buzz Aldrin had separated from the module, where Michael Collins remained.[40]

The first big moment of the day came in the afternoon when the lunar module, named the *Eagle*, landed on the moon's surface. As that event grew close, it became clear that ABC and CBS had each hired a professional actor to play Armstrong. During the simulation, these two men—each dressed in a spacesuit—sat at their respective replica control panel and moved their arms exactly as Armstrong was moving his as he piloted the module. NBC didn't use an actor, relying on correspondents to describe what was happening in space.[41]

All three networks were careful to place the words "This is a simulation" on the screen the entire time the mock landing was shown. As TV viewers watched the images, live audio from the module provided the sound. Armstrong was heard calmly saying, "The *Eagle* has landed," when the module came to rest on the surface.[42]

The even bigger moment on that historic day came about 9 P.M. when Armstrong left the module and stepped onto the moon's surface. An image of that epic event aired live. Viewers saw the astronaut's left leg moving out from the bottom rung of the ladder, followed by his foot stepping onto the moon's

One of the magical moments during the July 1969 lunar mission came when Buzz Aldrin saluted the American flag that he and Neil Armstrong had planted on the moon. Courtesy of NASA.

surface. A few more heart-stopping seconds later, the world heard Armstrong say, "That's one small step for man, one giant leap for mankind."[43]

People who were tuned to CBS also heard Walter Cronkite breathing heavily with excitement and gasping, "Man on the moon!" and then "Oh, geez!" and "Oh, boy!"[44]

Soon after Armstrong took his first step, Aldrin joined him on the surface. The two men were then seen testing methods for getting around, including two-footed kangaroo hops. Before long, it became clear that loping was their movement of choice. They told the world that the dust on the surface was "very fine-grained" and "almost like a powder."[45]

Viewers remained in front of their TV sets, watching the two men roam the surface and set up scientific instruments to record data. One particularly poignant moment came when they planted an American flag on the lunar surface. President Richard Nixon also spoke to the men by phone, saying, "For every American, this has to be the proudest day of our lives."[46]

After two and a half hours of walking on the surface, the space pioneers returned to the module, carrying forty-nine pounds of soil and rock samples they'd collected. Then they slept for seven hours before rejoining Collins in the command module and heading back to Earth.[47]

The next day's newspapers were unrestrained in praising TV's coverage. The *Los Angeles Times* pronounced it "first rate," and the *Washington Post* wrote, "Television performed splendidly. And our world is better off because of it."[48]

Even more satisfying than the praise was the number that Nielsen soon reported. That figure of 600 million viewers worldwide set a new record as the largest audience ever to have witnessed a televised event.[49]

More live coverage followed, first of the splashdown and then of a string of celebrations. Highlights included parades in New York, Chicago, and Los Angeles, as well as a White House state dinner where America's three new heroes were awarded Presidential Medals of Freedom.[50]

PROPELLING AMERICA TOWARD A GLOBAL TRIUMPH

The moon landing effectively ended the Space Race, with the United States standing alone as the undisputed winner. News organizations eventually reported details about how the Soviets had attempted to compete but hadn't come anywhere close to the mark.[51]

Various scholars have credited American TV with having been instrumental in the nation's glorious victory. One wrote, "Television helped create a national fervor for the venture into space," and several others observed that TV's extensive coverage was instrumental in NASA receiving the congressional funding it needed. Indeed, those scholars questioned if America would have succeeded in putting a man on the moon in 1969 if it hadn't been for the networks helping to turn the Space Race into a national obsession.[52]

Achieving Justice for Japanese Americans Interned during World War II

In the early 1940s, some 120,000 Americans of Japanese descent were removed from their homes and placed in internment camps. Three decades later, a small group of activists began an effort to see that these wronged individuals received an apology and financial compensation for the losses they'd suffered. When the proposal was first put forward, political observers said the chances of it being enacted were nil.

Those skeptics didn't factor in, however, that the news media would take up the cause. That is, those observers didn't know that American journalism would, for the next several years, be relentless in reporting on the issue. Nor did the doubters anticipate that the country's newspapers would support the proposal on their editorial pages while also keeping the topic on the minds of the public through a steady stream of human-interest stories. Indeed, the nation's news outlets wouldn't end their crusade until justice was achieved.

The executive order that President Franklin D. Roosevelt issued in February 1942 applied to Japanese Americans living on the West Coast. It directed the U.S. military to remove the men, women, and children from their homes and place them in internment camps. These facilities were located in remote and desolate areas of the country, generally hundreds of miles from where the internees had been living.[1]

About 77,000 of the internees—which meant almost two-thirds of them—were U.S. citizens. The others were residents of this country, with many of them not having set foot in Japan for several decades.[2]

A large number of the internees lost homes and businesses because they weren't able to pay their mortgages once they were taken to the camps. They also were forced to sell their cars, furniture, and personal belongings at a fraction of what the items were worth, as all they were allowed to take with them to the internment camps was what they could carry.[3]

The government's actions came three months after Japanese forces had bombed the U.S. naval base at Pearl Harbor. Officials in the White House and Congress justified the internment based on "military necessity," saying Japanese Americans were disloyal to the United States and therefore were likely to be involved in acts of espionage and treason.[4]

When some Japanese Americans filed a lawsuit to protest how they were being treated, the country's legal system sided with the government. The U.S. Supreme Court ruled that the actions taken by the president and supported by Congress were fully within the powers these elected officials were granted by the Constitution.[5]

The internment camps consisted of tar-papered military barracks that were surrounded by barbed-wire fences and guarded by armed soldiers. Living quarters were often cramped because each family, regardless of its size, was assigned to a single room. These living spaces didn't have plumbing, so internees had to use communal bathrooms and showers. At mealtimes, everyone ate in large mess halls.[6]

The internees remained in the camps until the facilities were closed, some in 1944 but others not until 1946.[7]

PROPOSING REPARATIONS

Beginning in the early 1970s, activist members of the Japanese American Citizens League discussed, during the organization's annual convention, the possibility of seeking a formal apology and financial reparations for the internees.[8]

League members who spearheaded these efforts met, in the late 1970s, with members of Congress and representatives from the White House to discuss their grievances. In 1980, President Jimmy Carter created a congressional commission to study the internment and make recommendations regarding possible action by the U.S. government.[9]

Scholars who've studied the topic have said that neither an apology nor reparations were thought to have any possibility of being approved. In the

Armed soldiers kept close watch over Japanese Americans as they arrived at the relocation camps in 1942. Courtesy of Getty Images/Popperfoto.

words of the author of one book on the subject, "Many factors seemed to portend political disaster for the initiative."[10]

First on the list of obstacles was that Japanese Americans represented only a tiny fraction of the country's population—about three-tenths of 1 percent—so they had minuscule political clout. Second was that many politicians feared that granting reparations for this one group would prompt similar appeals from African Americans because of slavery and Native Americans because of the land that had been taken from them. Timing also worked against the proposal, as the federal deficit was at an all-time high in the early 1980s.[11]

TELLING POIGNANT STORIES OF HARDSHIP AND LOSS

During the summer and fall of 1981, the Commission on Wartime Relocation and Internment of Civilians conducted public hearings in six cities across the country. Most of the 750 people who testified were former internees, and their powerful stories helped propel the country's journalists into committing themselves to righting the wrong that Japanese Americans had experienced four decades earlier.

One human drama that came to life on the front page of the *Chicago Tribune* was that of Tokujiro Murakami. After arriving penniless in the United States, he'd earned a living as a fisherman, catching tuna and mackerel in the waters off the California coast. He'd prospered to the point that, by February 1942, he'd been able to buy a house, $50,000 worth of fishing nets, and a brand-new Plymouth.[12]

But then Murakami, his wife, and their two sons were sent to an internment camp in North Dakota. They had to sell the house at far below its market value, and they never received any money whatsoever for the fishing nets or the car—military officials promised at the time that the items would be returned after the family left the camp, but that never happened. The *Tribune*'s story about the 1981 public hearing quoted the eighty-one-year-old Murakami as saying, simply and eloquently, "The way the United States treated us wasn't right."[13]

A story in the *St. Louis Post-Dispatch* focused on Henry Tanaka. He was an eighteen-year-old U.S. citizen living in Oregon when he and his parents were sent to a camp. His relocation forced him to give up his scholarship and drop out of Willamette University, where he'd been studying. Tanaka was angry and bitter when he testified before the commissioners, insisting on referring to the internment camps as "concentration camps."[14]

The nation's three TV networks also broadcast stories that the internees shared during the public hearings. On the *CBS Evening News*, anchor Dan Rather introduced viewers to John Tateishi, who was sent to a camp when he was three years old. Tateishi didn't focus on the financial losses that he and other internees suffered but on the emotional impact of the experience. "The depth of psychological harm can be seen in the fact that, until a few years ago, Japanese Americans were unable to talk publicly about the internment," he said. "For forty years, we have lived with the stigma of disloyalty as the reason for how we were treated."[15]

REPORTING ON INTERNMENT DEFENDERS

Not every witness at the hearings spoke about personal suffering. Instead, some argued that the government's actions had been fully justified. The nation's journalistic voices dutifully reported what these individuals said.

John McCloy, an assistant secretary of war in the 1940s, told the commission that the Japanese Americans had to be placed in the camps "because government officials feared they might engage in subversive activities," according to the *New York Times*. He also argued that the internees were removed from the West Coast partly for their own protection. Residents of the region felt so much hostility toward them following the bombing of Pearl Harbor, McCloy said, that they might have been physically harmed if they hadn't been relocated to the camps.[16]

With regard to how the internment program was implemented, the *Times* quoted McCloy as testifying that it was "reasonably undertaken and thoughtfully and humanely conducted." The story also reported that McCloy described the living conditions in the camps as "very pleasant."[17]

Another defender of the internment was the retired army officer who'd led the relocation. When Colonel Karl Bendetsen appeared as a guest on the ABC news program *Nightline*, he said, "After the attack in Hawaii, the anti-Japanese feeling was intense, particularly on the West Coast. Violence was near at hand." Bendetsen also said, "The sweeping condemnations recently made of the responsible officials cannot be condoned."[18]

News organizations also reported statements by Senator S. I. Hayakawa. The *New York Times* quoted the Republican from California as having told the commission that Japanese Americans asking for financial reparations "fills me with shame and embarrassment"—Hayakawa was of Japanese ancestry but was born in Canada, so he wasn't sent to a camp. The *Chicago Tribune* was among the news outlets that quoted Hayakawa as also saying the internment amounted to "a three-year vacation" for the Japanese Americans.[19]

EXPOSING RACISM AND POLITICS AS MOTIVATING FACTORS

After the hearings ended, the *Washington Post* published a series of stories on the internment program. Each of the five pieces began on page one under the heading "Internment: The 'Enemy' 40 Years Ago."[20]

The most powerful of the articles was one that challenged the argument that the White House and Congress had made in 1942 that Americans of Japanese descent had shown signs of being disloyal to the United States. "There never was any truth to it," *Post* reporter Fred Barbash stated unequivocally. "Not a single example of espionage or disloyalty by a Japanese American was ever documented during World War II. Government officials up to President Roosevelt received intelligence reports specifically refuting the charge."[21]

To support its accusation that FDR and Congress uprooted Japanese Americans despite counsel from many experts that the action wasn't called for, the *Post* quoted from a February 1942 report written by FBI director J. Edgar Hoover. "The call for mass evacuation is based primarily upon public and political pressure rather than on factual data," Hoover had told the president. The *Post* reported that intelligence officials had offered Roosevelt similar advice.[22]

The primary factor that led to Japanese Americans being interned was "unconcealed racism," the *Post* argued. To support this charge, the paper reproduced a memo written in early 1942 by General John L. DeWitt, one of the military officers in charge of removing families from their homes. "The Japanese race is an enemy race," DeWitt wrote.[23]

Roosevelt's reelection effort played a role in the decision-making, according to the *Post*, with the paper stating, "Internment continued for largely political reasons." For evidence, the paper summarized notes from a May 1944 meeting FDR had with his closest political advisers. According to the notes, these men "doubted the wisdom" of allowing the internees to return home "before the election." In other words, the anti-Japanese sentiment was so strong among American voters that the officials counseling FDR on his political strategy thought releasing the internees would harm the president's chances of being reelected in November 1944. For this reason, the *Post* stated, Roosevelt kept the camps open until a month *after* the election.[24]

LABELING INTERNMENT A "GRAVE INJUSTICE"

The commission charged with studying the internment program spent 1982 reviewing documents—including those that the *Washington Post* series had reported on—and the testimony given during the public hearings. And then, in February 1983, the nine commissioners released their summary report.

TV news gave prominent play to the findings. *NBC Nightly News* anchor Roger Mudd, for example, introduced the story by saying, "Today the Commission on Wartime Relocation and Internment of Civilians said the U.S. government committed a grave injustice against Japanese Americans during World War II." Mudd then turned the story over to correspondent Jamie Gangel, who showed photos of internees at the camps and footage from a press conference held earlier that day. "The commission found that there was

Many Japanese-American children were confused and frightened when they had to leave their homes and were placed in relocation camps. Courtesy of Getty Images/Apic.

no military justification for the internment," Gangel reported. "Instead, it was the result of racism, war hysteria and politics."[25]

The *Houston Post* was one of a long list of newspapers that placed the story on page one. It reported that the commissioners had condemned the internment as a "shameful page in American history." The paper also quoted a member of the commission as saying the internment was "a case study of what happens when public policy is built on racism."[26]

Another paper that highlighted the story by placing it on the front page was the *Washington Post*, which paid particular attention to what the commissioners said about the conditions the internees were forced to endure. Quoting from the report, the *Post* said, "The camps were short on medical and educational facilities, space and especially privacy, but amply supplied with armed guards and barbed wire."[27]

SHOWCASING THE RECOMMENDATIONS

In June 1983, the commission announced its recommendations as to what the nation should do in response to Japanese Americans being mistreated four decades earlier. The nation's news media again gave high-profile coverage to what the group had to say.

In its page-one story, the *Philadelphia Inquirer* began, "Calling for 'an act of national apology,' a congressional commission yesterday recommended that Congress pay $1.5 billion in reparations to 60,000 surviving Japanese-Americans who were interned." The *Inquirer* went on to report that the commission proposed that each living internee be given $20,000.[28]

Some papers recognized that the financial recommendation would be controversial, so they published the details that the commission released regarding the economic losses the internees had sustained. The *San Francisco Chronicle* was among these papers, reporting that the losses were estimated, when calculated in 1983 dollars, to have been $6.2 billion—four times the amount the commission was proposing that the survivors be paid.[29]

SUPPORTING REPARATIONS THROUGH EDITORIALS

In addition to America's newspapers printing articles about the internment on page one, they were also publishing statements of support for reparations on their editorial pages.

Some papers began calling for an apology and compensation after the commission's 1981 public hearings. "The internment was an injustice of great magnitude," the *Los Angeles Times* wrote. "Thousands of loyal Americans were imprisoned simply because of their ancestry and not for anything they did." In the final paragraph of the editorial titled "A Matter of Justice," the *Times* endorsed monetary payments. "We believe that compensation, generous enough to make it meaningful, is due," the paper stated. "The government committed a wrong against thousands of its loyal citizens. That wrong must be rectified."[30]

More news outlets endorsed reparations in February 1983 after the commission released its report on the internment. The *Boston Globe* wrote, "The legitimate resentments of Japanese-Americans must not be minimized. Neither German-Americans nor Italian-Americans were detained; only the loyalties of Japanese-Americans were unfairly challenged." The *Globe* ended its editorial by adding its name to the list of journalistic voices supporting both a national apology and monetary compensation. "Measures can and should be taken," the paper said.[31]

A third round of editorials appeared after the commission made its recommendations in June 1983. Among the papers that joined the chorus in support of giving money to the internees at this point was the *Philadelphia Inquirer*. "The $20,000 figure, modest in terms of each victim, should be held to," the paper said. "The Congress should accept the commission's recommendation and move forward with an appropriation."[32]

KEEPING THE ISSUE IN THE PUBLIC EYE

Beyond taking up the cause on the front page and editorial page, papers also campaigned on behalf of the internees in their feature sections. From 1983 to 1988, a handful of U.S. senators and representatives worked behind the scenes to turn the commission's proposals into legislation, lobbying their colleagues in Congress one by one. Therefore, for five years, journalists had relatively little concrete news to report on the topic. To make sure the public didn't forget about the internees, papers printed a steady stream of human-interest stories about them.

Many of the pieces were profiles of people who'd been interned in their youth but who'd succeeded despite the unjust treatment. One such story in the *Chicago Tribune* began with the statement, "Noby Yamakoshi is the embodiment of the American dream." Yamakoshi had been in his early teens when his family had been removed from their California farm—"a brand new tractor fetched a mere $50." The *Tribune* story described how the industrious young man's "years of 80-hour work weeks" had paid off, as he now employed 325 workers in his print graphics firm that had brought in $22 million in sales the previous year. The paper maintained a positive tone throughout the piece, telling readers that Yamakoshi "speaks without a trace of bitterness" about the years he spent in the camp.[33]

Other features were about activists who'd been working to see that former internees were compensated. An example was a *Los Angeles Times* profile of Frank Emi, whose efforts had begun in 1943 when he'd been sent to a camp in Wyoming. "For the government to pull people out of their homes and put them in concentration camps just didn't seem right," he said. And so, Emi founded the Fair Play Committee, which held protests in the camp, an action that led to him being sent to federal prison. He was released at the end of the war, and he then helped organize the National Coalition for Redress/Reparations. When the *Times* ran its profile in 1987, Emi was serving as spokesman for the group's Los Angeles chapter.[34]

Some features took broader brushstrokes. A piece in the *Washington Post* reported that men of Japanese descent were a highly successful American subgroup. "An extraordinary 33.5 percent of Japanese-American males," the article said, "hold professional or managerial positions—as doctors, engineers, pharmacists, dentists and business executives. The national median is 23.6 percent." The fact that many of these men had spent their youth in internment camps was introduced in the third paragraph. "The wartime confinement made Japanese Americans even more patriotic, law-abiding and accommodating than before the war," the *Post* observed. The reporter attributed this reality to the men's desire to erase any perception that Japanese Americans deserved to have been interned.[35]

POLITICIANS TAKING ACTION

At the same time that the nation's news organizations were making sure, between 1983 and 1988, that the public didn't forget about the internees, efforts were being made on Capitol Hill. Four Japanese-American members of Congress were leading the charge, gradually gaining support for legislation that would put the commission's recommendations into place.

In the Senate, Daniel Inouye and Spark Matsunaga from Hawaii were widely respected, partly because they'd both served in the U.S. military. Indeed, Inouye served in the 442nd Regimental Combat Team, which consisted entirely of Japanese Americans and was the most highly decorated unit in U.S. military history. Inouye lost his right arm on an Italian battlefield and later was awarded two Purple Hearts and the Medal of Honor.[36]

Two other men of Japanese heritage led the effort in the House. Norman Mineta and Robert Matsui, who both represented California, were compelling voices on the topic because they'd both, as children, been confined to internment camps.[37]

Only after the four Democrats had persuaded significant numbers of their colleagues to support the bills they sponsored did quotes from them begin to appear in the country's leading news outlets. In 1987, the *New York Times* published a story about Mineta and his family being relocated to a camp in

Wyoming when he was ten years old. "No one ever explained to me what threat I posed," Mineta said. "The only organizations I belonged to were the Cub Scouts and the Methodist youth group."[38]

PROPELLING POSITIVE CHANGE

The efforts by the members of Congress and the nation's journalistic outlets finally paid off in 1988 when Congress passed a bill expressing a national apology to the men, women, and children who'd been removed from their homes and placed in camps. The legislation also authorized $20,000 to be paid to each internee who was still living.[39]

The bill passed the Senate by a vote of 69 to 27 and the House by a vote of 257 to 156. President Ronald Reagan then signed it.[40]

Many of the news organizations that had labored long and hard in support of reparations published editorials commemorating the signing. The *Washington Post* wrote, "Tens of thousands of American citizens have been waiting for an apology for almost 50 years. It is evidence that the United States can confess error, attempt to make amends to those who suffered and resolve publicly that this kind of injustice will not happen again."[41]

Stopping Catholic Priests from Sexually Abusing Little Boys

Thousands of boys were sexually abused by Catholic priests from the 1950s through the early 2000s. These innocent children—some of them as young as four years old—carried the scars of their betrayal for decades after the acts took place. Indeed, many of the victims were so psychologically damaged that they were never able to live normal lives. Although many Church officials were aware of the abuse, they allowed it to continue.

It wasn't until 2002 that the despicable behavior became widely known. The Boston Globe *published the first stories about the abuse and cover-up, and then the paper was joined by dozens of other news outlets around the country in reporting on the topic. The high-profile coverage pushed officials of the Catholic Church both to punish the offending priests and to enact policies aimed at protecting other children from suffering similar harm.*

The news outlet that deserved the most credit for exposing the vile behavior of Catholic priests and their superiors was the *Boston Globe*. When the paper was awarded the Pulitzer Prize for Public Service in 2003, the citation read: "For its courageous, comprehensive coverage of sexual abuse by priests, an effort that pierced secrecy, stirred local, national, and international reaction, and produced changes in the Roman Catholic Church."[1]

In the *Globe*'s first article on the topic, published on Sunday, January 6, 2002, the paper focused on one particularly egregious case. "Since the mid-1990s," the first paragraph read, "more than 130 people have come forward with horrific childhood tales about how former priest John J. Geoghan allegedly fondled or raped them during a three-decade spree through a half-dozen Greater Boston parishes."[2]

A photo of Geoghan accompanied the front-page story that described how he'd targeted boys who were in vulnerable circumstances. "The affable Geoghan usually befriended Catholic mothers struggling to raise large families, often alone," the story stated. "His offers to help, often by taking the children for ice cream or praying with them at bedtime, were accepted without suspicion."[3]

The *Globe* also quoted one of the victims. Geoghan first made contact with Patrick McSorley soon after the twelve-year-old boy's father had committed suicide and while his mother was being treated for schizophrenia. When the priest was alone with the youngster, he touched the boy's crotch. "Then he put his hand on my genitals and started masturbating me," the *Globe* quoted the adult McSorley as saying. "I was petrified."[4]

McSorley was twenty-eight years old when the *Globe* reporter interviewed him. He said that first incident was one of many and that he'd battled depression and alcoholism since his early teens.[5]

Cardinal Bernard F. Law's reprehensible misdeeds were also reported in that initial article. Law, the head of the Boston archdiocese, was identified as having repeatedly approved Geoghan's placement in positions in which the priest worked closely with children. Law approved the transfers to new parishes even though he was fully aware of the priest's history of having molested numerous boys while working in previous assignments.[6]

The story reported that Geoghan and Law had refused the *Globe*'s requests for interviews.[7]

CATHOLIC OFFICIALS PAYING "HUSH MONEY"

An article published in late January 2002 made it dramatically clear that the wrongdoing extended far beyond one priest and one cardinal. "Under an extraordinary cloak of secrecy," the piece began, "the Archdiocese of Boston in the last 10 years has quietly settled child molestation claims against at least 70 priests."[8]

Church officials paid the accusers and their parents large amounts of money, the *Globe* reported, to avoid the sex offenders being tried in the court system and, therefore, the abuse becoming known to Church members or the public. "The archdiocese paid what amounted to 'hush money' to settle cases," the paper stated. "Their motive was to avoid scandal and hope it would all go away."[9]

As an example of the kind of arrangement that Church officials negotiated, the *Globe* described an instance in the 1990s when a mother and father were paid $400,000 in exchange for keeping secret the fact that a priest had sexually abused their sons.[10]

Each financial agreement required that the abused boy and his parents sign a legal contract stipulating they wouldn't discuss the case with law enforcement authorities. For their part, Church officials promised that the offending priest would undergo treatment and wouldn't be allowed near children again, being assigned to serve as a prison chaplain or to fulfill administrative duties.[11]

The *Globe* documented, however, that church officials often didn't hold up their end of the bargain, as many priests were transferred to other parishes where they again worked closely with altar boys or served as advisers to youth groups.[12]

One compelling source in the story was Raymond P. Sinibaldi. Years earlier, he and his parents had accepted a financial settlement in exchange for not telling police that he'd been sexually assaulted by Rev. Ernest E. Tourigney. "I'm ashamed we took their money," the adult Sinibaldi said. "We should have gone and reported it to the police, or filed a lawsuit and called a press conference to announce it. If we had done that, this problem would have been exposed long ago."[13]

OTHER PUBLICATIONS EXPAND THE COVERAGE

After the *Globe* broke the sexual abuse story, other news outlets quickly joined the paper in reporting on the topic.

The *New York Times* took the lead among these journalistic voices, with the scandal appearing on page one of the country's newspaper of record for forty-one consecutive days. Several of the stories focused on the issue of the statute of limitations, as many of the accusations involved incidents that dated back several decades. Another important *Times* article placed the total price tag for the "hush money" the Catholic Church had paid to victims and their families at a minimum of $350 million, and possibly as much as $1 billion.[14]

Two other major papers that were soon devoting sizeable amounts of attention to the story were the *Los Angeles Times* and *Washington Post*. The

Times criticized the large number of Catholic bishops who blamed the child sex abuse not on the priests and the church but on "a too-permissive secular society." One *Washington Post* story told the jaw-dropping details about how a woman who'd accused a priest of having molested her sons, aged seven and ten, was being sued by the Catholic Church; officials claimed that *she* was the one who'd been negligent because she'd allowed her boys to spend so much time with the priest.[15]

Dozens of other papers around the country also were soon running articles about the scandal. The *Milwaukee Journal Sentinel* reported that sexual abuse charges had been filed against six Wisconsin priests, the *Detroit News* published a similar story about sixteen men in Michigan, and the *San Francisco Chronicle* ran a piece about forty priests in California.[16]

A *Time* magazine article related to the scandal was titled "Is the Church Dying?" The personal essay was written by cultural commentator and blogger Andrew Sullivan, a devoted Catholic. "Some have argued that the current sex-abuse scandal in the church is the crisis. They're wrong," Sullivan wrote. "It is a symptom of a real and deeper one—the collapse of the moral credibility of the church hierarchy among its own laity." Sullivan reported that 49 percent of Catholics had been attending church regularly in 1972 but that the figure had dropped to 26 percent by 2000. Sullivan also told his readers that 1,000 young American men had entered the priesthood in 1965 but only 500 had done so in 2000. Sullivan followed these statistics with a devastating rhetorical question: "When so many church leaders could not treat even the raping of children as a serious offense, how can we trust them to tell us what to believe about the more esoteric questions of contraception, or homosexuality, or divorce?"[17]

TV NEWS EXPLORES MORE FACETS OF THE STORY

Television news outlets were soon trying to keep pace with their print counterparts. Local TV stations concentrated mostly on accusations of abuse against priests in their specific geographic areas, while the national networks took on broader issues.

A lengthy piece on the *NBC Nightly News* focused on the increasing number of lay Catholics who wanted to have more say in making Church decisions—a suggestion that many priests and bishops vehemently opposed. Correspondent Anne Thompson told viewers about an organization called

As the news media reported stories about Catholic priests sexually abusing little boys, public protests found some people criticizing the church and other people defending it. AP Photo/Rene Macura.

Voice of the Faithful, which had 8,600 members nationwide. "The group wants a more influential role for ordinary Catholics," Thompson said. She interviewed several members of the organization, including a Harvard University professor who spoke about how bishops were reacting to the proposal that nonclergy help set policy. "They are threatened by this," Mary Jo Bain said, "precisely because it is coming from such a moderate and mainstream group within the church."[18]

The other major networks also aired substantive stories about the scandal. ABC ran a lengthy piece on its evening news program about leaders of the Catholic Church pressuring abuse victims to stay silent, and CBS looked at the many worshipers who were expressing their displeasure by refusing to put money in the collection plate. CNN highlighted an international angle of the story by reporting that officials at the Vatican believed U.S. bishops were "overreacting" to the news stories and treating abusive priests too harshly.[19]

One PBS story on the scandal focused on how the *Boston Globe* found the information reported in its initial stories. The first step, according to the piece, came in July 2001 when the paper's new editor, Martin Baron, learned that the Catholic Church was keeping legal charges against priests from the public through a confidentiality order granted by the courts. So Baron asked a judge to open the files. "We thought there was a public interest at stake here," the editor said during the PBS program. It took *Globe* attorneys six months of legal wrangling before they succeeded in having the confidentiality order lifted and thousands of documents made public.[20]

Once the *Globe* gained access to the material and published its initial stories, the hundreds of other news outlets also began looking at the documents and writing literally thousands more stories. PBS media critic Terence Smith had it right when he said during the show, "The story has mushroomed."[21]

ONLINE VENUES TAKE THE STORY IN NEW DIRECTIONS

By 2002, the news media landscape wasn't limited to print and broadcast organizations, as online outlets were having an increasingly strong and vibrant presence. Those innovative venues took it upon themselves to move coverage of the child sex abuse scandal into new territory.

Salon argued that the most despicable acts weren't committed by the wayward priests but by the country's 195 bishops. "Average Catholics retain their faith in their church, but they have lost their confidence in that church's leaders," *Salon* stated in one story. "Catholics don't think it's rocket science for bishops to understand what people in the pews know so simply in their hearts: Truth and falsehood differ, as do openness and evasion, disclosure and cover-up—the elements that the robed monarchs seem to feel it is their right to mix and match with divinely granted impunity." The online magazine's stand vis-à-vis Church leaders was particularly powerful because a study had found that fully two-thirds of the bishops in the United States had concealed the fact that priests in their diocese had been accused of sexually abusing children.[22]

Salon also pointed out that, despite print and broadcast journalism's focus on young male victims, many sexual abuse cases involved Catholic priests assaulting either girls or women. The magazine's main source for the story was a Minneapolis psychologist named Gary Schoener, who had consulted in more than 2,000 such cases during the previous three decades. "Schoener says that in his practice," *Salon* reported, "he sees more female (both adolescent and adult) than male victims of abuse from priests."[23]

Slate was another online news venue that devoted a considerable amount of coverage to the scandal. In one provocative article, the magazine asked, "Does abstinence make the church grow fondlers?" The writer followed this playful opening line with a serious discussion of the role that the Catholic Church's insistence that priests refrain from all sexual activity had in the sexual abuse crisis. He synthesized the two sides of the question in a brief series of statements. "The simplest version of the blame-celibacy theory," he wrote, "is that repressing your sexual urges makes you resort, in the words of one suspended priest, to a 'sick outlet.'" The *Slate* writer then reported that defenders of the celibacy rule made two arguments. First, they noted that sexual abuse by clergymen occurred in all denominations, not just those demanding celibacy. Second, the celibacy supporters pointed out that pedophilia is fundamentally different from sexual attraction to adults. On that last point, the *Slate* writer quoted one expert as saying, "Most pedophiles don't find adult partners the least bit attractive sexually."[24]

Slate also was willing to take on the controversial subject of gay priests. The magazine reported that recent studies had found that at least 30 percent and possibly as many as 50 percent of Catholic priests in the United States were closeted gay men. Because of this revelation, the article continued, Church officials were using gay priests as a scapegoat. "The problem, they say, is homosexuality. If the church gets rid of gay priests, everything will be fine." But *Slate* didn't agree with this position, pointing out that 85 percent of the Catholic priests who'd been convicted of sexual abuse were straight.[25]

ALLOWING VICTIMS TO TELL THEIR STORIES

There's no question that the thousands of stories that were printed, broadcast, or posted online brought important facets of the scandal to light. It also can be argued, though, that the news outlets were performing an equally valuable service by providing a way that those boys who'd been sexually abused could tell their stories. Many of the victims had buried the details of their mistreatment under layers of guilt and shame for decades, allowing those memories to severely damage their emotional health. Finally being able to speak publicly about their experiences was enormously cathartic to them.

Mark Vincent Serrano shared his painful memories on the front page of the *New York Times*. "I can remember the first time he exposed himself to me," the thirty-seven-year-old man recalled, referring to an incident with Rev. James T. Hanley. The boy's interaction with the priest began with pizza parties when he was nine years old but later moved on to Hanley sodomizing him. "It's this horrible dichotomy," Serrano said. "This man is telling you, 'It's good, it's OK, it's our secret.' But I remember having this terrible feeling in my chest, when the adrenaline is rushing and your hair stands on end." The sexual abuse continued for seven years.[26]

When the *Omaha World Herald* allowed a victim to share his story, the paper agreed not to publish the man's name. The twenty-three-year-old said his parish priest went with him, when he was thirteen, on a trip to another city where he received a trophy for being an outstanding altar boy. Rev. Daniel Herek took the boy to a hotel room, gave him alcohol to drink, and told him to take off his clothes. Herek then fondled the boy. "Here is this priest standing over me in his underwear," the victim said. "I'm now naked. But I'm thinking, 'This is a priest. This is somebody I trust. I can't be defensive against a priest.'" During the next five years, Herek sexually assaulted the boy twenty times, often on Church property.[27]

Perhaps the most heart-wrenching of all the personal stories was one published in the *Boston Globe*. The front-page article began with Thomas Fulchino talking about being molested in the 1960s and then continued with his son, Christopher Fulchino, recalling how he'd also been abused in the 1990s. The father said he was overwhelmed less by what happened to him than by the guilt he felt because he hadn't prevented his son from suffering similar pain. "You block it," Thomas Fulchino told the *Globe*. "You just totally put it behind Door Number 6 in your mind." Both victims said they were still plagued by nightmares.[28]

PROPELLING POSITIVE CHANGE

Within a year after the *Boston Globe* began its exposé, many actions had been taken. The subject of the paper's first article, John J. Geoghan, had been sentenced to nine years behind bars for having sexually assaulted a ten-year-old boy. In addition, the man the *Globe* had identified as having allowed Geoghan to molest dozens of children, Cardinal Bernard F. Law, had been forced to resign from his position as the head of the Boston archdiocese.[29]

On a larger scale, 450 Catholic priests across the country had been removed from their parishes because of sexual abuse charges. Father Andrew

M. Greeley was among the many observers who saw a direct connection between the *Globe*'s coverage and the actions taken to prevent these men from preying on more children. "Without the paper's stories," Greeley said, "the abuse would have gone right on. There would have been no crisis, no demand from the laity that the church cut out this cancer of irresponsibility, corruption, and sin."[30]

The outrage that Catholic laypersons expressed after learning about the abuse forced Church officials to make fundamental changes. Before the news coverage began in 2002, the bishop in each diocese decided how he would respond—or would *not* respond—to allegations of child sexual abuse. After journalists reported that many of these men chose merely to shuffle accused priests from one parish to another, leaders of the Catholic Church implemented procedures aimed at preventing further mistreatment.[31]

Specifically, in June 2002 the U.S. Conference of Catholic Bishops adopted a zero-tolerance policy. The new rules stipulated that every priest who was found to have abused a child would be permanently barred from working as a pastor in a parish or as a chaplain in a school or hospital. There was no statute of limitations on the incidents, meaning that a priest would be punished no matter how many years had passed since the incident had taken place.[32]

In addition, every bishop in the country was required to alert civil authorities to any accusation against a clergyman for sexually abusing a child. An investigation of the charge would then be undertaken, and the police and court officials would prosecute the man if the allegations were found to be true. If convicted, the priest would be sent to prison.[33]

Another significant facet of the policy was that laypersons would have an important role in the procedures. That is, an outside review board was established to make sure the bishops and other Church authorities complied with the new rules. Oklahoma Governor Frank Keating, a lifelong Catholic, was appointed chair of the board.[34]

Although these measures certainly didn't guarantee that no child would ever again be sexually abused, observers applauded them as a major step forward. The *Boston Globe* was among the news organizations that praised the new policy, saying, "The Catholic bishops have devised a structure of oversight, supervision, and monitoring that will prevent any number of future cases of abuse."[35]

Redefining the American Lesbian

Throughout most of American history, lesbians were largely invisible. On the rare occasion that gay women appeared, they were defined by stereotypes that most of society perceived as negative. That is, lesbians were thought of as overweight and unattractive creatures who had masculine mannerisms and dressed in flannel shirts and work boots. Their personality traits were seen as unpleasant, too, with most people thinking of lesbians as humorless scolds.

In the final years of the twentieth century, the country's news media began to shine their spotlight on a very different representative of Lesbian America. Ellen DeGeneres was slender and had lustrous blond hair, perfect skin, and pale blue eyes. What's more, news outlets portrayed the comedian as an amazingly talented and big-hearted person who was so charming and personable that millions of fans were eager to spend their afternoons hanging out with her.

Ellen Lee DeGeneres was born in New Orleans in 1958. Her father worked as an insurance company executive and her mother as a speech therapist. When Ellen was fourteen years old, her parents divorced. Betty DeGeneres soon married a salesman, taking her daughter with her when she moved into her new husband's home in Texas.[1]

After Ellen graduated from high school, she attended the University of New Orleans for one semester but then dropped out. She next worked at a variety of jobs, from painting houses to shucking oysters. This was also the period when DeGeneres realized she was a lesbian, telling her mother—who was instantly supportive—and various other close friends and relatives.[2]

DeGeneres spent much of her free time, during her late teens and early twenties, doing stand-up comedy at small clubs and coffeehouses. In 1984, she entered a humor competition sponsored by the Showtime cable channel and won the top prize, thereby being named "the Funniest Person in America."[3]

That victory prompted DeGeneres to commit herself full-time to working as a comedian. So she relocated to Southern California, an area known for its many comedy clubs and for its TV and movie studios.[4]

For the next four years, DeGeneres performed stand-up routines in and around Los Angeles. She gained a reputation as one of the few comedians who avoided getting laughs by ridiculing other people, preferring to find humor in everyday activities.[5]

In 1986, a producer from *The Tonight Show* saw her act and invited her to appear on the program hosted by Johnny Carson. She was such a hit that she returned half a dozen more times in the next two years. Other career highlights that soon followed included landing a minor role on a TV sitcom that lasted two seasons and appearing on an HBO special with comics Howie Mandel and Robin Williams.[6]

An even bigger break came in 1994 when ABC signed DeGeneres to star in her own sitcom that debuted as *These Friends of Mine* but was later renamed *Ellen.* DeGeneres played Ellen Morgan, the neurotic manager of a bookstore/coffee shop, and the plot lines revolved around her interaction with three close friends.[7]

Reviews of the show provided plenty of early examples of news outlets being enamored by the rising star. The *St. Louis Post-Dispatch* wrote, "DeGeneres, with a sweet face and gentle way of making even the most outrageous comments, is a real treat," while the *Atlanta Constitution* chimed in with, "She has a goofy likeability that wears well," and the *Pittsburgh Post-Gazette* stated unequivocally, "DeGeneres is a gifted comedian."[8]

The show's ratings were strong for the first three seasons, but they fell off sharply in the fourth. ABC's executives then told DeGeneres that the series had grown stale, warning her that if something significant didn't change, her show would be canceled.[9]

COMING OUT ON TV—AND GETTING LOTS OF APPLAUSE

DeGeneres suggested to the network that Ellen Morgan come out as a lesbian. This would be a major event, as it would mark the first time a TV show featured a gay or lesbian lead character. DeGeneres further proposed that Morgan's coming out coincide with her own public announcement that she was a lesbian—she'd previously dodged questions about her sexuality for fear it would damage her career. ABC quickly signed on to the plan.[10]

When the news media got wind of what was happening, they turned it into the most public exit from the closet in American history. The *Los Angeles Times* ran sixty articles on various aspects of DeGeneres's revelation, and *Time* magazine splashed an image of her across its cover, next to the headline "Yep, I'm Gay." ABC featured the comedian on its *Primetime Live* news magazine show, with DeGeneres saying, "I don't have to worry anymore about some reporter trying to find out information. I don't have anything to be scared of, which outweighs whatever else happens in my career."[11]

The widely anticipated *Ellen* episode, which aired in April 1997, was built around Ellen Morgan being attracted to another woman for the first time and then working through the process of acknowledging her sexuality to herself and her friends. Among the guest stars on the one-hour segment were Oscar-winning actress Helen Hunt, Emmy-winner Julianna Margulies, and talk show queen Oprah Winfrey.[12]

DeGeneres and the show's writers played the moment everyone was waiting for to its maximum comic effect. Morgan was standing in an airport waiting room, surrounded by dozens of people, as she stumbled over her words while trying to tell the woman she was talking to that she was a lesbian. "Susan, I think maybe I'm . . . ," the anxious Morgan begins. "I am, . . . uh . . . I guess what I'm trying to say is . . ." She's so nervous she gasps for breath. "This is so hard, but I think . . . I think I've realized that I am . . ." Morgan twitches and fidgets, barely able to speak. "Why can't I just say the word?" Struggling to steady herself, she leans on the ticket agent's podium, accidentally tripping the switch to a microphone so that her next two words—in a complete surprise to her—are broadcast over the airport's loudspeaker system: *"I'm gay!"*

Yikes! Morgan made her statement not in the soft whisper to Susan that she'd planned but in an amplified voice that reverberated throughout the building. "That felt great," Morgan says, smiling broadly. "It felt great, and it felt . . . *loud.*"

Reviews of the segment, which was later awarded an Emmy, were uniformly positive. The *Los Angeles Times* led the applause, calling the episode "a positive milestone" that was "very smart" and "very funny." Other papers agreed. The *Washington Post* said the segment was "well written and full of laughs," and the *Boston Globe* dubbed it "one of *the* great sitcom episodes of all time."[13]

The most remarkable of the comments appeared in the *New York Times*, as the country's most influential news organization devoted its lead editorial, on the day after the broadcast, not to national politics or the global economy but to a TV sitcom. "The 'coming out' of the title character on 'Ellen' was accomplished with wit and poignancy," the *Times* stated, "which should help defuse the antagonism toward homosexuals still prevalent in society."[14]

A hefty slice of America was subject to that defusing, as an eye-popping 42 million viewers had tuned in to *Ellen* that particular night, tripling the show's average audience and ranking it as one of the most widely viewed hours of TV that year.[15]

EXPERIENCING TOUGH TIMES—BUT NOT WITH THE NEWS MEDIA

Despite the episode's success, *Ellen*'s viewership dropped dramatically during the next season. Observers said the show was placing too much emphasis on the main character being a lesbian, with an official of the Gay and Lesbian Alliance Against Defamation criticizing the program as being "too gay-specific."[16]

ABC canceled *Ellen* in April 1998. DeGeneres then returned for a second interview on *Primetime Live*. When Diane Sawyer asked the star why she'd focused so much of the series on her character's sexuality, DeGeneres responded by reading letters she'd received from gay teenagers. "Thank you for letting me realize that I'm not a nasty, sick person," one boy wrote, and "I was going to kill myself, but, because of you, I didn't," a girl said. After DeGeneres stopped reading, Sawyer asked, "So you made the decision that you would rather be a pioneer than be renewed?" DeGeneres instantly replied, "Yes. If I just had this one year of doing what I did on national television, I'll take that over ten more years of just being funny."[17]

DeGeneres's sitcom being taken off the air didn't stop journalists from praising her. She appeared in several films in the two years after *Ellen* ended, and the nation's news outlets ran flattering reviews of those performances. The *Washington Post* pronounced DeGeneres "bubbly" and "likable" in *The Love Letter*, for example, while the online magazine *Salon* wrote that "Ellen DeGeneres virtually steals the show" in the film *EDtv*.[18]

Journalistic voices again had DeGeneres's back when she starred in another TV sitcom, this one on CBS. *The Ellen Show* had her playing an openly lesbian Internet executive who returns to her hometown in search of a quieter life. The reviews were positive, with the *Washington Post* calling it "a sweetheart of a show." Nevertheless, the series failed to attract a large audience, and it was canceled after thirteen episodes.[19]

HELPING TO HEAL A NATION

In November 2001, DeGeneres accepted a challenge that had the potential to put her back on top. Her task was to host the annual *Emmy Awards* show on CBS just two months after the 9/11 terrorist attacks. The event had been postponed twice because network executives didn't think it was wise to air such a festive event in the wake of attacks that killed 3,000 Americans. Now it was up to DeGeneres to strike a balance between being funny but also being mindful of the tragic events.[20]

The comedian, dressed in a dark gray suit, set the tone for the awards show with a statement in her opening monologue. "I'm in a unique position as host

Ellen DeGeneres was widely praised for her success at hosting the Emmy Awards two months after the 9/11 terrorist attacks. Courtesy of Getty Images/Michael Caulfield Archive.

because—think about it," she said, setting up what became the most memorable line of the night: "What would bug the Taliban more than seeing a gay woman in a suit surrounded by a room full of Jews?"[21]

Perfect.

DeGeneres delivered various jokes about the TV industry. She began one of them by saying, with a straight face, "I think it's important for us to be here. It shows that the terrorists can't take away our creativity, our striving for excellence, our joy." Then came a brief pause and the punch line: "Only network executives can do that."[22]

For three hours, DeGeneres skillfully mixed such laser-sharp comments with a generous amount of heartfelt respect for the difficult times the country was going through. An example of the latter began with her saying, in a serious tone, "To all of you watching tonight, not just as Americans but as citizens of the world, we thank you." She followed that statement with a video collage of scenes from twenty-five countries showing people expressing their support for the United States.[23]

At the end of the show, the audience gave DeGeneres a prolonged standing ovation. "That's unbelievably kind," she said, waving her arms in an effort to cut off the applause.[24]

News organizations were soon singing DeGeneres's hosannas. The *Denver Post* said, "Ellen DeGeneres pulled it off. The tone was patriotic and somber with flashes of comic relief, funny but respectful." More praise came from the *New York Daily News*, which wrote that DeGeneres "walked the tightrope of humor and seriousness adeptly," and the *Hollywood Reporter*, which ended its laudatory review by saying, "Thanks, Ellen. We needed that."[25]

TRIUMPHING AS A TALK SHOW HOST

DeGeneres's success with the awards program coupled with the news media applauding her performance propelled her into discussions with producers about starring on her own syndicated daytime talk show. The star was determined to make her return to series television work this time, so she spent two years developing *The Ellen DeGeneres Show* into exactly what she wanted it to be.[26]

A big part of her plan was to maintain a consistently upbeat feel on the show. As she told Matt Lauer of *The Today Show* just before her program premiered, "There's not as much respect for one another as there needs to be.

I think we all want to change the world in a positive way. For me, changing the world would mean making people nicer to one another."[27]

With regard to content, DeGeneres decided on a mix of comedy, celebrity interviews, musical guests, human-interest stories, and games involving members of her studio audience. Another light touch would be that, after her opening monologue, DeGeneres would segue into the rest of the hour-long show by dancing. The show debuted in September 2003, mostly on local NBC channels.[28]

News outlets were soon raving about both the program and its host. The *Philadelphia Inquirer* communicated its approval with the headline that ran above the paper's exuberant review: "Just Being Herself, DeGeneres Has a Talk-Show Winner." Other organizations also were quick to pronounce the show a hit. The online magazine *PopMatters* praised the program's "pleasant, cheery feel" that "invites us to kick up our feet and relax," while the *Minneapolis Star-Tribune* gushed, "Aside from a nap, there are few more attractive callings in the afternoon than The Ellen DeGeneres Show."[29]

Even more important to DeGeneres's success as a talk-show host was what came after that initial flurry of positive critiques. That is, news outlets that cover TV typically publish a review of a new program when it debuts and then say nothing more about it. With DeGeneres's show, however, the news media couldn't stop talking about it, keeping the program in the media spotlight long after it was launched.

The day that actress Gwyneth Paltrow came on the program and the host threw her a surprise baby shower, for example, *USA Today* published a story about the event. Likewise, when DeGeneres stunned the 200 people in her studio audience by giving them all TiVo DVRs, *Slate* reported her generosity in a news article, as did the *Philadelphia Inquirer* when DeGeneres promised on her show that she'd raise $1.5 million for Hurricane Katrina relief.[30]

The Ellen DeGeneres Show soon amassed a loyal audience of 4 million viewers and, at the end of its first season, won the Emmy for outstanding daytime talk show. From that point on, the program remained a perennial winner, eventually filling its trophy case with more than thirty of the prized statues.[31]

COUPLING WITH HER "PERFECT FIT"

A big moment in the star's personal life came in early 2004 when she met and was immediately attracted to actress Portia de Rossi. DeGeneres had previously

Ellen DeGeneres wore a white suit and Portia de Rossi wore a princess-style pink halter gown on their wedding day in 2008. Courtesy of Getty Images.

been involved with two other women, but this would ultimately prove to be the longest and most substantial romantic relationship in her life.[32]

When the behemoths of American journalism learned in 2006 that DeGeneres and the beautiful actress had become a couple, they decided it was news the public needed to know. The *New York Times* reported, in a lengthy article about DeGeneres's career, that "she shares a home with the actress Portia de Rossi." *People* magazine devoted an entire story to the women's relationship, quoting DeGeneres as saying, "There's happiness and there's love, and then there's completion. I feel like I've found my perfect fit." The *Chicago Sun-Times* went so far as to consult a woman who'd written a book on "reading auras" and then quoted her as saying of DeGeneres and de Rossi, "They have the body language of one of the most in-love couples you will ever have the privilege of meeting. They practically melt into each other, as though they were one body."[33]

Online venues posted lots of stories about the couple, too. *Salon* wrote that "Ellen seems much better matched with Portia de Rossi than with either of her two earlier girlfriends." *PopMatters* reported that de Rossi's career wasn't suffering now that the public knew she was living with a woman, even though she often was cast in romantic roles playing opposite men. The *Huffington Post* was among the first outlets to break the news, in May 2008, that the women planned to marry.[34]

When it came time for their wedding three months later, however, DeGeneres and de Rossi gave the exclusive rights to photograph their special day to a publication known mostly for its print edition. *People* magazine not only put the couple on its cover but also ran several more photos inside. "Saturday evening was full of love, laughter and a few tears for Ellen DeGeneres and Portia de Rossi," the story began, "who exchanged personal wedding vows in front of their closest family and friends." *People* went on to quote the comedian as saying, "I'm the luckiest girl in the world. She's officially off the market. No one else gets her." DeGeneres then paused and smiled before adding, "And now she'll cook and clean for me."[35]

Other news outlets filled in details about the wedding. The *Jezebel* blog focused on the fashion angle, telling readers that DeGeneres wore a "white tuxedo-style ensemble" and de Rossi chose a "beautiful princess-style backless pink halter gown." The *Washington Post* stuck to the basic facts, including that the event took place at the couple's Beverly Hills home and that "just 19 people attended." *Salon* scored a coup, getting a quote from one of the guests, who said, "I only wish someone from one of those anti-gay marriage groups could have witnessed the great outpouring of love and respect between Ellen and Portia. Then they might better understand that love is not about gender—it's about two people who are totally dedicated to each other."[36]

PROPELLING POSITIVE CHANGE

While the coverage of DeGeneres's wedding was extensive, that wasn't the last event in the star's life that the news media played to the hilt. One development that drew lots of headlines came later in 2008 when cosmetics industry giant Cover Girl hired DeGeneres—at age fifty—to be the new face of its products, with *USA Today* quoting a company spokesman as saying that she'd been chosen "because she is smart, confident, natural, and beautiful from the inside out." Other news outlets reported on her humanitarian work, such as the *Huffington Post* commending her efforts on behalf of animal rights and the *Daily Beast* giving her kudos for her financial support of programs designed to reduce the suicide rate among gay teens.[37]

Another topic that made it onto the news media's radar screen was the pivotal role that DeGeneres had played in the increasing visibility of lesbians. In 2009, the *New York Times* ran a story reporting that DeGeneres's success had opened the door for other gay women to succeed on TV. The list included MSNBC political talk show host Rachel Maddow, CNBC financial guru Suze Orman, and comedian and actress Wanda Sykes.[38]

It wasn't possible to provide such tangible evidence of the role that DeGeneres's success had played in changing how the public viewed gay women. In other words, no one could create a list of all the people whose perception of lesbians had been redefined. And yet, after the comedian's many triumphs and the news media's enthusiastic coverage of them, there's no question that DeGeneres had become the most visible gay woman in the country. Beyond that, it was clear that people loved her. When the Harris polling organization asked members of the public, in 2008, to name their favorite TV personality, the most frequent choice was Ellen "Yep, I'm Gay" DeGeneres.[39]

Conclusion

I've now piloted my readers through sixteen of the many instances in which the American news media used their power to propel positive change. At this point, I'd like to identify and briefly discuss some of the recurring themes that emerge when these case studies aren't looked at as separate episodes but as a unified whole.

First on my list is motivation. The individual chapters have generally focused on *what* the news outlets did rather than *why* they did it. When the why question is considered, it's clear that those organizations—time and time again—were driven by a desire to improve society.

In several instances, this effort to make America a better place to live involved seeing that some of the most vulnerable members of society weren't mistreated but were allowed to enjoy the quality of life that other citizens were experiencing.

The earliest example of such an initiative came in chapter 1 with the chronicling of Nellie Bly's daring adventure, in 1887, that led to proper care for women confined to a New York insane asylum. Following close on the heels of this case study came the one detailing how three publications worked to improve society by campaigning for regulations to protect the 2 million children who were part of the nation's labor force.

Such efforts weren't limited to the nineteenth and early twentieth century, as others played out in the years that followed. Among the later crusades to improve the lives of vulnerable groups were CBS airing its powerful *Harvest of Shame* documentary to illuminate the plight of migrant farmworkers and the *Boston Globe* leading an initiative aimed at stopping Catholic priests from sexually abusing little boys.

In several instances, journalism's motivation was to make American society more inclusive. One example came in 1945 when newspapers waged an assault on the rampant anti-Semitism of the period by providing extensive and relentlessly positive coverage of the young Jewish woman who won the Miss America crown. That same year, several of those same papers turned their spotlight on a talented ballplayer named Jackie Robinson, transforming No. 42 into a squeaky clean role model. Yet another example of celebrating inclusiveness occurred more recently when the nation's news outlets, including many online venues, portrayed a lesbian named Ellen DeGeneres as an extraordinarily likeable and talented comedian.

Perhaps as important as what motivated news organizations to propel positive change is a factor that *didn't* play a prominent role. Specifically, the journalistic voices leading the charge in the various case studies generally weren't driven by a desire to make an enormous financial profit. Yes, every news outlet discussed in this book was a business, which means it had to earn enough money to stay afloat, but the fiscal bottom line didn't appear to be the paramount factor in deciding what content was published or broadcast. In short, the news media's function as a public trust repeatedly trumped their function as a profit maker.

Indeed, with regard to economics, several chapters demonstrate that news organizations weren't trying to make money for themselves but were working to help raise the financial status of the people involved in the cause they were championing. When Robert S. Abbott encouraged African-American men and women in the South to relocate to the North, for example, he hoped to raise the earning power of the readers who heeded his call. Likewise, when the news media took up the cause of Japanese Americans who'd been removed from their homes and confined to internment camps during World War II, those journalistic voices spoke out in favor of the former internees receiving financial reparations for the businesses and possessions they'd lost.

Economics of a different sort was a factor in the news coverage of the Space Race. This time, the consistently complimentary portrayal by the TV networks helped build the public support that contributed to Congress repeatedly increasing NASA's annual budget.

The second item on my list of recurring themes isn't a positive one. Specifically, when the case studies are examined closely, there's evidence that news organizations highlighted in this book sometimes behaved in ways that a critic could label as either unethical or in violation of standard journalistic practice.

One example came in the 1930s when some of the nation's most influential newspapers allowed J. Edgar Hoover to play too large of a role in how they portrayed his Bureau of Investigation. It was absolutely wrong for the titans of American journalism such as the *New York Times* and *Washington Star* to publish articles that weren't written entirely by reporters but were the joint products of Hoover and complicit journalists.

Another ethical breach played out between 1945 and 1947 when a group of papers committed themselves to portraying Jackie Robinson in an unfailingly favorable light. While it's commendable that these journalistic outlets helped break the color barrier in professional baseball, they can be faulted for downplaying how many times the racial pioneer was mistreated. By minimizing the fact that players from opposing teams yelled racial slurs at Robinson and dug the spikes of their shoes into his leg or foot, the papers weren't merely sugarcoating reality but were keeping factual details about his experience from their readers.

TV news organizations sometimes joined their print counterparts in crossing ethical lines. When CBS broadcast the *Harvest of Shame* documentary in 1960, the network was clearly being manipulative when it juxtaposed certain statements. One example came when Edward R. Murrow said, "A family of six will move into this room"—while the TV screen showed a filthy, ten-foot-by-twelve-foot space furnished with a crude table consisting of boards that had been nailed together—and then Murrow immediately said, "Nearby, a trotting raceway has new stables for horses. They cost $500,000"—while the screen was filled with images of a modern, spotlessly clean building where men were meticulously grooming handsome thoroughbred racehorses. Likewise, CBS and NBC were being dishonest with their viewers when, a year later, they failed to properly identify prerecorded footage from the NASA control center that they'd mixed in with live shots of Gus Grissom's flight.

A third common thread running through many of the case studies involves the limitations of the efforts the news media have made while seeking to propel positive change.

Two examples that come immediately to mind are the pair of undertakings that, as noted in the chapters about them, ultimately fell short. Despite any number of American news organizations warning readers that they were killing themselves by smoking cigarettes, millions of people kept puffing away their lives; journalism was no match for the tobacco industry that devoted huge resources to promoting cigarette use. Likewise, *Harvest of Shame* failed to improve the lives of migrant farmworkers, despite the high quality of the documentary; in this instance, it was the farm lobby that blocked the attempt to make changes that could have reduced the challenges facing these downtrodden American laborers.

A limitation of a very different ilk involved the changes that came about with regard to giving average citizens more say in choosing their president. While TV news started this shift during the 1952 national conventions and campaign, that change was superseded two decades later when the major political parties expanded the role of the presidential primaries in choosing their nominees.

In several other case studies, the news media succeeded in bringing about worthy change, but the particular problem has resurfaced with the passage of time. One example involved the Ponzi scheme. There's no question that the *Boston Post* triumphed, in 1920, in exposing the fallacies inherent in Charles Ponzi's get-rich-quick plan, sending the errant financier to jail and winning a Pulitzer Prize for its work. And yet, there's also no question that a long list of other charlatans have bilked huge sums of money out of millions more investors since that time.

It's been a similar story with other of the chapter topics. The compelling stories and photos that Jacob Riis created during the late nineteenth century led to the destruction of the squalid urban slums that he found so vile, but anyone with a social conscience knows that disgraceful living conditions continued to be a persistent problem in the wealthiest nation in the world. Also distressing is that while the *Boston Globe* fully deserved the Pulitzer Prize for exposing the wrongdoing by Catholic priests in 2002, many stories since that time have documented the sad reality that reprehensible men of the cloth continue to sexually abuse little boys.

The fourth and final theme I want to highlight is more positive. What I have in mind can best be summarized in a single word: connections. That is, when I look back over the various chapters, I'm struck by how many of the episodes from the distant past have much in common with events occurring either today or just a few years ago.

For instance, the chapter about 1930s news organizations glorifying the G-men who gunned down a long list of notorious criminals sounds very similar to contemporary journalistic enterprises praising U.S. Navy SEALs. When members of this elite military group killed Osama bin Laden in 2011, the country's leading news voices were unstinting in their praise of the men. Print and online outlets such as the *New York Times* and *Slate* called the SEALs "heroes," and *ABC World News* anchor Diane Sawyer dubbed them "super-human."[1]

Likewise, I can see a parallel between how news outlets of the 1920s through the 1950s reported that cigarette smoking was doing serious damage to the health of millions of Americans and how news outlets today are reporting that climate change is harming the environment. What's unclear at this point is whether the public will heed journalism's warnings vis-à-vis how we're contributing to global warming or will ignore those cautionary words and continue to behave as we have been—just as millions of smokers didn't pay attention to the articles that newspapers and magazines published.

A third parallel between the distant past and today that can be drawn from one of the chapters involves technology and the American presidency. Chapter 10, "Giving Average Citizens More Say in Choosing Their President," documented how Dwight Eisenhower benefited enormously, in 1952, from recognizing that TV news would play a major role in the election process. How Eisenhower adapted to that new medium resonates with how, sixty years later, Barack Obama gained a major advantage over his opponents by incorporating the Internet and social media into his successful presidential campaigns.

I want to end this book with one final observation that relates not to a recurring theme in the chapters but to a statement I made in the introduction. Specifically, I said that the topics covered in *A Force for Good* were ones that "aren't classified as milestones in American history but are what I think of as *cultural phenomena*." I further noted that these topics aren't talked about in standard American history books.

Now I'd like to say: Maybe they should be.

In other words, I propose that some of the episodes I've illuminated in this book are of such significance that they deserve to be designated "historic events." And, as such, they merit being part of the narrative told in standard American history textbooks.

One topic that definitely qualifies is the Great Migration. Hundreds of thousands of African Americans abandoning the South and relocating to the North had a massive impact not only on the lives of the individuals who moved but also on their children and their children's children—ultimately numbering in the tens of millions. What's more, the Great Migration's influence wasn't limited to the individuals themselves, as those African Americans and their descendants became a transformative social and political force that forever changed the cities that they began calling home, such as Chicago and Detroit.

An argument can be made that the birth control pill, for completely different reasons, also deserves a place in the textbooks that purport to synthesize the history of this nation. As mentioned in chapter 12, the ten-milligram dose of synthetic hormones changed the sex lives of men and women while also dramatically reducing the national birthrate. But the ramifications were much greater than that. In 1960 when the pill was introduced, professional occupations were overwhelmingly a male domain. But then, with women being able to limit and postpone childbirth, huge numbers of them stopped restricting themselves to short-term jobs and began thinking in terms of lifelong careers. Indeed, the pill made such a difference in the lives of so many people that it can be argued that its availability was every bit as important to the advancement of American women as winning the right to vote had been four decades earlier.

Another topic that's discussed at length in *A Force for Good* and deserves more attention in U.S. history textbooks is Jackie Robinson breaking the color barrier in major league baseball. Yes, yes, yes, I can hear many of my fellow historians huffing and puffing at the audacity of my suggesting that anything that happened on a baseball diamond belongs between the covers of a history textbook. Nevertheless, I believe a case can be made—as mentioned at the end of chapter 9—that Robinson joining the ranks of white players in this highly visible American pastime paved the way for the U.S. Supreme Court outlawing segregated public schools in the *Brown v. Board of Education* case. To repeat the quote from a scholar that I cited earlier in this book: "The integration of baseball represented both a symbol of imminent racial challenge and a direct agent of social change."[2]

An added benefit of raising these topics from their current designations as cultural phenomena to the stature of historic events would come if, in each case, the role of the news media were incorporated into the summaries that were added to the history textbooks. Indeed, if future students became aware of the role that, for example, the *Chicago Defender* played in the Great Migration and the country's leading outlets played in popularizing the birth control pill, maybe tomorrow's news consumers wouldn't be quite so inclined as their contemporary counterparts to treat journalism as a punching bag.

Notes

CHAPTER 1: SECURING HUMANE CARE FOR THE MENTALLY ILL

1. *New York Times*, "Charges against Physicians," August 14, 1887, 9; "The City Workhouse," August 18, 1887, 4.

2. On Elizabeth Cochran's early years, see Brooke Kroeger, *Nellie Bly: Daredevil, Reporter, Feminist* (New York: Times Books/Random House, 1994), 3–26; "Nellie Bly, Journalist, Dies of Pneumonia," *New York Times*, January 28, 1922, 11; Jean Marie Lutes, *Front Page Girls: Women Journalists in American Culture and Fiction, 1880-1930* (Ithaca, N.Y.: Cornell University Press, 2006), 94–95; Ishbel Ross, *Ladies of the Press: The Story of Women in Journalism by an Insider* (New York: Harper & Brothers, 1936), 48–49.

3. Kroeger, *Nellie Bly*, 34–36; David Randall, *The Great Reporters* (Ann Arbor, Mich.: Pluto, 2005), 95–96; Ross, *Ladies of the Press*, 49.

4. Kroeger, *Nellie Bly*, 38–39; "Nellie Bly, Journalist," 11; Randall, *Great Reporters*, 96; Ross, *Ladies of the Press*, 49.

5. Kroeger, *Nellie Bly*, 43–44; Marion Marzolf, *Up from the Footnote: A History of Women Journalists* (New York: Hastings House, 1977), 23; Randall, *Great Reporters*, 97; Ross, *Ladies of the Press*, 49.

6. For the quote, see Kroeger, *Nellie Bly*, 44–45. See also Ross, *Ladies of the Press*, 49.

7. Nellie Bly, "Perilous Paths," *Pittsburgh Dispatch*, February 8, 1885, 12.

8. Kroeger, *Nellie Bly*, 49–56; Randall, *Great Reporters*, 97. For stories on the flower show, see Nellie Bly, *Pittsburgh Dispatch*, "Scenes among the Roses," April 16, 1885, 5; "Farewell to the Flowers," April 19, 1885, 2. For the profile of the owner of the opera company, see Nellie Bly, "A Plucky Woman," *Pittsburgh Dispatch*, May 31, 1885, 7. For stories about fashion, see Nellie Bly, *Pittsburgh Dispatch*, "Hand and Headwear,"

May 3, 1885, 7; "Styles for the Little Tots," May 6, 1885, 4; "A Princess' Dresses," May 10, 1885, 9; "Some Lovely Laces," May 11, 1885, 3.

9. For the quote, see Nellie Bly, *Six Months in Mexico* (New York: John W. Lovell, 1886), 5; Kroeger, *Nellie Bly*, 56.

10. Randall, *Great Reporters*, 98; Ross, *Ladies of the Press*, 49.

11. Kroeger, *Nellie Bly*, 75; Randall, *Great Reporters*, 98; Ross, *Ladies of the Press*, 49.

12. Kroeger, *Nellie Bly*, 79–80; Lutes, *Front Page Girls*, 15–16.

13. Denis Brian, *Pulitzer: A Life* (New York: John Wiley & Sons, 2002), 124; Kroeger, *Nellie Bly*, 84–86; "Nellie Bly, Journalist," 11; "Nellie Bly, Noted Writer, Dead at 56," *Washington Post*, January 28, 1922, 11; Randall, *Great Reporters*, 94, 99; Ross, *Ladies of the Press*, 50.

14. Brian, *Pulitzer*, 124; Kroeger, *Nellie Bly*, 85–86; Lutes, *Front Page Girls*, 12; Marzolf, *Up from the Footnote*, 23; Randall, *Great Reporters*, 99.

15. Kroeger, *Nellie Bly*, 89; Randall, *Great Reporters*, 99; Ross, *Ladies of the Press*, 50.

16. For the quote, see Nellie Bly, "Behind Asylum Bars," *New York World*, October 9, 1887, 25. See also Brian, *Pulitzer*, 124; Brooke Kroeger, *Undercover Reporting: The Truth about Deception* (Evanston, Ill.: Northwestern University Press, 2012), 176–77; Randall, *Great Reporters*, 99.

17. For the quote, see Bly, "Behind Asylum Bars," 25. See also Brian, *Pulitzer*, 124; Kroeger, *Nellie Bly*, 90–91; Randall, *Great Reporters*, 93, 99; Ross, *Ladies of the Press*, 48.

18. For the quote, see Bly, "Behind Asylum Bars," 25. See also Brian, *Pulitzer*, 125; Randall, *Great Reporters*, 100–101; Ross, *Ladies of the Press*, 50.

19. For the quote, see Bly, "Behind Asylum Bars," 25. See also Brian, *Pulitzer*, 125.

20. Nellie Bly, "Inside the Madhouse," *New York World*, October 16, 1887, 25; Brian, *Pulitzer*, 125.

21. Bly, "Inside the Madhouse," 25.

22. Ibid.

23. Ibid.

24. Ibid., 26.

25. Brian, *Pulitzer*, 126; Marzolf, *Up from the Footnote*, 23; Ross, *Ladies of the Press*, 51.

26. Bly, "Inside the Madhouse," 25.

27. Ibid.

28. Ibid.

29. Ibid.

30. Ibid.

31. Brian, *Pulitzer*, 125; Marzolf, *Up from the Footnote*, 23; Ross, *Ladies of the Press*, 51.

32. Bly, "Inside the Madhouse," 25.

33. Ibid., 26.

34. Ibid.

35. Ibid.

36. Bly, "Behind Asylum Bars," 25–26; Bly, "Inside the Madhouse," 25–26. Kroeger, *Nellie Bly*, 93; Marzolf, *Up from the Footnote*, 23.

37. "Playing Mad Woman," *New York Sun*, October 14, 1887, 1; Ross, *Ladies of the Press*, 51.

38. "The Famous Nellie Bly," *New Haven Evening Register*, November 2, 1887, 4; "Personal and General Notes," *New Orleans Daily Picayune*, October 17, 1887, 4; "In Gotham," *Fort Worth Daily Gazette*, October 29, 1887, 6; "The Same Old Opponents," *Salt Lake Herald*, December 9, 1887, 4; Lutes, *Front Page Girls*, 13; Ross, *Ladies of the Press*, 51.

39. "A Work of Humanity," *New York World*, October 18, 1887, 4.

40. Brian, *Pulitzer*, 127; Kroeger, *Undercover Reporting*, 176–77; Marzolf, *Up from the Footnote*, 23; "The World Their Savior," *New York World*, October 28, 1887, 12.

41. Brian, *Pulitzer*, 127; Kroeger, *Undercover Reporting*, 176–77; *New York Times* articles: "Taken Up by the Grand Jury," October 20, 1887, 2; "City and Suburban News," November 2, 1887, 3; "Due to Lack of Money," November 3, 1887, 4; "The Mayor on the Island," December 18, 1887, 2; Randall, *Great Reporters*, 103; Ross, *Ladies of the Press*, 51.

42. Brian, *Pulitzer*, 127; Agnes Hooper Gottlieb, "Women and Exposé: Reform and Housekeeping," in *The Muckrakers: Evangelical Crusaders*, ed. Robert Miraldi (Westport, Conn.: Praeger, 2000), 80; Lutes, *Front Page Girls*, 13; Randall, *Great Reporters*, 101.

CHAPTER 2: WAGING WAR ON URBAN SLUMS

1. On Riis's early years, see Tom Buk-Swienty, *The Other Half: The Life of Jacob Riis and the World of Immigrant America* (New York: W. W. Norton, 2008), 13–33; "Jacob A. Riis, Reformer, Dead," *New York Times*, May 27, 1914, 1; Louise Ware, *Jacob A. Riis: Police Reporter, Reformer, Useful Citizen* (New York: D. Appleton-Century, 1939), 1–15; Bonnie Yochelson and Daniel Czitrom, *Rediscovering Jacob Riis: Exposure Journalism and Photography in Turn-of-the-Century New York* (New York: New Press, 2007), 3. Riis's parents were Niels and Carolina Riis.

2. Buk-Swienty, *Other Half*, 49–55; "Jacob A. Riis," 1; Ware, *Jacob A. Riis*, 12–15; Yochelson and Czitrom, *Rediscovering Jacob Riis*, 3–4.

3. Buk-Swienty, *Other Half*, 102–10; "Jacob A. Riis," 1; Ware, *Jacob A. Riis*, 16–30; Yochelson and Czitrom, *Rediscovering Jacob Riis*, 4–9.

4. Buk-Swienty, *Other Half,* 123–58; "Jacob A. Riis," 1; Ware, *Jacob A. Riis,* 31–36; Yochelson and Czitrom, *Rediscovering Jacob Riis,* 7–8.

5. Buk-Swienty, *Other Half,* 133–34; "Jacob A. Riis," 1; Ware, *Jacob A. Riis,* 37–39; Yochelson and Czitrom, *Rediscovering Jacob Riis,* 8.

6. Buk-Swienty, *Other Half,* 162; "Jacob A. Riis," 1; Ware, *Jacob A. Riis,* 39–48; Yochelson and Czitrom, *Rediscovering Jacob Riis,* 8–10.

7. Buk-Swienty, *Other Half,* 165; "Jacob A. Riis," 1; Ware, *Jacob A. Riis,* 49–59; Yochelson and Czitrom, *Rediscovering Jacob Riis,* 10–13.

8. Jacob Riis, "Life's Struggles Too Hard," *New York Tribune,* July 9, 1881, 8.

9. Jacob Riis, "Visiting Tenement Houses," *New York Tribune,* July 18, 1881, 8.

10. Buk-Swienty, *Other Half,* 150; "Jacob A. Riis," 1; Ware, *Jacob A. Riis,* 49–59; Yochelson and Czitrom, *Rediscovering Jacob Riis,* 20, 23.

11. Jacob Riis, *The Making of an American* (New York: Macmillan, 1901), 266.

12. Ibid., 267.

13. Buk-Swienty, *Other Half,* 203.

14. Ibid., 204–9.

15. Ware, *Jacob A. Riis,* 66; Yochelson and Czitrom, *Rediscovering Jacob Riis,* 86–87.

16. Buk-Swienty, *Other Half,* 215; Yochelson and Czitrom, *Rediscovering Jacob Riis,* 86–97.

17. For the quotes, see "The Remarkable Storm," *Long Island Democrat,* March 13, 1888, which is quoted in Buk-Swienty, *Other Half,* 220–21. See also, Buk-Swienty, *Other Half,* 220–21, 231; Yochelson and Czitrom, *Rediscovering Jacob Riis,* 86–97.

18. The photos can be found at the Library of Congress in the Jacob Riis Collection.

19. Ware, *Jacob A. Riis,* 66–67.

20. Jacob Riis, "How the Other Half Lives: Studies Among the Tenements," *Scribner's,* December 1889, 643–62; Ware, *Jacob A. Riis,* 67–68; Yochelson and Czitrom, *Rediscovering Jacob Riis,* 103–4.

21. Buk-Swienty, *Other Half,* 234; Yochelson and Czitrom, *Rediscovering Jacob Riis,* 103–4.

22. Buk-Swienty, *Other Half,* 233–34; Yochelson and Czitrom, *Rediscovering Jacob Riis,* 103–4.

23. Riis, "How the Other Half Lives," 647.

24. For the quote, see Riis, "How the Other Half Lives," 662. See also, Buk-Swienty, *Other Half,* 234.

25. The photos can be found at the Library of Congress in the Jacob Riis Collection.

26. Buk-Swienty, *Other Half,* 230–31; Ware, *Jacob A. Riis,* 68–69.

27. Buk-Swienty, *Other Half,* 234–35; "Jacob A. Riis," 1; Ware, *Jacob A. Riis,* 68–70.

28. Riis, *How the Other Half Lives,* 15.

29. Ibid., 160, 171.

30. The photos can be found at the Library of Congress in the Jacob Riis Collection.

31. For the quotes, see Buk-Swienty, *Other Half*, 242.

32. Buk-Swienty, *Other Half*, 245; Ware, *Jacob A. Riis*, 129–30.

33. Buk-Swienty, *Other Half*, 248; Ware, *Jacob A. Riis*, 129–30.

34. Buk-Swienty, *Other Half*, 253; "Jacob A. Riis," 1; Ware, *Jacob A. Riis*, 129–30.

35. For the quote, see Jacob Riis, *Theodore Roosevelt: The Citizen* (New York: Macmillan, 1904), 144. See also, "Jacob A. Riis," 1; Ware, *Jacob A. Riis*, 130–33.

36. Buk-Swienty, *Other Half*, 254; Ware, *Jacob A. Riis*, 133–39.

37. Buk-Swienty, *Other Half*, 254; "Rear Tenements Must Go," *New York Times*, June 23, 1896, 9; Ware, *Jacob A. Riis*, 133–39.

38. For the quote, see Riis, *Making of an American*, 349. See also, "Jacob A. Riis," 1.

39. For the quote, see "Mulberry Park Opened," *New York Times*, June 16, 1897, 7. See also Ware, *Jacob A. Riis*, 159. The speaker was George Waring, a New York City sanitation official.

40. "Jacob A. Riis," 1.

CHAPTER 3: PROTECTING AMERICA'S CHILDREN

1. "Child Labor in Pennsylvania," *Los Angeles Times*, December 17, 1902, 6; "A Children's Strike," *New York Evening Post*, December 21, 1904, 14.

2. "Child Labor in Factories," *Harper's Weekly*, September 13, 1902, 1280.

3. Mrs. John Van Vorst, "The Cry of the Children: Human Documents in the Case of the New Slavery," *Saturday Evening Post*, 1906, running March 10, 1–3, 28–29; April 14, 3–4, 5; April 28, 10–11; May 5, 11–13; May 19, 12–13, 26–27; July 7, 12–13; July 28, 17–18; August 18, 17–18. On the significance of the series, see Louis Filler, *The Muckrakers* (University Park: Pennsylvania State University Press, 1976), 271; Walter I. Trattner, *Crusade for the Children* (Chicago: Quadrangle, 1970), 48.

4. Van Vorst, "Cry of the Children," March 10, 1906, 1.

5. Ibid., 2.

6. Ibid., 3.

7. Van Vorst, "Cry of the Children," April 28, 1906, 10.

8. Ibid.

9. *Chicago Tribune* series: "Nation's Shame Is Child Labor," July 22, 1906, 1, 5; "Child Labor Not Always Wicked," July 23, 1906, 1, 7; "Child Labor Law Works Hardship," July 24, 1906, 1, 7; "Ills of Poverty in Child Labor," July 25, 1906, 1, 4; "Relief Plan for Children of Toil," July 26, 1906, 1, 4; "Wise Charity Is Slums' Bulwark," July 27, 1906, 1, 4; "Sweatshop Evil Is Hard to Kill," July 28, 1906, 1, 7; "Peril of Disease in Child Labor," July 30, 1906, 1, 5; "Would Divorce Home and Shop," July 31, 1906, 1,

5; "Burden of Toil for Breaker Boy," August 6, 1906, 1, 7; "Boys' Lot Dreary in Coal Breakers," August 7, 1906, 1, 7; "Mine Boys' Hope in Age Limit Act," August 8, 1906, 1, 5; "Boy Killing Pace Glass Works' Evil," August 9, 1906, 1, 5; "Glass Factories Place for Boys," August 10, 1906, 1, 5; "Girl Child's Toil Tragedy of Yards," August 11, 1906, 1, 6; "Law Often Hard on Child Worker," August 12, 1906, 1, 4; "Work of a Child Often Last Hope," August 13, 1906, 1; "Children's Abuse in Lack of School," August 14, 1906, 1, 7; "Brains Stunted by Child Labor," August 15, 1906, 1, 5.

10. "Nation's Shame Is Child Labor," 1.

11. Ibid.

12. "Peril of Disease in Child Labor," 1.

13. "Brains Stunted by Child Labor," 5.

14. "Boy Killing Pace Glass Works' Evil," 1.

15. "Mine Boys' Hope in Age Limit Act," 1.

16. For the quote, see "Glass Factories Place for Boys," 1. "Boys' Lot Dreary in Coal Breakers," 1.

17. Edwin Markham, "The Hoe-Man in the Making," *Cosmopolitan*, September 1906, 480–87; October 1906, 567–74. On the significance of the series, see Bruce J. Evensen, "Edwin Markham," in *Encyclopedia of American Journalism*, ed. Stephen L. Vaughn (New York: Routledge, 2008), 293–94; Bruce J. Evensen, "The Muckrakers as Evangelicals," in *The Muckrakers: Evangelical Crusaders*, ed. Robert Miraldi (Westport, Conn.: Praeger, 2000), 16–17; Trattner, *Crusade for the Children*, 48, 99. Arthur Weinberg and Lila Weinberg, eds., *The Muckrakers: The Era in Journalism That Moved America to Reform—the Most Significant Magazine Articles of 1902–1912* (New York: Simon and Schuster, 1961), 359.

18. For the quote, see Markham, "Hoe-Man," October 1906, 567.

19. Ibid., 570.

20. Ibid.

21. Ibid., 571–72.

22. Ibid., 572.

23. Ibid., 573–74.

24. Van Vorst, "Cry of the Children," August 18, 1906, 18.

25. Markham, "Hoe-Man," October 1906, 574.

26. "Child Labor," B4.

27. "Brains Stunted by Child Labor," 1.

28. Laurie Collier Hillstrom, *The Muckrakers and the Progressive Era* (Detroit: Omnigraphics, 2009), 43–44.

29. "Child Labor Ills Issues for States," *Chicago Tribune*, January 25, 1907, 1, 7; "Child Labor in the States," *New York Times*, February 9, 1907, 8; "Child Labor

Law Enforced," *Baltimore Sun*, August 31, 1907, 8; "Child Labor Laws," *New York Times*, January 28, 1907, 6; "Child Labor Laws in Force," *New York Times*, October 1, 1907, 11; "Child-Labor Law," *Los Angeles Times*, May 14, 1907, B7; "Child-Labor Law Change," *Washington Post*, February 5, 1907, 16; "Defect in Child Labor Law," *Baltimore Sun*, May 20, 1907, 6; "Drastic Proviso on Child Labor," *Chicago Tribune*, February 8, 1907, 10; "Enforces Child Labor Law," *Baltimore Sun*, July 16, 1907, 14; "Keep Children Out of Shops and Factories," *Chicago Tribune*, February 3, 1907, F2; "Must Obey Child Labor Law," *New York Times*, December 13, 1907, 4; "New Child-Labor Laws," *Baltimore Sun*, January 27, 1907, 15; "Regulation of Child Labor," *Baltimore Sun*, January 7, 1907, 12; "To Stop Child Labor," *New York Times*, October 10, 1907, 5; "To Teach Mine Workers," *New York Times*, September 22, 1908, 2; "Unique Southern School," *Los Angeles Times*, January 13, 1907, E17.

30. Evensen, "Edwin Markham," 294; Weinberg and Weinberg, *Muckrakers*, 360.

31. For the quotes, see Weinberg and Weinberg, *Muckrakers*, 359; Filler, *Muckrakers*, 270–71. For the impact of the articles about child labor, see also Bruce J. Evensen, "The Media and Reform, 1900–1917," in *The Age of Mass Communication*, ed. William David Sloan (Northport, Ala.: Vision, 1998), 349; Louis Filler, "Marie Louise Van Vorst," in *Notable American Women, 1607–1950*, vol. 2, *A Biographical Dictionary*, eds., Edward T. James, Janet Wilson James, and Paul S. Boyer (Cambridge, Mass.: Belknap Press of Harvard University Press, 1971), 515; Hillstrom, *Muckrakers*, 43; Hugh D. Hindman, *Child Labor: An American History* (Armonk, N.Y.: M. E. Sharpe, 2002), 53; Trattner, *Crusade for the Children*, 99.

CHAPTER 4: CREATING A BETTER LIFE FOR AFRICAN AMERICANS

1. For the quote, see Alan D. Desantis, "A Forgotten Leader: Robert S. Abbott and the *Chicago Defender* from 1910–1920," *Journalism History* 23 (Summer 1997): 64. See also Metz T. P. Lochard, "Robert S. Abbott—'Race Leader,'" *Phylon* 8 (1947): 124; Roi Ottley, *The Lonely Warrior: The Life and Times of Robert S. Abbott* (Chicago: Regnery, 1955), 24, 66–67, 76; Isabel Wilkerson, *The Warmth of Other Suns: The Epic Story of America's Great Migration* (New York: Random House, 2010), 191. Abbott's mother was Flora Abbott Sengstacke, and his stepfather was John Sengstacke.

2. Desantis, "Forgotten Leader," 64; Ottley, *Lonely Warrior*, 88–93.

3. Desantis, "Forgotten Leader," 65; Ottley, *Lonely Warrior*, 105–7.

4. Desantis, "Forgotten Leader," 65; Henry Walker, "Southern White Gentlemen Burn Race Boy at Stake," *Chicago Defender*, May 20, 1916, 1; "White Man Rapes Colored Girl," *Chicago Defender*, April 29, 1916, 1.

5. Ottley, *Lonely Warrior*, 130.

6. James R. Grossman, "Blowing the Trumpet: The *Chicago Defender* and Black Migration during World War I," *Illinois Historical Journal* 78 (Summer 1985): 88; James R. Grossman, *Land of Hope: Chicago, Black Southerners, and the Great Migration* (Chicago: University of Chicago Press, 1989), 79; Wilkerson, *Warmth of Other Suns*, 191.

7. Desantis, "Forgotten Leader," 65.

8. *Chicago Defender*, "Eye for an Eye, Tooth for a Tooth," January 8, 1916, 1; "When the Mob Comes and You Must Die, Take at Least One with You," January 23, 1915, 1; "Call the White Fiends to the Door and Shoot Them Down," January 23, 1915, 1.

9. Ottley, *Lonely Warrior*, 159.

10. Desantis, "Forgotten Leader," 65; Grossman, "Blowing the Trumpet," 84; Ottley, *Lonely Warrior*, 139; Roland E. Wolseley, *Black Press, U.S.A.*, 2nd ed. (Ames: Iowa State University Press, 1971), 54.

11. Desantis, "Forgotten Leader," 66; Grossman, "Blowing the Trumpet," 88.

12. Emmett J. Scott, "Letters of Negro Migrants of 1916–1918," *Journal of Negro History* 4 (1919): 333; Emmett J. Scott, *Negro Migration during the War* (New York: Oxford, 1920), 30; Ottley, *Lonely Warrior*, 8.

13. Desantis, "Forgotten Leader," 66; Wilkerson, *Warmth of Other Suns*, 191.

14. Ottley, *Lonely Warrior*, 136.

15. *Chicago Defender*, Henry E. Reed, "Below the Mason-Dixon Line," May 6, 1916, 1; "Woman Brutally Murdered by Memphis," September 11, 1915, 1; "Paducah Horror!" October 21, 1916, 1.

16. *Chicago Defender*, Robert S. Abbott, "How Much Longer," February 12, 1916, 8; "Invites All North," February 10, 1917, 3.

17. Desantis, "Forgotten Leader," 66; Ottley, *Lonely Warrior*, 161.

18. For the quotes, see Robert S. Abbott, "Blazing the Way," *Chicago Defender*, October 12, 1918, 16; "Our Industrial Opportunity," *Chicago Defender*, August 12, 1916, 12. See also, Ottley, *Lonely Warrior*, 160.

19. Scott, *Negro Migration*, 29.

20. Grossman, *Land of Hope*, 86.

21. "Trooper of Troop K," *Chicago Defender*, October 7, 1916, 4.

22. "Clubs and Societies," *Chicago Defender*, November 6, 1915, 6.

23. *Chicago Defender*, "World's Champion Is Jack of All Trades," February 20, 1915, 6; "American Giants Close Season with Victory," October 20, 1917, 10.

24. Quoted in Grossman, *Land of Hope*, 86.

25. For the quote, see Florette Henri, *Black Migration: Movement North, 1900–1920* (Garden City, N.Y.: Anchor, 1975), 64. See also Ottley, *Lonely Warrior*, 162–63.

26. For the quote, see "The Exodus," *Chicago Defender*, September 2, 1916, 1. See also Desantis, "Forgotten Leader," 66–67; Ottley, *Lonely Warrior*, 160–61.

27. *Chicago Defender*, "300 Leave for North," November 18, 1916, 2; "Farewell, Dixie Land," October 7, 1916, 12; "Thousands Leave Memphis," June 2, 1917, 3; "200 Leave for the North," February 10, 1917, 5; "Down in Georgia," March 10, 1917, 2.

28. *Chicago Defender*, "Millions Prepare to Leave the South Following Brutal Burning of Human," May 26, 1917, 1; "Lynching of Crawford Causes Thousands to Leave the South," October 7, 1916, 3.

29. For the quote, see Ottley, *Lonely Warrior*, 165. See also Wilkerson, *Warmth of Other Suns*, 191.

30. Ottley, *Lonely Warrior*, 165; Wilkerson, *Warmth of Other Suns*, 163, 216.

31. "Emigration Worries South; Arrests Made to Keep Labor from Going North," *Chicago Defender*, March 24, 1917, 1.

32. For the quote, see *The Black Press: Soldiers without Swords* (video), produced and directed by Stanley Nelson (New York: Half Nelson Productions, 1998). Ottley, *Lonely Warrior*, 145, 167; Henri, *Black Migration*, 64; Desantis, "Forgotten Leader," 69.

33. Ottley, *Lonely Warrior*, 142.

34. Abbott, "Farewell, Dixie Land," 12.

35. Ottley, *Lonely Warrior*, 161.

36. Ibid., 170–71.

37. Desantis, "Forgotten Leader," 69.

38. Ottley, *Lonely Warrior*, 160; "Riot Sweeps Chicago," *Chicago Defender*, August 2, 1919, 1.

39. Desantis, "Forgotten Leader," 69.

40. Ibid., 70.

41. For the Sandburg quote, see Ottley, *Lonely Warrior*, 159; for the quote beginning "Chicago's image," see Grossman, "Blowing the Trumpet," 84; the quote beginning "The *Defender* became" is by Charles S. Johnson, president of Fisk University, and is quoted in Ottley, *Lonely Warrior*, 9.

CHAPTER 5: CLOSING DOWN THE ORIGINAL PONZI SCHEME

1. On Ponzi's early years, see "Doubles the Money Within Three Months," *Boston Post*, July 24, 1920, 4; Herbert A. Kennedy, *Newspaper Row: Journalism in the Pre-Television Era* (Chester, Conn.: Globe Pequot, 1987), 185; "Ponzi Dies in Rio in Charity Ward," *New York Times*, January 19, 1949, 56; Mitchell Zuckoff, *Ponzi's Scheme: The True Story of a Financial Legend* (New York: Random House, 2005), 19–23.

2. "Doubles the Money," 4; Kennedy, *Newspaper Row*, 185; "Ponzi Dies," 56; Zuckoff, *Ponzi's Scheme*, 26–27.

3. Kennedy, *Newspaper Row*, 187; "Ponzi Dies," 56; Zuckoff, *Ponzi's Scheme*, 28–30.

4. Kennedy, *Newspaper Row*, 187; Zuckoff, *Ponzi's Scheme*, 45–46.

5. "Doubles the Money," 4; Kennedy, *Newspaper Row*, 187; Zuckoff, *Ponzi's Scheme*, 78–85.

6. "Doubles the Money," 4; Kennedy, *Newspaper Row*, 188; Zuckoff, *Ponzi's Scheme*, 87–88.

7. "Doubles the Money," 4; Kennedy, *Newspaper Row*, 188; Zuckoff, *Ponzi's Scheme*, 89.

8. "Doubles the Money," 4; Roy J. Harris Jr., *Pulitzer's Gold: Behind the Prize for Public Service Journalism* (Columbia: University of Missouri Press, 2007), 125; Zuckoff, *Ponzi's Scheme*, 93–94.

9. Harris, *Pulitzer's Gold*, 125; Kennedy, *Newspaper Row*, 188.

10. "Doubles the Money," 4; Harris, *Pulitzer's Gold*, 125; Zuckoff, *Ponzi's Scheme*, 94.

11. "Doubles the Money," 4; Harris, *Pulitzer's Gold*, 125; "Pulitzer Prize Is Awarded to Post," *Boston Post*, May 30, 1921, 1; Zuckoff, *Ponzi's Scheme*, 95.

12. "Doubles the Money," 4; Harris, *Pulitzer's Gold*, 125; "Pulitzer Prize Is Awarded," 1; Zuckoff, *Ponzi's Scheme*, 95.

13. "Doubles the Money," 4; Harris, *Pulitzer's Gold*, 125; Kennedy, *Newspaper Row*, 189; "Ponzi Dies," 56; Zuckoff, *Ponzi's Scheme*, 98, 106–7.

14. Harris, *Pulitzer's Gold*, 124–25; Zuckoff, *Ponzi's Scheme*, 11.

15. Harris, *Pulitzer's Gold*, 124–25; Zuckoff, *Ponzi's Scheme*, 107.

16. Kennedy, *Newspaper Row*, 189; Zuckoff, *Ponzi's Scheme*, 111–13.

17. Kennedy, *Newspaper Row*, 189; Zuckoff, *Ponzi's Scheme*, 116, 118.

18. Kennedy, *Newspaper Row*, 189; Zuckoff, *Ponzi's Scheme*, 115, 123.

19. Kennedy, *Newspaper Row*, 189; Zuckoff, *Ponzi's Scheme*, 113.

20. Zuckoff, *Ponzi's Scheme*, 113, 125.

21. Kennedy, *Newspaper Row*, 187, 191; Zuckoff, *Ponzi's Scheme*, 134, 155.

22. Harris, *Pulitzer's Gold*, 127; Kennedy, *Newspaper Row*, 194; Zuckoff, *Ponzi's Scheme*, 162.

23. "Doubles the Money," 1, 4.

24. Ibid.

25. Ibid., 4.

26. Kennedy, *Newspaper Row*, 191.

27. *Boston Post*, August 2, 1920: "Film Men Keep Ponzi Busy," 6; "Ponzi Home Mecca of Curious," 6.

28. Kennedy, *Newspaper Row*, 192; Zuckoff, *Ponzi's Scheme*, 186.

29. Zuckoff, *Ponzi's Scheme*, 186–87, 190.

30. Kennedy, *Newspaper Row*, 187, 191; Zuckoff, *Ponzi's Scheme*, 187.

31. Kennedy, *Newspaper Row*, 193.

32. Harris, *Pulitzer's Gold*, 127; Kennedy, *Newspaper Row*, 191; Zuckoff, *Ponzi's Scheme*, 162.

33. William H. McMasters, "Declares Ponzi Is Now Hopelessly Insolvent," *Boston Post*, August 2, 1920, 1, 6.

34. McMasters, "Declares Ponzi," 1.

35. Ibid., 1, 6.

36. Ibid., 6.

37. "Great Run on Ponzi Continues Until Office Is Closed for the Day," *Boston Post*, August 3, 1920, 1; "Mobs Flock to Ponzi's Office," *Boston Post*, August 3, 1920, 1; Kennedy, *Newspaper Row*, 195.

38. "All Demands Met by Ponzi," *Boston Globe*, August 3, 1920, 1; "Hundreds Paid by Ponzi," *Boston American*, August 2, 1920, 1.

39. Kennedy, *Newspaper Row*, 195; "Pulitzer Prize Is Awarded," 1; Zuckoff, *Ponzi's Scheme*, 234–35, 243.

40. "Pulitzer Prize Is Awarded," 1.

41. Harris, *Pulitzer's Gold*, 130–31; "Pulitzer Prize Is Awarded," 1.

42. Kennedy, *Newspaper Row*, 197; Zuckoff, *Ponzi's Scheme*, 255–56.

43. Herbert L. Baldwin, "Canadian 'Ponsi' Served Jail Term," *Boston Post*, August 11, 1920, 1.

44. Harold Wheeler, "Ponzi Arrested: Admits Now He Cannot Pay—$3,000,000 Short," *Boston Post*, August 13, 1920, 1.

45. "Ponzi Is Arrested by U.S. and State," *Philadelphia Inquirer*, August 13, 1920, 1; "Bondsman for Money Wizard Gives Him Up," *San Francisco Chronicle*, August 14, 1920, 1; "To Get 30 Cents on the Dollar," *Wall Street Journal*, December 8, 1920, 13.

46. "Ponzi Sentenced to 5 Years in Jail," *New York Times*, December 1, 1920, 9; "Guilty on 14 Counts," *Boston Globe*, February 26, 1925, 1; "Ponzi Deported, Leaves in Tears," *Boston Globe*, October 8, 1934, 1.

47. "Ponzi's Residence and Autos Seized," *Washington Post*, August 28, 1920, 2; "Mrs. Ponzi Gets Divorce from Deported Husband," *Chicago Tribune*, December 11, 1936, 25.

48. "Ponzi Dies," 56.

49. Harris, *Pulitzer's Gold*, 131; Kennedy, *Newspaper Row*, 197; "Ponzi Award of Merit," *Boston Post*, June 1, 1921, 14; "Pulitzer Prize Is Awarded," 1; "Richard Grozier, 59, Head of Boston Post," *New York Times*, June 20, 1946, 23; "Richard Grozier Dies," *Boston Globe*, June 20, 1946, 17; "Richard Grozier Dies Suddenly," *Boston Post*, June 20, 1946, 1, 2; Zuckoff, *Ponzi's Scheme*, 300–301.

50. Harris, *Pulitzer's Gold*, 123; Kennedy, *Newspaper Row*, 189, 191; Zuckoff, *Ponzi's Scheme*, 118, 187.

51. "Pulitzer Prize Is Awarded," 1; "Sims's Book Wins Columbia Prize," *New York Times*, May 30, 1921, 14.

52. Harris, *Pulitzer's Gold*, 124; Kennedy, *Newspaper Row*, 197; "Pulitzer Prize Is Awarded," 1; "Richard Grozier, 59," 23; Zuckoff, *Ponzi's Scheme*, 300–301.

CHAPTER 6: ASSURING CITIZENS THAT "G-MEN" WERE KEEPING THEM SAFE

1. Bryan Burroughs, *Public Enemies: America's Greatest Crime Wave and the Birth of the FBI, 1933–34* (New York: Penguin, 2004), 16; *Official Records of the National Commission on Law Observance and Enforcement: Enforcement of the Prohibition Laws of the United States*, Vol. 1 (Washington, D.C.: Government Printing Office, 1931), 422–23; Claire Bond Potter, *War on Crime: Bandits, G-Men and the Politics of Mass Culture* (New Brunswick, N.J.: Rutgers University Press, 1998), 68.

2. Burroughs, *Public Enemies*, 16.

3. *New York Times*, "20,000 at Meeting Protest Gang Reign," August 25, 1931, 1; "$175,000 Is Sought for Scout Camps," April 10, 1932, 22. The scout leader was Frederic Kernochan.

4. "Two Women Shot in Front of Home," *Miami Herald*, September 2, 1930, 1; "Bank Robbers Shoot Woman, Kidnap Mate," *Sacramento Union*, October 2, 1930, 1.

5. Quoted in *Literary Digest*, October 31, 1931, 6.

6. "Kelly and His Wife Seized in Memphis in Urschel Case," *New York Times*, September 27, 1933, 1.

7. "Arrest Elates Cummings," *New York Times*, September 27, 1933, 2; "Kelly and His Wife Seized in Memphis in Urschel Case," 1.

8. "Arrest Elates Cummings," 2; "Kelly and His Wife Seized in Memphis in Urschel Case," 1.

9. "Gunman Kelly Trapped in Hideaway," *Atlanta Constitution*, September 27, 1933, 1; "Raid Traps Desperado," *Los Angeles Times*, September 27, 1933, 1.

10. "Kelly and His Wife Seized in Memphis in Urschel Case," 1; Richard Gid Powers, *Secrecy and Power: The Life of J. Edgar Hoover* (New York: Free Press, 1987), 188; Athan G. Theoharis and John Stuart Cox, *The Boss: J. Edgar Hoover and the Great American Inquisition* (Philadelphia: Temple University Press, 1988), 124.

11. "Kellys Sentenced to Prison for Life," *New York Times*, October 13, 1933, 10.

12. "Barrow and Woman Are Slain by Police in Louisiana Trap; The War on Crime," *New York Times*, May 24, 1934, 1, 3; "Killer Barrow and Woman Bandit Slain in Police Net," *Washington Post*, May 24, 1934, 1, 4; Potter, *War on Crime*, 77–78.

13. "Barrow and Girl Slain in Trap by Louisiana Posse," *Philadelphia Inquirer*, May 24, 1934, 1, 18; "Barrow and Woman Are Slain," 1, 3; "Killer Barrow and Woman Bandit," 1, 4.

14. "Barrow and Woman Are Slain," 1, 3; "Killer Barrow and Woman Bandit," 1, 4.

15. "Barrow and Woman Are Slain," 1, 3; "Killer Barrow and Woman Bandit," 1, 4.

16. "Barrow and Woman Are Slain," 1, 3; "Killer Barrow and Woman Bandit," 1, 4.

17. "Clyde Barrow and Bonnie Parker Trapped and Killed," *Dallas Morning News*, May 24, 1934, 1; "Texas Bad Man and His Gun Girl Slain by Posse," *Chicago Tribune*, May 24, 1934, 2.

18. "Dillinger Had Hectic, Violent Crime Career," *San Francisco Chronicle*," July 23, 1934, 1, 3; "Dillinger's Death Ends Long Career of Daring Crimes," *Atlanta Constitution*, July 23, 1934, 1, 2.

19. "Dillinger Had Hectic," 1, 3; "Dillinger's Death," 1, 2.

20. Robert C. Albright, "House Bill Puts $25,000 'Price' on Big Bandits," *Washington Post*, May 6, 1934, M1.

21. "New Dillinger Hunt On," *Chicago Tribune*, March 10, 1934, 1; "20,000 Police on Dillinger's Trail," *Washington Post*, March 4, 1934, 1; "Dillinger Had Hectic," 1, 3; "Dillinger's Death," 1, 2.

22. Richard Gid Powers, *G-Men: Hoover's FBI in American Popular Culture* (Carbondale: Southern Illinois University Press, 1983), 123–24.

23. "Dillinger Killed by U.S. Agents," *Minneapolis Tribune*, July 23, 1934, 1, 2; "John Dillinger Shot to Death by Federal Marksmen," *New Orleans Times-Picayune*, July 23, 1934, 1; Powers, *G-Men*, 123–24.

24. "Dillinger Killed," 1, 2; "John Dillinger Shot," 1.

25. Robert Talley, "Capital's Famous Hoover Brothers," *Washington Post*, October 7, 1934, SM13.

26. Ibid., SM12, SM13.

27. Ibid., SM13.

28. Rex Collier, "Why Uncle Sam's Agents Get Their Men," *New York Times*, August 19, 1934, SM4.

29. Ibid.

30. Hal H. Smith, "Agents of Justice 'Got' Dillinger," *New York Times*, July 29, 1934, XX2.

31. "Sleuth School," *Time*, August 5, 1935, 1, 12.

32. Ibid., 16.

33. For the quote, see Powers, *G-Men*, 113. See also, Matthew Cecil, *Hoover's FBI and the Fourth Estate: The Campaign to Control the Press and the Bureau* (Lawrence: University Press of Kansas, 2014), 43–75.

34. Cecil, *Hoover's FBI*, 48.

35. Ibid., 61–62. For the stories, see Collier, "Why Uncle Sam's Agents," SM4; "Justice Agents Brush Up on Sharpshooting," *Washington Star*, June 19, 1934, B1;

"Was the G-Man Execution of Dillinger Wanton, or Justified," *Milwaukee Journal*, August 5, 1936, 1, 3.

36. For the quote, see Powers, *G-Men*, 131. See also Powers, *G-Men*, 129.

37. "Floyd, No. 1 Outlaw, Slain by Federal Agents," *Cleveland Plain Dealer*, October 23, 1934, 1.

38. "'Baby Face' Nelson Found Dead in Roadside Ditch, Victim of Bullets Fired by U.S. Agents," *Atlanta Constitution*, November 29, 1934, 1.

39. "U.S. Agents Slay 'Ma' and Fred Barker," *Philadelphia Inquirer*, January 17, 1935, 1.

40. For the quote, see Burroughs, *Public Enemies*, 521. On the crime wave ending, see also Burroughs, *Public Enemies*, 517–21; Powers, *G-Men*, 178.

41. Burroughs, *Public Enemies*, 521.

42. Burroughs, *Public Enemies*, 517–21; Cecil, *Hoover's FBI*, 1–2; Potter, *War on Crime*, 126, 154; Powers, *G-Men*, xix, 19; Athan G. Theoharis, ed., *The FBI: A Comprehensive Reference Guide* (Phoenix: Oryx, 1999), 176.

43. Burroughs, *Public Enemies*, 518.

44. "Hard-Boiled Patriotism Triumphs in 'G Men,'" *Kansas City Star*, May 19, 1935, D1; "Close Finish Looms in Race between Studios' 'G-Men,'" *Los Angeles Times*, April 14, 1935, 1. On the six more FBI-themed films released by the end of 1935, see Burroughs, *Public Enemies*, 518. The titles of the other FBI-themed films released in 1935 are *Let 'Em Have It*; *Mary Burns, Fugitive*; *Public Enemy's Wife*; *Public Hero Number One*; *Show Them No Mercy*; and *Whipsaw*.

CHAPTER 7: STOPPING SMOKERS FROM KILLING THEMSELVES

1. Reprinted as "Defends Cigarettes," *Washington Post*, July 17, 1904, E4.

2. Reprinted as "My Lady Nicotine," *Washington Post*, September 20, 1917, 6.

3. "Smokers Steady Workers," *San Francisco Chronicle*, October 17, 1926, 4.

4. "'Index' Tells to What Age Man May Live," *Des Moines Register*, February 25, 1938, 1.

5. Ibid.

6. Ibid.

7. For the quote, see "Pearl Denies Ickes' Charge Papers Suppressed Findings," *Baltimore Sun*, January 14, 1939, 1. See also, "Biological Index Is Discovered Predicting Person's Life Span," *Washington Post*, February 25, 1938, X20; "Biologist Develops Index to Predict Length of Life," *Los Angeles Times*, February 25, 1938, 1; "Hopkins Savant Reveals Index to Forecast Length of Life," *Baltimore Sun*, February 25, 1938, 22; "Index Foretells Human Life Span," *Cleveland Plain Dealer*, February 25, 1938, 15; "Science Foretells Human Life Span," *New York Times*, February 25, 1938, 19.

8. William L. Laurence, "Lung Cancer Rise Laid to Cigarettes," *New York Times*, October 26, 1940, 17.

9. Ibid.

10. Ibid.

11. Ibid.

12. "Doctor Reports Cigarets Cause Cancer of Lung," *Miami Herald*, October 26, 1940, 16; "Doctor Says Smoking Is Cancer Cause," *Minneapolis Tribune*, October 26, 1940, 36.

13. "Study Links Lung Deaths to Smoking," *Atlanta Constitution*, December 12, 1952, 3; "Smoking Tied to Cancer Rise," *Baltimore Sun*, December 12, 1952, 10; "Cancer of Lungs Linked to Smoking," *Los Angeles Times*, December 12, 1952, 11.

14. See, for example, "Study Links," 3; "Cancer of Lungs Linked," 11.

15. "Report Cancer of Lung Rises with Smoking," *Chicago Tribune*, December 12, 1952, B13.

16. "Lung Cancer Rises as Smoking Increases, British Study Finds," *St. Louis Post-Dispatch*, December 12, 1952, B8.

17. Ibid.

18. "British Study Ties Cancer to Tobacco," *New York Times*, December 12, 1952, 22.

19. Irving Cutter, "How to Keep Well: Curtail Smoking in Peptic Ulcer," *Chicago Tribune*, October 14, 1938, 14.

20. "Anti-Smokers Meet," *Washington Post*, June 28, 1940, 21.

21. *Los Angeles Times*, Chapin Hall, "What Goes On?" July 11, 1939, A8; "Smoking's Bad for Everyone, Says Teamsters Chief Tobin," April 9, 1950, 13.

22. On *Reader's Digest*'s commitment to reporting on the dangers of smoking, see Elizabeth M. Whelan, *A Smoking Gun: How the Tobacco Industry Gets Away with Murder* (Philadelphia: George F. Stickley 1984), 79.

23. Irving Fisher, "Does Tobacco Injure the Human Body?" *Reader's Digest*, November 1924, 435–36.

24. Ibid.

25. For the quotes, see Robert Littell, "Cigarette Holders Put to the Test," *Reader's Digest*, November 1938, 45–46.

26. Gene Tunney, "Nicotine Knockout, or the Slow Count," *Reader's Digest*, December 1941, 21–24.

27. Roy Norr, "Cancer by the Carton," *Reader's Digest*, December 1952, 738–39.

28. Whelan, *Smoking Gun*, 88. On the importance of the "Cancer by the Carton" story, see also Tara Parker-Pope, *Cigarettes: Anatomy of an Industry from Seed to Smoke* (New York: New Press, 2001), 112; Thomas Whiteside, *Selling Death: Cigarette Advertising and Public Health* (New York: Liveright, 1970), 11–12.

29. "Trends in Tobacco Use," American Lung Association, Research and Program Services, Epidemiology and Statistics Unit, July 2011.

30. *Des Moines Register*, February 25, 1938, 5; *St. Louis Post-Dispatch*, December 12, 1952, A11.

31. Whiteside, *Selling Death*, 1.

32. Parker-Pope, *Cigarettes*, 83–86.

33. Randy James and Scott Olstad, "Cigarette Advertising," *Time*, June 15, 2009. http://www.time.com/time/magazine/article/0,9171,1905530,00.html.

34. Allan M. Brandt, *The Cigarette Century: The Rise, Fall, and Deadly Persistence of the Product That Defined America* (New York: Basic, 2007), 106.

CHAPTER 8: CELEBRATING A JEWISH MISS AMERICA

1. On Bess Myerson's early years, see Shana Alexander, *When She Was Bad: The Story of Bess, Hortense, Sukhreet & Nancy* (New York: Random House, 1990), 20–23; Susan Dworkin, *Miss America, 1945: Bess Myerson and the Year That Changed Our Lives* (New York: Newmarket, 1987), 10–13; Jennifer Preston, *Queen Bess: An Unauthorized Biography of Bess Myerson* (Chicago: Contemporary, 1990), 8–15. Bess Myerson's parents were Louis and Bella Myerson.

2. Alexander, *When She Was Bad*, 23–24; Dworkin, *Miss America*, 40–44; Preston, *Queen Bess*, 14–18.

3. Alexander, *When She Was Bad*, 26–27; Dworkin, *Miss America*, 50; Preston, *Queen Bess*, 19–20.

4. For the quote, see Preston, *Queen Bess*, 22. See also Alexander, *When She Was Bad*, 15; Dworkin, *Miss America*, 67–68.

5. Alexander, *When She Was Bad*, 27; Dworkin, *Miss America*, 69; Preston, *Queen Bess*, 23.

6. Dworkin, *Miss America*, 69–70; Preston, *Queen Bess* 24–25.

7. Dworkin, *Miss America*, 71; "Nice Pickin', Eh?" *New York World-Telegram*, August 16, 1945, 5; Earl Wilson, "It Happened Last Night," *New York Post*, August 17, 1945, 11; "New York's Entrant," *Washington Post*, August 17, 1945, 2.

8. Alexander, *When She Was Bad*, 30; Dworkin, *Miss America*, 93; Preston, *Queen Bess*, 24–25.

9. For the quote, see Dworkin, *Miss America*, 93. See also Preston, *Queen Bess*, 24–25.

10. For the quote, see Dworkin, *Miss America*, 94, 109. See also Alexander, *When She Was Bad*, 30; Preston, *Queen Bess*, 24–25.

11. Dworkin, *Miss America*, 91; Preston, *Queen Bess*, 27–28.

12. Frank Deford, *There She Is: The Life and Times of Miss America* (New York: Viking, 1971), 160; Dworkin, *Miss America*, 130, 134; Preston, *Queen Bess*, 29.

13. Morley Cassidy, "40 Rival Beauties Show the Judges Their Skill in Social Graces," *Philadelphia Bulletin*, September 8, 1945, E3; "Air Veterans Select Bronx Beauty Queen," *Los Angeles Times*, September 6, 1945, 2; "Vets' Choice," *Philadelphia Inquirer*, September 6, 1945, 12.

14. For the quote, see Dworkin, *Miss America*, 124. See also Preston, *Queen Bess*, 30–31.

15. Dworkin, *Miss America*, 146–47; Preston, *Queen Bess*, 31–32. The judges who reported receiving threatening phone calls were Arthur Williams Brown, Harry Conover, Dean Cornwell, Brad Crandall, and Vincent Trotta.

16. "Bronx Girl, 21, Wins Miss America Title," *New York Times*, September 9, 1945, 44; Dworkin, *Miss America*, 165; Preston, *Queen Bess*, 32–33.

17. Dworkin, *Miss America*, 165.

18. On the news media consistently casting Bess Myerson in a flattering light, see Deford, *There She Is*, 161–62.

19. "N.Y. Girl Wins Beauty Title," *Miami Herald*, September 9, 1945, 1. Venus Ramey was crowned on September 9, 1944; no coverage of the event was published in the *Miami Herald* on September 10, 11, or 12, 1944.

20. "New Miss America," *Minneapolis Tribune*, September 10, 1945, 1; "New York City Coed Wins 19th Miss America Contest," *Seattle Post-Intelligencer*, September 9, 1. Venus Ramey was crowned on September 9, 1944; no coverage of the event was published in the *Minneapolis Tribune* or *Seattle Post-Intelligencer* on September 10, 11, or 12, 1944.

21. For *Los Angeles Times* stories about Myerson, see "Air Veterans Select Bronx Beauty Queen," September 6, 1945, 2; "Beauty's Royal Family," August 25, 1946; "Fund of $100,443 Raised for Soldier," September 8, 1945, 4; "Los Angeles Beauty Crowned Miss America," September 8, 1946, 3; "Miss America of 1945 Shuns Career in Film," September 10, 1945, 2; "Miss America Packs 'Em in for Lectures," April 28, 1946, 3; "New York Girl Is Miss America," September 9, 1945, 12; "Tarzana Girl Still in Beauty Crown Race," September 7, 1945, 2. For *Los Angeles Times* stories about Ramey, see "Miss America of 1944 Plans Bond Tour," September 11, 1944, 12; "Miss America Title Won by Washington Girl," September 10, 1944, 8. For *Chicago Tribune* stories about Myerson, see "American Beauties," September 23, 1945, G7; "Bess Myerson," August 11, 1946, D1; "Luncheon Speaker," June 4, 1946, 2; "Meet Beauteous Miss America of 1945," October 27, 1946, E9; "Miss America," September 9, 1945, 5; "Miss America '45 Comes to Talk to City's Youth," June 3, 1946, 6; "Miss America Beauty Plus!" August 11, 1946, C10; "Miss America in City," February 26, 1946, 8; "Model in Recital," January 31, 1946, 15. For *Chicago Tribune* stories about Ramey, see "Buy War Bonds," November 11, 1944, 11; "Miss America 1944," September 24, 1944, F12. For *New York Times* stories about

Myerson, see "Bronx Girl, 21, Wins Miss America Title," September 9, 1945, 44; "Bronxites Rally to Aid War Fund," September 24, 1945, 17; "Launching Tour of Nation's Army and Navy Hospitals," July 31, 1946, 29; "Music for Miss America," September 12, 1945, 27; "Music Notes," May 31, 1946, 27; "Pop Concert Role for Bess Myerson," June 1, 1946, 21; "Truly 'a Very Serious Type' Is Miss America of 1945," September 10, 1945, 10.

22. "Miss America of 1945 Shuns Career in Film," 2; "New York City Coed Wins 19th Miss America Contest," 1; "Miss America to Study; Declines Hollywood Offer," *Atlanta Constitution*, September 10, 1945, 2; "Miss America Tells of Plans," *New York Post*, September 10, 1945, 5.

23. "Miss America," *Cleveland Plain Dealer*, September 10, 1945, 5; "Music Comes First with Miss America," *Pittsburgh Post-Gazette*, September 10, 1945, 2; "Bronx Gal New Miss America," *New York Daily News*, September 9, 1945, 4.

24. "Miss New York Wins Nation's Beauty Title," *Philadelphia Inquirer*, September 9, 1945, 1.

25. "Miss America Tells of Plans," 5; "Music Comes First with Miss America," 2.

26. "Miss America to Study; Declines Hollywood Offer," 2; "Beauty Queen for 1945," *Philadelphia Daily News*, September 9, 1945, 1.

27. Earl Wilson, "It Happened Last Night," *New York Post*, September 10, 1945, 26. On Wilson's column appearing in 175 newspapers, see Glenn Fowler, "Earl Wilson Dies at 79," *New York Times*, January 17, 1987, 15.

28. Deford, *There She Is*, 162.

29. "Miss America of 1945 Shuns Career in Films," *Los Angeles Times*, September 10, 1945, 2; "Miss America to Study; Declines Hollywood Offer," 2.

30. "New Miss America Spurns Talent Scouts," *New York Journal-American*, September 10, 1945, 3.

31. "Miss America Didn't Know She Was in New York Contest," *Baltimore Sun*, September 10, 1945, 9.

32. "Bronxites Rally to Aid War Fund," 17.

33. "Miss America Comes to D.C. to Aid Victory Bond Drive," *Washington Post*, November 5, 1945, 1.

34. Alexander, *When She Was Bad*, 33; Dworkin, *Miss America*, 190–92; Preston, *Queen Bess*, 41.

35. Dworkin, *Miss America*, 197; Preston, *Queen Bess*, 42.

36. Philip King, "Miss America Speaks on Tolerance," *Chicago Daily News*, February 13, 1946, 1; "Miss America Warns of Hate," *Chicago Herald-American*, February 25, 1946, 22.

37. For the quote, see Dennis Horkins, "Bigotry Breeds Hurt," *Buffalo News*, April 12, 1946, 1. See also, Dworkin, *Miss America*, 198–99; Preston, *Queen Bess*, 42.

38. Miles Kastendieck, *Brooklyn Eagle*, June 1, 1946, 11.

39. "Named Miss America of 1945," *Des Moines Register*, September 9, 1945, 1; "N.Y. Girl Wins Beauty Title," 1; "New Miss America," 1; "Beauty Queen for 1945," 1; "New York City Coed Wins 19th Miss America Contest," 1.

40. Dworkin, *Miss America*, 7.

CHAPTER 9: BREAKING THE COLOR BARRIER IN MAJOR LEAGUE BASEBALL

1. Bob Addie, "Jackie Robinson, First Black in Major Leagues, Dies at 53," *Washington Post*, October 25, 1972, A1; Dave Anderson, "Jackie Robinson, First Black in Major Leagues, Dies," *New York Times*, October 25, 1972, A1; Arnold Rampersad, *Jackie Robinson: A Biography* (New York: Knopf, 1997), 15–18, 33–35.

2. Addie, "Jackie Robinson," A1; Anderson, "Jackie Robinson," A1; Jonathan Eig, *Opening Day: The Story of Jackie Robinson's First Season* (New York: Simon and Schuster, 2007), 11.

3. Addie, "Jackie Robinson," A1; Anderson, "Jackie Robinson," A1; Rampersad, *Jackie Robinson*, 75–80, 85–86.

4. Addie, "Jackie Robinson," A1; Anderson, "Jackie Robinson," A1; Rampersad, *Jackie Robinson*, 89–112.

5. Addie, "Jackie Robinson," A1; Anderson, "Jackie Robinson," A1; Larry Lester and Sammy J. Miller, *Black Baseball in Kansas City* (Dover, N.H.: Arcadia, 2000), 55; Rampersad, *Jackie Robinson*, 113.

6. Jules Tygiel, *Baseball's Great Experiment: Jackie Robinson and His Legacy* (New York: Vintage, 1984), 8.

7. For the quote, see Jackie Robinson, *I Never Had It Made: An Autobiography* (New York: HarperCollins, 1972), 33. For the meeting with Rickey, see also Addie, "Jackie Robinson," A1; Anderson, "Jackie Robinson," A1.

8. "Montreal Signs Negro Shortstop," *New York Times*, October 24, 1945, 17; "Robinson Hailed as Great All-Around Star," *Los Angeles Times*, October 24, 1945, 10.

9. "Brooklyn Signs Negro Player, First in Organized Baseball," *Baltimore Sun*, October 24, 1945, 1; "Baseball Gives Contract to 1st Negro Player," *Chicago Tribune*, October 24, 1945, 1.

10. "Robinson Hailed," 10; Hy Turkin, "Dodgers Sign Jack Robinson," *Los Angeles Times*, October 24, 1945, 10.

11. "Rickey Doesn't Want to Be Called Crusader," *Baltimore Sun*, October 24, 1945, 15.

12. Sheehan, "Montreal Winner," 22.

13. "Negro Stars in First Tilt," *Baltimore Sun*, April 19, 1946, 21; "Robinson Clouts Three-Run Homer as Montreal Wins," *Washington Post*, April 19, 1946, 12; "Smash Hit!" *Chicago Tribune*, April 19, 1946, 27.

14. Ralph Roden, "Robinson on Way to Majors, Hopper Says," *Washington Post*, August 11, 1946, M6; "Batting King Jackie Robinson Knocks at Major League Door," *Washington Post*, September 15, 1946, M6. See also "Jackie Robinson Loop Bat Champ," *Los Angeles Times*, September 15, 1946, A7; "Robinson Tops League," *New York Times*, September 15, 1946, 12; Bob Myers, "Jackie Robinson Views Ball Chances with Hope," *Los Angeles Times*, February 23, 1947, 6.

15. "Robinson to Play for Dodgers," *Washington Post*, April 11, 1947, 1.

16. Joe Reichler, "Robinson Makes Debut as Dodger," *Washington Post*, April 12, 1947, 8.

17. "Jackie Robinson Becomes Dodger," *Los Angeles Times*, April 11, 1947, A8.

18. Louis Effrat, "Royals' Star Signs with Brooks Today," *New York Times*, April 11, 1947, 20.

19. "J. Robinson, Ballplayer," *New York Times*, April 12, 1947, 16.

20. "Rickey Cites Wire to Refute Critics," *New York Times*, October 26, 1945, 14.

21. Roscoe McGowen, "Robinson, Wright, Negro Players, Start Training at Sanford Camp," *New York Times*, March 5, 1946, 28; Bob Myers, "Jackie Robinson Views Ball Chances with Hope," *Los Angeles Times*, February 23, 1947, A6.

22. "Robinson to Play," 1.

23. Morris Siegel, "Jackie Robinson Plans Retirement in 3 Years," *Washington Post*, October 25, 1947, 14.

24. McGowen, "Robinson, Wright," 28.

25. Bob Myers, "Jackie Robinson Views Ball Chances with Hope," *Los Angeles Times*, February 23, 1947, A6.

26. Braven Dyer, "The Sports Parade," *Los Angeles Times*, May 11, 1947, A5.

27. "Negro Stars," 21.

28. Arthur Daley, "Sports of the Times," *New York Times*, October 25, 1945, 16; Myers, "Jackie Robinson Views," A6; "A Colored Recruit to Big League Baseball," *Baltimore Sun*, October 25, 1945, 14.

29. Myers, "Jackie Robinson Views," A6.

30. Ibid.

31. "Brooklyn Celebrates Baseball Pennant with Victory Parade," *Chicago Tribune*, September 27, 1947, 24.

32. Siegel, "Jackie Robinson Plans," 14.

33. "Board Prohibits Negro Star in Florida Game," *Chicago Tribune*, March 22, 1946, 24.

34. Anderson, "Jackie Robinson," A1; "Card Strike Plan Denied," *Los Angeles Times*, May 9, 1947, 8.

35. Shirley Povich, "This Morning," *Washington Post*, April 27, 1947, M12. For the exact words the Philadelphia player used, see Eig, *Opening Day*, 73.

36. "Jackie Robinson Relates Career, Future Plans," *Los Angeles Times*, November 19, 1947, 16.

37. "Robinson Threatened Thru Mails, Branch Rickey Reveals," *Chicago Tribune*, May 10, 1947, 17. See also, "Robinson Reveals Written Threats," *New York Times*, May 10, 1947, 16.

38. "Rookie of the Year," *Time*, September 22, 1947, 72-78. On other African-American players joining Major League Baseball teams, see "Player Joins Team Tomorrow," *New York Times*, July 4, 1947, 16; Rampersad, *Jackie Robinson*, 813. On other professional sports adding African-American players, see, for example, Anderson, "Jackie Robinson," A1.

39. Braven Dyer, "The Sports Parade," *Los Angeles Times*, May 11, 1947, A5.

40. For the quotation, see Tygiel, *Baseball's Great Experiment*, 9. On scholars connecting baseball's integration to the *Brown* decision, see, for example, Eig, *Opening Day*, 64; Tygiel, *Baseball's Great Experiment*, 303.

CHAPTER 10: GIVING AVERAGE CITIZENS MORE SAY IN CHOOSING THEIR PRESIDENT

1. James S. Chase, *Emergence of the Presidential Nominating Convention, 1789–1832* (New York: Houghton Mifflin, 1973), 216, 263.

2. James A. Hagerty, "19 Party Leaders Make Caucus Call to Block Truman," *New York Times*, July 4, 1948, A1; James A. Hagerty, "Dewey Is Gaining as Top Contender in Republican Race," *New York Times*, May 24, 1948, A1.

3. Sig Mickelson, *From Whistle Stop to Sound Bite: Four Decades of Politics and Television* (New York: Praeger, 1989), 33–34.

4. Jack Gould, "The X of the Campaign—TV Personality," *New York Times*, June 22, 1952, SM14.

5. Robert J. Donovan and Ray Scherer, *Unsilent Revolution: Television News and American Public Life, 1948–1991* (New York: Press Syndicate of the University of Cambridge, 1992), 220; Mickelson, *From Whistle Stop*, 36–37.

6. John Crosby, "Radio and Television," *New York Herald Tribune*, July 7, 1952, 17.

7. Donovan and Scherer, *Unsilent Revolution*, 221.

8. Donovan and Scherer, *Unsilent Revolution*, 221; Kurt Lang and Gladys Engel Lang, *Politics and Television* (Chicago: Quadrangle, 1968), 79; Mickelson, *From Whistle Stop*, 39.

9. Lang and Lang, *Politics and Television*, 104; William S. White, "Struggle Is Bitter," *New York Times*, July 21, 1952, A1.

10. Donovan and Scherer, *Unsilent Revolution*, 221; Johnson Kanady, "Party Looks to Adlai; He Looks Away," *Chicago Tribune*, July 22, 1952, A1; Lang and Lang, *Politics and Television*, 109; James Reston, "Stevenson Speech Sends Him to Fore," *New York Times*, July 22, 1952, A1.

11. Jeff Broadwater, *Adlai Stevenson and American Politics: The Odyssey of a Cold War Liberal* (New York: Twayne: 1994), 113; John Bartlow Martin, *Adlai Stevenson of Illinois: The Life of Adlai E. Stevenson* (New York: Doubleday, 1976), 587.

12. Kanady, "Party Looks to Adlai," A1; Martin, *Adlai Stevenson*, 585–86.

13. Broadwater, *Adlai Stevenson*, 114; Martin, *Adlai Stevenson*, 586.

14. Holmes Alexander, "Stevenson Speech Sparks Convention," *Los Angeles Times*, July 22, 1952, 2; Earl C. Behrens, "Big Swing to Stevenson," *San Francisco Chronicle*, July 22, 1952, A1; Broadwater, *Adlai Stevenson*, 113; Kanady, "Party Looks to Adlai," A1; Anne O'Hare McCormick, "Kick-Off by Illinois," *New York Times*, July 22, 1952, 14; Kyle Palmer, "Stevenson Drive Booming," *Los Angeles Times*, July 23, 1952, 1; James Reston, "Stevenson Boom Abetted by Speech," *Los Angeles Times*, July 22, 1952, 4.

15. Broadwater, *Adlai Stevenson*, 113–14; Donovan and Scherer, *Unsilent Revolution*, 221–22; Martin, *Adlai Stevenson*, 585–87.

16. Behrens, "Big Swing to Stevenson," A1; Broadwater, *Adlai Stevenson*, 113–14; Donovan and Scherer, *Unsilent Revolution*, 221–22; Martin, *Adlai Stevenson*, 585–87; James Reston, "Stevenson Speech Sends Him to Fore," *New York Times*, July 22, 1952, A1; Gerry Robichaud, "Rush to Get Ride on Adlai's Kite," *Chicago Sun-Times*, July 22, 1952, A1.

17. Donovan and Scherer, *Unsilent Revolution*, 221–22; Kanady, "Party Looks to Adlai," A1; Martin, *Adlai Stevenson*, 585–87; Reston, "Stevenson Speech," A1.

18. Mickelson, *From Whistle Stop*, 47.

19. Stephen E. Ambrose, *Eisenhower: Soldier, General of the Army, President-Elect, 1890-1952* (New York: Simon and Schuster, 1983), 538–39; Donovan and Scherer, *Unsilent Revolution*, 218; James A. Hagerty, "Lodge Cites Plan," *New York Times*, July 7, 1952, A1; Lang and Lang, *Politics and Television*, 85–86.

20. Ambrose, *Eisenhower*, 538–39; Donovan and Scherer, *Unsilent Revolution*, 218–19; Lang and Lang, *Politics and Television*, 87–88.

21. For the quotes, see Russell Porter, "Eisenhower Scores Taft 'Chicanery,'" *New York Times*, July 5, 1952, A1. See also Ambrose, *Eisenhower*, 538–40; Lang and Lang, *Politics and Television*, 87–88; William Manchester, *The Glory and the Dream: A Narrative History of America, 1932-1972* (Boston: Little, Brown, 1973), 617; Porter, "Eisenhower Scores," A1.

22. Donovan and Scherer, *Unsilent Revolution*, 219; Lang and Lang, *Politics and Television*, 88–89; A. M. Sperber, *Murrow: His Life and Times* (New York: Bantam, 1986), 385.

23. Donovan and Scherer, *Unsilent Revolution*, 219; Lang and Lang, *Politics and Television*, 88–89; Sperber, *Murrow*, 385.

24. Donovan and Scherer, *Unsilent Revolution*, 219; Lang and Lang, *Politics and Television*, 88–89; Mickelson, *From Whistle Stop*, 37; Sperber, *Murrow*, 385.

25. For the quote, see Ambrose, *Eisenhower*, 539. See also, Robert C. Albright, "Dixie Steal 'Shocks' Ike," *Washington Post*, July 8, 1952, M1; Ambrose, *Eisenhower*, 538–40; Donovan and Scherer, *Unsilent Revolution*, 220; Lang and Lang, *Politics and Television*, 90–91; W. H. Lawrence, "Eisenhower in First Test Wins on Disputed Delegates," *New York Times*, July 8, 1952, A1; Charles McDowell, "Television Politics: The Medium in the Revolution," in *Beyond Reagan: The Politics of Upheaval*, ed. Paul Duke (New York: Warner Books, 1986), 237–39; Mickelson, *From Whistle Stop*, 42–43.

26. Ambrose, *Eisenhower*, 539–41; Donovan and Scherer, *Unsilent Revolution*, 220; Lang and Lang, *Politics and Television*, 90–91; W. H. Lawrence, "Eisenhower Nominated on the First Ballot," *New York Times*, July 12, 1952, A1; McDowell, "Television Politics," 237–39; Kyle Palmer, "Ike Passes Taft with Georgia, Texas Wins," *Los Angeles Times*, July 10, 1952, 1; Mickelson, *From Whistle Stop*, 42–43; "The Voice of the Convention," *New York Times*, July 10, 1952, 30.

27. John Crosby, "Convention 'Gets' Even the TV Crowd," *Washington Post*, July 9, 1952, 33.

28. For the quote, see Donovan and Scherer, *Unsilent Revolution*, 222. See also Lang and Lang, *Politics and Television*, 87.

29. Broadwater, *Adlai Stevenson*, 115; Martin, *Adlai Stevenson*, 601.

30. Donovan and Scherer, *Unsilent Revolution*, 222; Mickelson, *From Whistle Stop*, 55, 75.

31. Ambrose, *Eisenhower*, 539–40; Donovan and Scherer, *Unsilent Revolution*, 222; Mickelson, *From Whistle Stop*, 55, 75.

32. Donovan and Scherer, *Unsilent Revolution*, 222.

33. For the quote, see "Texts of Governor Stevenson's Speeches during His Invasion of Ohio," *New York Times*, October 4, 1952, A10. See also, Edwin Diamond and Stephen Bates, *The Spot: The Rise of Political Advertising on Television*, rev. ed. (Cambridge, Mass.: MIT Press, 1988), 60; Martin, *Adlai Stevenson*, 614.

34. Ambrose, *Eisenhower*, 538–41; Craig Allen, *Eisenhower and the Mass Media: Peace, Prosperity, and Prime-Time TV* (Chapel Hill: University of North Carolina Press, 1993), 20–21; Mickelson, *From Whistle Stop*, 55, 75.

35. Diamond and Bates, *The Spot*, 60.

36. Donovan and Scherer, *Unsilent Revolution*, 223; "Texts of Eisenhower Tampa, Birmingham and Little Rock Talks Assailing Administration," *New York Times*, September 4, 1952, A20.

37. Donovan and Scherer, *Unsilent Revolution*, 223; Mickelson, *From Whistle Stop*, 71. The political adviser was Rosser Reeves.

38. Donovan and Scherer, *Unsilent Revolution*, 223.

39. William R. Conklin, "Eisenhower Scores Rivals as Party of 'Stand-Patters,'" *New York Times*, October 23, 1952, A1; Donovan and Scherer, *Unsilent Revolution*, 224.

40. Diamond and Bates, *The Spot*, 60; Donovan and Scherer, *Unsilent Revolution*, 218–24.

41. Ambrose, *Eisenhower*, 538–41; Broadwater, *Adlai Stevenson*, 113–16; Diamond and Bates, *The Spot*, 60; Donovan and Scherer, *Unsilent Revolution*, 218–24; Martin, *Adlai Stevenson*, 584–587.

CHAPTER 11: IMPROVING THE LIVES OF MIGRANT FARMWORKERS

1. Chad Raphael, *Investigated Reporting: Muckrakers, Regulators, and the Struggle over Television Documentary* (Urbana: University of Illinois Press, 2005), 18. On Murrow's life and career, see Alexander Kendrick, *Prime Time: The Life of Edward R. Murrow* (Boston: Little Brown, 1969); A. M. Sperber, *Murrow: His Life and Times* (New York: Bantam, 1986).

2. Robert Miraldi, *Muckraking and Objectivity: Journalism's Colliding Traditions* (New York: Greenwood, 1990), 88; Raphael, *Investigated Reporting*, 18; Sperber, *Murrow*, 594–95.

3. Michael Curtin, *Redeeming the Wasteland: Television Documentary and Cold War Politics* (New Brunswick, N.J.: Rutgers University Press, 1995), 191–92; Miraldi, *Muckraking and Objectivity*, 88; Sperber, *Murrow*, 595.

4. "The Excluded Americans," *Time*, December 5, 1960, 52; Fred W. Friendly, *Due to Circumstances beyond Our Control* (New York: Random House, 1967), 121; Miraldi, *Muckraking and Objectivity*, 88.

5. Miraldi, *Muckraking and Objectivity*, 90.

6. For the quote, see Miraldi, *Muckraking and Objectivity*, 91. See also Sperber, *Murrow*, 595.

7. Curtin, *Redeeming the Wasteland*, 168.

8. "Conference to Produce 10-Yr. Migrant Aid Plan," *Washington Post*, November 12, 1960, C6.

9. Miraldi, *Muckraking and Objectivity*, 96–99; Sperber, *Murrow*, 595.

10. Miraldi, *Muckraking and Objectivity*, 99.

11. Ibid.

12. Jack Gould, "TV: 'Harvest of Shame,'" *New York Times*, November 26, 1960, 43.

13. Jack Gould, "Television Documentaries," *New York Times*, December 4, 1960, X17.

14. Jack Anderson, "A Night of Migrants," *Miami Herald*, November 26, A14; "TV Key Previews," *Washington Evening Star*, November 25, 1960, B15; Cecil Smith, "The TV Scene," *Los Angeles Times*, November 25, 1960, A14.

15. "The Excluded Americans," 52.

16. Miraldi, *Muckraking and Objectivity*, 100; David L. Protess, Fay Lomax Cook, Jack C. Doppelt, James S. Ettema, Margaret T. Gordon, Donna R. Leff, and Peter Miller, *The Journalism of Outrage: Investigative Reporting and Agenda Building in America* (New York: Guilford, 1991), 47.

17. For the quotes, see *Congressional Record—Senate*, February 6, 1961, 2216; William Moore, "Senator Raps CBS for Show on Migrants," *Chicago Tribune*, February 7, 1961, B20. On Williams introducing legislation, see Peter Braestrup, "Aid Proposals Set on Migrant Labor," *New York Times*, February 5, 1961, 37; "Sen. Williams Asks Migrant Wage Floor," *Washington Post*, March 1, 1961, B10.

18. On the Senate approving legislation, see "Child Farm-Work Curb," *New York Times*, September 2, 1961, 8; "An End to Farm Peonage," *New York Times*, January 28, 1962, 142; "Senate Unit Votes Help for Migrants," *New York Times*, May 10, 1963, 21; "Senate Votes Help for Migrant Labor," *New York Times*, June 11, 1963, 7. On the House defeating legislation, see "Justice for Migrants," *Washington Post*, January 20, 1962, A8; "Progress on Migrants," *Washington Post*, June 18, 1963, A16; Raphael, *Investigated Reporting*, 25–26. On editorials supporting migrant aid, see "An End to Farm Peonage," 142; "Justice for Migrants," A8.

19. For the quote, see Miraldi, *Muckraking and Objectivity*, 100. See also Friendly, *Due to Circumstances*, 122; Philip L. Martin and David A. Martin, *The Endless Quest: Helping America's Farm Workers* (Boulder, Colo.: Westview, 1994), 22–23; Miraldi, *Muckraking and Objectivity*, 101–2; Raphael, *Investigated Reporting*, 23–24.

20. For the quote, see Raphael, *Investigated Reporting*, 18. On the documentary's significance, see also Friendly, *Due to Circumstances*, 122; Martin and Martin, *Endless Quest*, 22–23; Miraldi, *Muckraking and Objectivity*, 81–122; Michael D. Murray, *The Political Performers: CBS Broadcasts in the Public Interest* (Westport, Conn.: Praeger, 1994), 82; Protess et al., *Journalism of Outrage*, 47.

CHAPTER 12: POPULARIZING THE BIRTH CONTROL PILL

1. "Contraceptive Pill?" *Time*, May 6, 1957, 83.

2. Ibid.

3. Ibid.

4. "Birth Control Pills on Way," *Washington Post*, July 11, 1957, B9; "Pill Held Success as Contraceptive," *New York Times*, September 19, 1958, 25.

5. "Progress on Birth Control Pill," *New York Times*, July 12, 1959, E9.

6. "U.S. Clears Pill for Contraceptive Use," *San Francisco Chronicle*, May 10, 1960, 26; "Birth Control Pill O.K.'d by Drug Administration," *Boston Globe*, May 10, 1960, 18; "Birth Control Pill Wins U.S. Approval for Safety," *Atlanta Constitution*, May 10, 1960, 8.

7. "U.S. Food, Drug Agency Declares Birth Control Pill Non-Dangerous," *Minneapolis Tribune*, May 10, 1960, 1.

8. "Birth Control Pill O.K.'d," 18.

9. "Birth Control Pill Gets U.S. OK on Safety," *Pittsburgh Post-Gazette*, May 10, 1960, 4.

10. "The Remarkable Pill," *Newsweek*, 30 January 1961, 71; J. D. Ratcliff, "An End to Woman's 'Bad Days'?" *Reader's Digest*, December 1962, 73; "Contraception: Freedom from Fear," *Time*, April 7, 1967, 78; Jane E. Brody, "The Pill: Revolution in Birth Control," *New York Times*, 31 May 1966, A1.

11. Joan Beck, "The Pill," *Chicago Tribune*, March 4, 1962, C18.

12. Edwin DeCosta, "Birth-Control Pills—Have They Side-Effects?" *Baltimore Sun*, July 12, 1964, WM14.

13. George Getze, "Birth Control Pills Cleared in Sex Deaths," *Los Angeles Times*, August 5, 1962, A2.

14. "Enovid Exonerated," *Newsweek*, June 29, 1964, 81.

15. David Boroff, "Sex: The Quiet Revolution," *Esquire*, July 1961, 96.

16. Ibid., 96, 98.

17. Jean White, "College 'Sex Revolution' Overstressed," *Washington Post*, May 1, 1966, E1; Lynn Lilliston, "Sex? 'Discretion Is Watchword,'" *Los Angeles Times*, April 26, 1966, C1.

18. For the quote, see "The Pill: How It Is Affecting U.S. Morals, Family Life," *U.S. News & World Report*, July 11, 1966, 63; for the story, see 62–65.

19. Gloria Steinem, "The Moral Disarmament of Betty Coed," *Esquire*, September 1962, 97, 153–57.

20. Ibid., 156–57.

21. Ibid., 157.

22. Andrew Hacker, "The Pill and Morality," *New York Times Magazine*, November 21, 1965, 138–39; "Contraception: Freedom from Fear," 80.

23. "Birth Control: The Pill and the Church," *Newsweek*, July 6, 1964, 51.

24. Ibid., 51, 55.

25. Ibid., 52.

26. Ibid., 54.

27. Ibid., 52.

28. Muriel Dobbin, "Rock, Catholic Birth Control Expert, Asks Church Speed," *Baltimore Sun*, June 30, 1965, 5.

29. For the quote, see Elizabeth Siegel Watkins, *On the Pill: A Social History of Oral Contraceptives, 1950–1970* (Baltimore: Johns Hopkins University Press, 1998), 41. On the central role the media played in popularizing the birth control pill, see also Loretta McLaughlin, *The Pill, John Rock, and the Church: The Biography of a Revolution* (Boston: Little, Brown, 1982), especially 137–39, 154–55, 165–66, 172–73; Watkins, *On the Pill*, especially 6, 35–36, 41–49.

30. Brody, "Pill," A1, A34.

31. Ibid., A1.

CHAPTER 13: FUELING THE SPACE RACE

1. Robert J. Donovan and Ray Scherer, *Unsilent Revolution: Television News and American Public Life, 1948–1991* (New York: Press Syndicate of the University of Cambridge, 1992), 49; Seymour Topping, "Thousands March in Moscow to Cheer Man-in-Space Flight," *New York Times*, April 13, 1961, 16.

2. Michael Allen, *Live from the Moon: Film, Television and the Space Race* (New York: I. B. Tauris, 2009), 78; Mary Ann Watson, *The Expanding Vista: American Television in the Kennedy Years* (New York: Oxford University Press, 1990), 114.

3. Allen, *Live from the Moon*, 78; Watson, *Expanding Vista*, 114.

4. *Washington Post*, May 6, 1961, A1: Edward T. Folliard, "Astronaut Has Perfect Flight"; Carroll Kilpatrick, "Kennedy Leads Congratulations"; John G. Norris, "Flight Proves Man Can Control Space Ship Outside Gravity Pull."

5. Edwin Diamond, "Perfect Match: TV and Space," *Columbia Journalism Review* (Summer 1965): 20.

6. John Catchpole, *Project Mercury: NASA's First Manned Space Programme* (Chichester, UK: Springer-Praxis, 2001), 282.

7. Jack Gould, "Radio-TV: Well Done!" *New York Times*, May 6, 1961, 63.

8. Watson, *Expanding Vista*, 115.

9. Richard Witkin, "U.S. Hurls Man 115 Miles into Space," *New York Times*, May 6, 1961, A1.

10. Watson, *Expanding Vista*, 115.

11. Ibid., 114.

12. For the quote, see Watson, *Expanding Vista*, 114.

13. Allen, *Live from the Moon*, 82; Donovan and Scherer, *Unsilent Revolution*, 49; Watson, *Expanding Vista*, 117.

14. John F. Kennedy, "Special Message to the Congress on Urgent National Needs," May 25, 1961; Chalmers M. Roberts, "Kennedy Asks Approval of New Projects," *Washington Post*, May 26, 1961, A1.

15. Kennedy, "Special Message"; Roberts, "Kennedy Asks Approval," A1.

16. Allen, *Live from the Moon*, 83; Watson, *Expanding Vista*, 119.

17. Allen, *Live from the Moon*, 83–84; Watson, *Expanding Vista*, 119; Richard Witkin, "U.S. Again Fires Man into Space," *New York Times*, July 22, 1961, A1.

18. Allen, *Live from the Moon*, 83; John W. Finney, "Unplanned Swim Leaves Grissom a 'Little Uneasy,'" *New York Times*, July 22, 1961, A1; Watson, *Expanding Vista*, 119.

19. For the quote, see Jack Gould, "Fakery in Space," *New York Times*, July 30, 1961, X11. See also, Fred Danzig, "Remorse Follows 'Cape Tape Jape,'" *Washington Post*, July 27, 1961, A23; Jack Gould, "2 Networks Used Rehearsal Shots," *New York Times*, July 22, 1961, A8.

20. Watson, *Expanding Vista*, 120.

21. Allen, *Live from the Moon*, 86–87; Howard E. McCurdy, *Space and the American Imagination*, 2nd ed. (Baltimore: Johns Hopkins University Press, 2011), 105–6.

22. Allen, *Live from the Moon*, 87.

23. Allen, *Live from the Moon*, 87; McCurdy, *Space and Imagination*, 106.

24. For the quote, see McCurdy, *Space and Imagination*, 86. See also Allen, *Live from the Moon*, 87–88; McCurdy, *Space and Imagination*, 105–6; Watson, *Expanding Vista*, 121.

25. Allen, *Live from the Moon*, 87; Donovan and Scherer, *Unsilent Revolution*, 53; Watson, *Expanding Vista*, 121.

26. For the quote, see Watson, *Expanding Vista*, 124. See also Allen, *Live from the Moon*, 91; Watson, *Expanding Vista*, 123.

27. Allen, *Live from the Moon*, 94–95, 97, 99–100.

28. Diamond, "Perfect Match," 19.

29. Ibid., 18.

30. Allen, *Live from the Moon*, 111–12, 115.

31. For the quote, see James A. Skardon, "The Apollo Story: The Concealed Patterns," *Columbia Journalism Review* (Winter 1967/1968): 34. See also Skardon, "Concealed Patterns," 34–39; Skardon, "The Apollo Story: What the Watchdogs Missed," *Columbia Journalism Review* (Fall 1967): 11–15.

32. For the quote, see Skardon, "Concealed Patterns," 37. See also Skardon, "Concealed Patterns," 34–37.

33. Allen, *Live from the Moon*, 116–21.

34. Ibid., 124–39.

35. Fred Farrar, "Apollo Units Linked Up," *Chicago Tribune*, March 4, 1969, A1.

36. Victor K. McElheny, "Crew Assembles Moon Ship in Space," *Boston Globe*, March 4, 1969, A1; "Apollo, Moonship Dock in Space; Crew's 1st Day in Orbit 'Flawless,'" *Philadelphia Inquirer*, March 4, 1969, A1; Marvin Miles, "Space Rescue? It's Possible if Maneuver Fails," *Washington Post*, March 4, 1969, A1.

37. Allen, *Live from the Moon*, 141.

38. Ibid., 143.

39. Allen, *Live from the Moon*, 145; Gould, "TV: Awesome," 67.

40. Allen, *Live from the Moon*, 158; Gould, "TV: Awesome," 67; John Noble Wilford, "Astronauts Land on Plain," *New York Times*, July 21, 1969, A1.

41. Allen, *Live from the Moon*, 145; Gould, "TV: Awesome," 67.

42. Allen, *Live from the Moon*, 145; Gould, "TV: Awesome," 67; Wilford, "Astronauts Land," A1.

43. Allen, *Live from the Moon*, 151; Gould, "TV: Awesome," 67; Wilford, "Astronauts Land," A1.

44. Allen, *Live from the Moon*, 157; Wilford, "Astronauts Land," A1.

45. Allen, *Live from the Moon*, 151; Gould, "TV: Awesome," 67.

46. Allen, *Live from the Moon*, 154; Wilford, "Astronauts Land," A1.

47. Wilford, "Astronauts Land," A1.

48. Cecil Smith, "Man on the Moon: It Was TV's Show All the Way," *Los Angeles Times*, July 22, 1969, C1; Lawrence Laurent, "Greatest Show off Earth," *Washington Post*, July 22, 1969, C1.

49. Allen, *Live from the Moon*, 155.

50. Joseph Lelyveld, "Surging Crowds Fill the Streets in New York," *New York Times*, August 14, 1969, A1; James T. Wooten, "Astronauts Back from Moon," *New York Times*, July 25, 1969, A1.

51. Jonathan Brown, "Recording Tracks Russia's Moon Gatecrash," *The Independent*, July 3, 2009.

52. For the quote, see Donovan and Scherer, *Unsilent Revolution*, 47. On TV coverage being instrumental in NASA receiving its funding, see Allen, *Live from the Moon*, 91; Diamond, "Perfect Match," 20; McCurdy, *Space and Imagination*, 106; Watson, *Expanding Vista*, 123–24.

CHAPTER 14: ACHIEVING JUSTICE FOR JAPANESE AMERICANS INTERNED DURING WORLD WAR II

1. Leslie T. Hatamiya, *Righting a Wrong: Japanese Americans and the Passage of the Civil Liberties Act of 1988* (Stanford, Calif.: Stanford University Press, 1993), xvii–xviii; Wendy Ng, *Japanese American Internment during World War II* (Westport, Conn.: Greenwood, 2002), 18, 31.

2. Lee May, "Japanese-Americans' Internment Unjust, U.S. Commission Concludes," *Los Angeles Times*, February 25, 1983, B4.

3. Hatamiya, *Righting a Wrong*, 15–16.

4. Ibid., 17.

5. Ibid., 168–69. The Supreme Court case was *Korematsu v. United States*. The decision was by a vote of 6–3, and it was announced on December 18, 1944.

6. Hatamiya, *Righting a Wrong*, 19; Ng, *Japanese American Internment*, 3–53.

7. Hatamiya, *Righting a Wrong*, xviii.

8. Ibid., xix.

9. Hatamiya, *Righting a Wrong*, xix–xx; "Votes in Congress," *New York Times*, July 27, 1980, 31. The panel was headed by Joan Z. Bernstein, a Washington attorney.

10. Hatamiya, *Righting a Wrong*, 2.

11. Ibid.

12. Ronald Yates, "For Nisei, Internment Still Hurts," *Chicago Tribune*, August 12, 1981, 1.

13. Ibid.

14. Martha Shirk, "Bitter Memories of Internment," *St. Louis Post-Dispatch*, August 3, 1981, A13.

15. *CBS Evening News*, July 13, 1981.

16. "Ex-Aide Calls Japanese Internment 'Humane,'" *New York Times*, November 4, 1981, A18.

17. Ibid.

18. *Nightline*, July 16, 1981.

19. "Hayakawa Denounces Claims of Nisei for Internment Pay," *New York Times*, August 5, 1981, A18; Ronald Yates, "Hayakawa Calls Nisei Internment a 'Vacation,'" *Chicago Tribune*, August 5, 1981, 2.

20. Fred Barbash, *Washington Post*, "'Evacuation' of the Japanese Americans," December 5, 1982, A1, A14, A15; "In Desert Camp, Life behind Barbed Wire," December 6, 1982, A1, A4; "Bearing the Brunt of 'Fifth-Column' Fears," December 7, 1982, A1, A14; "The West Coast Turns into a War Zone," December 8, 1982, A1, A18; "Is It Time to Make Apologies, Amends?" A1, A6.

21. Barbash, "Bearing the Brunt," A1.

22. Ibid.

23. Ibid.

24. Ibid.

25. *NBC Nightly News*, February 24, 1983.

26. "FDR Gets Much of Blame for Japanese Internment," *Houston Post*, February 25, 1983, 1, 15. The commissioner quoted was Arthur Fleming, former chair of the Civil Rights Commission.

27. Fred Barbash, "Wartime Internment Decried," *Washington Post*, February 25, 1983, A1.

28. James R. Carroll, "Panel Urges Reparations for Internees," *Philadelphia Inquirer*, June 17, 1983, 1, 2.

29. "Economic Losses of Interned U.S. Japanese," *San Francisco Chronicle*, June 16, 1983, 12.

30. "A Matter of Justice," *Los Angeles Times*, November 22, 1982, C6.

31. "Personal Justice Denied," *Boston Globe*, March 4, 1983, 16.

32. "A Case for Reparations," *Philadelphia Inquirer*, June 19, 1983, C6.

33. Matt O'Connor, "A Survivor in Graphics as in Life," *Chicago Tribune*, August 11, 1986, N9.

34. Frederick M. Muir, "40 Years Later, Ex-Internee Renews Fight for Jailed Japanese-Americans," *Los Angeles Times*, September 14, 1987, C1.

35. Jay Mathews, "Japanese Americans' Continuing Struggle," *Washington Post*, August 15, 1985, A26.

36. Hatamiya, *Righting a Wrong*, 22–23.

37. Ibid.

38. Nathaniel Nash, "Seeking Redress for an Old Wrong," *New York Times*, September 17, 1987, B13. See also, "Wartime Detentions Recalled," *New York Times*, April 29, 1986, A13.

39. "$20,000, Apology Voted for WWII Japanese Internees," *Los Angeles Times*, August 4, 1988, 1. On Congress approving the legislation, see also "Measures to Pay War Detainees Goes to Reagan," *New York Times*, August 5, 1988, A10; Tom Kenworthy, "Congress Approves War-Internee Fund," *Washington Post*, August 5, 1988, A1.

40. "$20,000, Apology Voted," 1; Irvin Molotsky, "Senate Votes to Compensate Japanese-American Internees," *New York Times*, April 21, 1988, A1; Paul Houston, "Reagan 'Rights' a Wrong, Signs Internee Reparation," *Los Angeles Times*, August 11, 1988, 1. On the signing, see also "Handclaps, Handclasps," *Washington Post*, August 11, 1988, A3; Julie Johnson, "President Signs Law to Redress Wartime Wrong," *New York Times*, August 11, 1988, A1.

41. "An Overdue Apology," *Washington Post*, August 6, 1988, A18.

CHAPTER 15: STOPPING CATHOLIC PRIESTS FROM SEXUALLY ABUSING LITTLE BOYS

1. Roy J. Harris, Jr., *Pulitzer's Gold: Behind the Prize for Public Service Journalism* (Columbia: University of Missouri Press, 2007), 87.

2. Globe Spotlight Team, "Church Allowed Abuse by Priest for Years," *Boston Globe*, January 6, 2002, A1. This article and many others about the abuse were

credited to a team of three reporters—Matt Carroll, Sacha Pfeiffer, and Michael Rezendes—and one editor, Walter V. Robinson. Rezendes wrote the article.

3. Ibid.

4. Ibid.

5. Ibid.

6. Ibid.

7. Ibid.

8. Globe Spotlight Team, "Scores of Priests Involved in Sex Abuse Cases," *Boston Globe*, January 31, 2002, A1. For this article, senior assistant metropolitan editor Stephen Kurkjian was listed as part of the team.

9. Ibid.

10. Ibid.

11. Ibid.

12. Ibid.

13. Ibid.

14. Michael Rezendes, "Scandal: The *Boston Globe* and Sexual Abuse in the Catholic Church," in Thomas G. Plante, ed., *Sin against the Innocents: Sexual Abuse by Priests and the Role of the Catholic Church* (Westport, Conn.: Praeger, 2004), xvii; Laurie Goodstein and Alessandra Stanley, "As Scandal Keeps Growing, Church and Its Faithful Reel," *New York Times*, March 17, 2002, A1; Dick Olin, "Pay the Victims, Protect the Church," *New York Times*, May 25, 2002, A17.

15. Carl M. Cannon, "The Priest Scandal," *American Journalism Review* (May 2002): 20; Michael Powell and Lois Romano, "Roman Catholic Church Shifts Legal Strategy," *Washington Post*, May 13, 2002, A1.

16. Tom Heinen, "6 More Priests Linked to Minors Uncovered," *Milwaukee Journal Sentinel*, May 14, 2002, A1; Ronald J. Hansen, "Duggan Targets 16 Priests in Abuse Inquiry," *Detroit News*, May 10, 2002, A1; Jaxon Van Derbeken and Peter Fimrite, "S.F. Archdiocese Lists 40 Accused of Abuse," *San Francisco Chronicle*, June 6, 2002, A1.

17. Andrew Sullivan, "Is the Church Dying?" *Time*, June 10, 2002. http://sullivan archives.theatlantic.com/faith.php.

18. *NBC Nightly News*, May 8, 2002; segment reported by Anne Thompson.

19. *ABC Evening News*, April 6, 2002; segment reported by Bill Blakemore; *CBS Evening News*, June 15, 2002; segment reported by Randall Pinkston; *CNN Evening News*, June 14, 2002; segment reported by John Allen.

20. *PBS Newshour*, March 26, 2002; segment reported by Terence Smith.

21. Ibid.

22. Eugene Cullen Kennedy, "See No Evil," *Salon*, April 26, 2002. http://www.salon.com/2002/04/26/kennedy_rome.

23. Cheryl L. Reed, "The Gay Purge," *Salon*, March 27, 2002. http://www.salon.com/2002/03/27/gay_purge.

24. William Saletan, "Priests, Pedophiles, and Celibacy," *Slate*, March 6, 2002. http://www.slate.com/articles/news_and_ politics/2002/03/06/saletan.

25. William Saletan, "Blaming Gays for Sex Abuse by Priests," *Slate*, April 24, 2002. http://www.slate.com/articles/news_and_politics/frame_game/2002/04/24/get_it_straight.html.

26. Richard Lezin Jones, "Former Altar Boys Describe Years of Abuse, Then Years of Silence," *New York Times*, March 18, 1002, A1.

27. Todd Cooper, "Man Tells of Herek's Betrayal of Trust," *Omaha World Herald*, June 6, 2002, A1.

28. Walter V. Robinson, "For Father and Son, a Shared Anguish," *Boston Globe*, February 3, 2002, A1.

29. Harris, *Pulitzer's Gold*, 85.

30. Ibid.

31. Laurie Goodstein and Sam Dillon, "Bishops Set Policy to Remove Priests in Sex Abuse Cases," *New York Times*, June 15, 2002, A1.

32. Ibid.

33. Ibid.

34. Ibid.

35. "Bishops' Partial Response," *Boston Globe*, June 16, 2002, E6.

CHAPTER 16: REDEFINING THE AMERICAN LESBIAN

1. On Ellen DeGeneres's early years, see Bill Carter, "Dialed God (Pause). He Laughed," *New York Times*, April 13, 1994, C1, C10; Lisa Iannucci, *Ellen DeGeneres: A Biography* (Westport, Conn.: Greenwood, 2009), 2–6; Sherry Beck Paprocki, *Ellen DeGeneres: Entertainer* (New York: Chelsea House, 2009), 18–23; Robert Wieder, "Ellen DeGeneres Is Proving She's 'Funniest,'" *San Francisco Chronicle*, November 30, 1986, Sunday Datebook, 35. Ellen DeGeneres's parents are Betty and Elliott DeGeneres. Her stepfather, whom her mother divorced in 1985, was Roy Gruessendorf.

2. Iannucci, *Ellen DeGeneres*, 11–15; Paprocki, *Ellen DeGeneres*, 25–28.

3. Carter, "Dialed God," C1; Iannucci, *Ellen DeGeneres*, 15–18; Paprocki, *Ellen DeGeneres*, 27–29, 31–32; Wieder, "Ellen DeGeneres," 35.

4. Iannucci, *Ellen DeGeneres*, 18; Paprocki, *Ellen DeGeneres*, 35; Wieder, "Ellen DeGeneres," 35.

5. Carter, "Dialed God," C1; Iannucci, *Ellen DeGeneres*, 15–16, 21; Paprocki, *Ellen DeGeneres*, 35.

6. Carter, "Dialed God," C10; Iannucci, *Ellen DeGeneres*, 22, 25–26; Paprocki, *Ellen DeGeneres*, 35; Wieder, "Ellen DeGeneres," 35.

7. Carter, "Dialed God," C10; Iannucci, *Ellen DeGeneres*, 27–28; Paprocki, *Ellen DeGeneres*, 41–45.

8. Gail Pennington, "'Seinfeld' West Has Its Fun with . . . Whatever," *St. Louis Post-Dispatch*, March 27, 1994, C8; Phil Kloer, "A Seinfeld from a Woman's Viewpoint," *Atlanta Constitution*, March 29, 1994, D1; Robert Bianco, "Viewers Ought to Bond with ABC's 'Friends of Mine,'" *Pittsburgh Post-Gazette*, March 27, 1994, TV2.

9. Iannucci, *Ellen DeGeneres*, 35; Paprocki, *Ellen DeGeneres*, 56.

10. Iannucci, *Ellen DeGeneres*, 35–36; Paprocki, *Ellen DeGeneres*, 57–58.

11. Bruce Handy, "Yep, I'm Gay," *Time*, April 14, 1997, 78; Paprocki, *Ellen DeGeneres*, 58–59; *Primetime Live*, ABC, April 25, 1997.

12. The episode aired on April 30, 1997.

13. Howard Rosenberg, "Honesty Is the Best Policy," *Los Angeles Times*, April 30, 1997, F8; Tom Shales, "Ellen's Night Out," *Washington Post*, April 30, 1997, D1; Frederic M. Biddle, "Tonight's Show Makes History," *Boston Globe*, April 30, 1997, C1, C8.

14. "Ellen and 'Ellen' Come Out," *New York Times*, May 1, 1997, A26.

15. Alan Bash, "42 Million Tuned In for a TV Coming-Out," *USA Today*, May 2, 1997, 2A.

16. John Gallagher, "Ellen DeGeneres: We're Not Coming Back," *The Advocate*, April 14, 1998. The official was Chastity Bono.

17. *Primetime Live*, May 5, 1998.

18. Rita Kempley, "'Love Letter' Doesn't Deliver," *Washington Post*, May 21, 1999, C5; Andrew O'Hehir, "EDtv," *Salon*, March 26, 1999.

19. Tom Shales, "Crossing Jordan and Ellen," *Washington Post*, September 24, 2001, C1; Iannucci, *Ellen DeGeneres*, 61–62.

20. Iannucci, *Ellen DeGeneres*, 62–63; Paprocki, *Ellen DeGeneres*, 77.

21. *Emmy Awards*, CBS, November 4, 2001.

22. Ibid.

23. Ibid.

24. Ibid.

25. Joanne Ostrow, "Awards Return with Low-Key, Respectful Show," *Denver Post*, November 5, 2001, C1; David Bianculli, "Ellen Makes Show Worth Wait," *New York Daily News*, November 5, 2001, B1; Ray Richmond, "The Miracle Worker," *Hollywood Reporter*, November 6, 2001, 12.

26. Paprocki, *Ellen DeGeneres*, 81–82.

27. *Today*, NBC, September 8, 2003.

28. Paprocki, *Ellen DeGeneres*, 82–85.

29. Gail Shister, "Just Being Herself, DeGeneres Has a Talk-Show Winner," *Philadelphia Inquirer*, October 21, 2003, E6; http://www.popmatters.com/com/tv/reviews/e/ellen-degeneres-show.shtml; Neal Justin, "Critic's Choice," *Minneapolis Star-Tribune*, September 6, 2004, E8.

30. Cesar G. Soriano, "Gwyneth Gets Buggy on 'Ellen,'" *USA Today*, December 9, 2003, D2; Dana Stevens, "Moyers Says Ciao to Now," *Slate*, December 14, 2004; "DeGeneres, Gray Give Aid and Comfort after Katrina," *Philadelphia Inquirer*, September 5, 2005, F4.

31. Iannucci, *Ellen DeGeneres*, 73; Paprocki, *Ellen DeGeneres*, 92.

32. Paprocki, *Ellen DeGeneres*, 87. DeGeneres's previous relationships had been with actress Anne Heche, from 1997 to 2000, and photographer Alexandra Hedison, from 2001 to 2004.

33. Jacques Steinberg, "Miss Congeniality Wants the Oscars to Be Fun," *New York Times*, October 5, 2006, E1; Tim Nudd, "Ellen DeGeneres: Portia Is 'My Perfect Fit,'" *People*, January 27, 2007; Paige Wiser, "Expert Analysis," *Chicago Sun-Times*, May 28, 2006, Fluff, 8. The author was Rose Rosetree.

34. Camille Paglia, "A Cause They've Long Ago Forgotten," *Salon*, May 9, 2007; Michael Abernethy, "Out Business," *PopMatters*, July 23, 2006; "Ellen Degeneres Announces Plans to Marry Portia de Rossi," *Huffington Post*, May 24, 2008.

35. Julie Jordan, "First Look: Ellen & Portia's Wedding Album," *People*, August 19, 2008.

36. "Ellen DeGeneres & Portia de Rossi: Weekend Wedding!" *Jezebel*, August 15, 2008; "Ellen & Portia Down the Aisle," *Washington Post*, August 18, 2008, C3; Kate Harding, "Quote of the Day," *Salon*, August 18, 2008.

37. Laura Petrecca, Theresa Howard, and Bruce Horovitz, "P&G Opt for Inner Beauty," *USA Today*, September 22, 2008, 7B ; J. R. Tungol, "LGBT History Month Icon of the Day: Ellen DeGeneres," *Huffington Post*, October 7, 2012; Louis Jordan, "The Bully Project Director Talks about Documenting Bullying in American Schools," *Daily Beast*, April 30, 2011.

38. Frank Bruni, "A Sapphic Victory, But Pyrrhic," *New York Times*, November 15, 2009, WK1.

39. "Ellen DeGeneres Tops Oprah as Favorite TV Personality," *Reuters News*, January 14, 2008.

CONCLUSION

1. Elisabeth Bumiller, "In Bin Laden's Compound, Seals' All-Star Team," *New York Times*, May 4, 2011; Josh Voorhees, "Osama's Shooter: 'Is This the Best Thing I've Ever Done, or the Worst Thing?'" *Slate*, February 11, 2013; *ABC World News*, May 3, 2011.

2. For the quote, see Jules Tygiel, *Baseball's Great Experiment: Jackie Robinson and His Legacy* (New York: Vintage, 1984), 9. On scholars connecting baseball being segregated to the *Brown* decision, see, for example, Jonathan Eig, *Opening Day: The Story of Jackie Robinson's First Season* (New York: Simon and Schuster, 2007), 64; Tygiel, *Baseball's Great Experiment*, 303.

Bibliography

The following list contains some of the sources that may be useful to readers interested in exploring the topics in this book in more depth.

CHAPTER 1: SECURING HUMANE CARE FOR THE MENTALLY ILL

Kroeger, Brooke. *Nellie Bly: Daredevil, Reporter, Feminist*. New York: Times Books/ Random House, 1994.

Lutes, Jean Marie. *Front Page Girls: Women Journalists in American Culture and Fiction, 1880–1930*. Ithaca, N.Y.: Cornell University Press, 2006.

Marzolf, Marion. *Up from the Footnote: A History of Women Journalists*. New York: Hastings House, 1977.

Randall, David. *The Great Reporters*. Ann Arbor, Mich.: Pluto, 2005.

Ross, Ishbel. *Ladies of the Press: The Story of Women in Journalism by an Insider*. New York: Harper & Brothers, 1936.

CHAPTER 2: WAGING WAR ON URBAN SLUMS

Buk-Swienty, Tom. *The Other Half: The Life of Jacob Riis and the World of Immigrant America*. New York: W.W Norton, 2008.

Ware, Louise. *Jacob A. Riis: Police Reporter, Reformer, Useful Citizen*. New York: D. Appleton-Century, 1939.

Yochelson, Bonnie, and Daniel Czitrom. *Rediscovering Jacob Riis: Exposure Journalism and Photography in Turn-of-the-Century New York*. New York: New Press, 2007.

CHAPTER 3: PROTECTING AMERICA'S CHILDREN

Evensen, Bruce J. "Edwin Markham." In *Encyclopedia of American Journalism*, ed. Stephen L. Vaughn, 293–94. New York: Routledge, 2008.

Filler, Louis. *The Muckrakers.* University Park: Pennsylvania State University Press, 1976.

Hillstrom, Laurie Collier. *The Muckrakers and the Progressive Era.* Detroit: Omnigraphics, 2009.

Trattner, Walter I. *Crusade for the Children.* Chicago: Quadrangle, 1970.

Weinberg, Arthur, and Lila Weinberg, eds. *The Muckrakers: The Era in Journalism That Moved America to Reform—the Most Significant Magazine Articles of 1902–1912.* New York: Simon and Schuster, 1961.

CHAPTER 4: CREATING A BETTER LIFE FOR AFRICAN AMERICANS

Desantis, Alan D. "A Forgotten Leader: Robert S. Abbott and the Chicago *Defender* from 1910–1920." *Journalism History* 23 (Summer 1997): 63–71.

Grossman, James R. "Blowing the Trumpet: The *Chicago Defender* and Black Migration during World War I." *Illinois Historical Journal* 78 (Summer 1985): 82–96.

Ottley, Roi. *The Lonely Warrior: The Life and Times of Robert S. Abbott.* Chicago: Regnery, 1955.

Wilkerson, Isabel. *The Warmth of Other Suns: The Epic Story of America's Great Migration.* New York: Random House, 2010.

CHAPTER 5: CLOSING DOWN THE ORIGINAL PONZI SCHEME

Harris, Roy J., Jr. *Pulitzer's Gold: Behind the Prize for Public Service Journalism.* Columbia: University of Missouri Press, 2007.

Kennedy, Herbert A. *Newspaper Row: Journalism in the Pre-Television Era.* Chester, Conn.: Globe Pequot, 1987.

Zuckoff, Mitchell. *Ponzi's Scheme: The True Story of a Financial Legend.* New York: Random House, 2005.

CHAPTER 6: ASSURING CITIZENS THAT "G-MEN" WERE KEEPING THEM SAFE

Burroughs, Bryan. *Public Enemies: America's Greatest Crime Wave and the Birth of the FBI, 1933–34.* New York: Penguin, 2004.

Cecil, Matthew. *Hoover's FBI and the Fourth Estate: The Campaign to Control the Press and the Bureau.* Lawrence: University Press of Kansas, 2014.

Potter, Claire Bond. *War on Crime: Bandits, G-Men and the Politics of Mass Culture.* New Brunswick, N.J.: Rutgers University Press, 1998.

Powers, Richard Gid. *G-Men: Hoover's FBI in American Popular Culture.* Carbondale: Southern Illinois University Press, 1983.

Theoharis, Athan G., and John Stuart Cox. *The Boss: J. Edgar Hoover and the Great American Inquisition.* Philadelphia: Temple University Press, 1988.

CHAPTER 7: STOPPING SMOKERS FROM KILLING THEMSELVES

Brandt, Allan M. *The Cigarette Century: The Rise, Fall, and Deadly Persistence of the Product That Defined America.* New York: Basic, 2007.

Parker-Pope, Tara. *Cigarettes: Anatomy of an Industry from Seed to Smoke.* New York: New Press, 2001.

Whelan, Elizabeth M. *A Smoking Gun: How the Tobacco Industry Gets Away with Murder.* Philadelphia: George F. Stickley, 1984.

Whiteside, Thomas. *Selling Death: Cigarette Advertising and Public Health.* New York: Liveright, 1970.

CHAPTER 8: CELEBRATING A JEWISH MISS AMERICA

Alexander, Shana. *When She Was Bad: The Story of Bess, Hortense, Sukhreet & Nancy.* New York: Random House, 1990.

Deford, Frank. *There She Is: The Life and Times of Miss America.* New York: Viking, 1971.

Dworkin, Susan. *Miss America, 1945: Bess Myerson and the Year That Changed Our Lives.* New York: Newmarket, 1987.

Preston, Jennifer. *Queen Bess: An Unauthorized Biography of Bess Myerson.* Chicago: Contemporary, 1990.

CHAPTER 9: BREAKING THE COLOR BARRIER IN MAJOR LEAGUE BASEBALL

Eig, Jonathan. *Opening Day: The Story of Jackie Robinson's First Season.* New York: Simon and Schuster, 2007.

Rampersad, Arnold. *Jackie Robinson: A Biography.* New York: Knopf, 1997.

Robinson, Jackie. *I Never Had It Made: An Autobiography.* New York: HarperCollins, 1972.

Tygiel, Jules. *Baseball's Great Experiment: Jackie Robinson and His Legacy.* New York: Vintage, 1984.

CHAPTER 10: GIVING AVERAGE CITIZENS MORE SAY IN CHOOSING THEIR PRESIDENT

Donovan, Robert J., and Ray Scherer. *Unsilent Revolution: Television News and American Public Life, 1948–1991.* New York: Press Syndicate of the University of Cambridge, 1992.

Lang, Kurt, and Gladys Engel Lang. *Politics and Television.* Chicago: Quadrangle, 1968.

Sig Mickelson, *From Whistle Stop to Sound Bite: Four Decades of Politics and Television.* New York: Praeger, 1989.

CHAPTER 11: IMPROVING THE LIVES OF MIGRANT FARMWORKERS

Curtin, Michael. *Redeeming the Wasteland: Television Documentary and Cold War Politics.* New Brunswick, N.J.: Rutgers University Press, 1995.

Friendly, Fred W. *Due to Circumstances beyond Our Control.* New York: Random House, 1967.

Martin, Philip L., and David A. Martin. *The Endless Quest: Helping America's Farm Workers.* Boulder, Colo.: Westview, 1994.

Raphael, Chad. *Investigated Reporting: Muckrakers, Regulators, and the Struggle over Television Documentary.* Urbana: University of Illinois Press, 2005.

CHAPTER 12: POPULARIZING THE BIRTH CONTROL PILL

McLaughlin, Loretta. *The Pill, John Rock, and the Church: The Biography of a Revolution.* Boston: Little, Brown, 1982.

Watkins, Elizabeth Siegel. *On the Pill: A Social History of Oral Contraceptives, 1950–1970.* Baltimore: Johns Hopkins University Press, 1998.

CHAPTER 13: FUELING THE SPACE RACE

Allen, Michael. *Live from the Moon: Film, Television and the Space Race.* New York: I. B. Tauris, 2009.

Diamond, Edwin. "Perfect Match: TV and Space." *Columbia Journalism Review* 4 (Summer 1965): 18–20.

Donovan, Robert J., and Ray Scherer. *Unsilent Revolution: Television News and American Public Life, 1948–1991.* New York: Press Syndicate of the University of Cambridge, 1992.

Watson, Mary Ann. *The Expanding Vista: American Television in the Kennedy Years.* New York: Oxford University Press, 1990.

CHAPTER 14: ACHIEVING JUSTICE FOR JAPANESE AMERICANS INTERNED DURING WORLD WAR II

Hatamiya, Leslie T. *Righting a Wrong: Japanese Americans and the Passage of the Civil Liberties Act of 1988.* Stanford, Calif.: Stanford University Press, 1993.

Ng, Wendy. *Japanese American Internment during World War II.* Westport, Conn.: Greenwood, 2002.

CHAPTER 15: STOPPING CATHOLIC PRIESTS FROM SEXUALLY ABUSING LITTLE BOYS

Cannon, Carl M. "The Priest Scandal." *American Journalism Review* 24 (May 2002): 18–25.

Harris, Roy J., Jr. *Pulitzer's Gold: Behind the Prize for Public Service Journalism.* Columbia: University of Missouri Press, 2007.

Rezendes, Michael. "Scandal: The Boston Globe and Sexual Abuse in the Catholic Church." In *Sin Against the Innocents: Sexual Abuse by Priests and the Role of the Catholic Church,* ed. Thomas G. Plante, 1–12. Westport, Conn.: Praeger, 2004.

CHAPTER 16: REDEFINING THE AMERICAN LESBIAN

Iannucci, Lisa. *Ellen DeGeneres: A Biography.* Westport, Conn.: Greenwood, 2009.

Paprocki, Sherry Beck. *Ellen DeGeneres: Entertainer.* New York: Chelsea House, 2009.

Index

About the Author

Rodger Streitmatter began his career as an award-winning journalist for Virginia's *Roanoke Times & World News*. He later earned a PhD in American history and is now a member of the School of Communication faculty at American University. His previous books include *Raising Her Voice: African-American Women Journalists Who Changed History*, *Mightier than the Sword: How the News Media Have Shaped American History*, and *Outlaw Marriages—the Hidden Histories of Fifteen Extraordinary Same-Sex Couples*.